THE
NEXT
EVOLUTION

A BLUEPRINT
FOR TRANSFORMING
THE PLANET

JACK REED

The Next Evolution:
a Blueprint for Transforming the Planet

Published by:
The Community Planet Foundation
1611 Olive Street
Santa Barbara, CA 93101-1114
www.communityplanet.org
Phone: 805-962-2038
Email: jack@communityplanet.org

Printed in the United States of America

Book Shepherding by Ellen Reid
www.smarketing.com

Cover design by David Sand

ISBN: 0-9740161-0-1
LCCN: 2003092802
Publisher's - Cataloging in Publication
Data available upon request

DEDICATION

This book is dedicated to Vicki, Mike, and Andrew for their
partnership in creating the vision, to John-Roger
for decades of support, and to all of you who hold the vision
of this planet working for the Highest Good of all life on the planet.

ABOUT THE BOOK

Very seldom does one hear about a viable plan to transform the planet and to address all its problems. *The Next Evolution: a Blueprint for Transforming the Planet* offers such a plan, a plan that could change everything. The author traces the challenges we face to the legacy of the everyone-for-themselves paradigm that has ruled this planet unquestioned for thousands of years.

But what if we instead choose to have this planet work for everyone and for all life on the planet? The heart of this book lays out that vision. The basic building block that is needed is how we live together and relate together in Community, and the author meticulously describes how that would look in a Highest Good for all model. Envision a world that enjoys the latest technology, yet respects the natural resources of the planet and keeps them intact. Imagine living in a diverse, sustainable Community where everyone is well cared for, with all their needs being met.

This is not a utopian fantasy. This *IS* the next evolution—literally a blueprint for transforming our world through realistic and practical solutions to the present-day political, environmental, economic, and social problems of the entire planet.

Jack Reed is a man who genuinely cares about the planet—as a whole, not just the separate aspects of it. He has the courage to stand up and say what is becoming increasingly obvious, yet is industriously being ignored: that our planet is in serious trouble, we are the cause of it, and we can fix it. He has spent nearly three decades studying, examining, considering and experimenting with ways to make this planet a better place, not just for the powerful few, but for everyone.

Jack's studies have taken him far beyond the theoretical; for fifteen years he lived in an urban cooperative community, where he took on various aspects of the active leadership. With this hands-on experience, he has developed a concept of Community that is generations apart from the commonly accepted process where individual power often drives the outcomes.

JACK REED

To support the evolved Community, Jack established, tested, and refined a consensus process that is practical and actually produces outcomes that are for the "Highest Good" of all concerned. He has taken that process on the road in the form of classes and workshops, and for a number of years has been consulting with corporations and non-profit organizations in the area of team building. Among his clients are The Educare Foundation, True North Leadership, The Wilderness Institute, The University of Southern California, Loyola-Marymount University, California State University at Northridge, California State Dept. of Rehabilitation, The Peace Theological Seminary, The Institute of Individual and World Peace, The Los Angeles Unified School District, and Amgen.

Jack is truly a visionary who sees the world as an interconnected whole. His first book, *The Next Evolution: A Blueprint For Transforming The Planet*, is a practical manual for creating Community and saving this planet, our home.

CONTENTS

by NEALE DONALD WALSCH

INTRODUCTION TO *THE NEXT EVOLUTION:*
A BLUEPRINT FOR TRANSFORMING THE PLANET

All the world is searching now for a New Tomorrow. We seek new and more effective ways to create ourselves as a human society. We may not have all of the answers to life's biggest mysteries, but we now know many of the questions. Why can't we get along? Why can't we harmonize? Why can't we find a way to live together in peace? What stops us from sharing in a way that provides something for all and misery for none?

Why can't the human race get its act together? What will it take for us to stop our own seemingly inexorable drive to self-destruction? If there were a way for us to co-habitate on this planet, to share the space we have been given by the gods, and to be with each other in joy and celebration, what would it be?

These are the questions that have confronted humanity from the beginning of time, and they are the questions that are confronting humanity now. But the answers are now more urgently needed than ever, for we have reached a point where the world can no longer tolerate another of humanity's temper tantrums. If one of us steps out of line now, we could bring an end to the entire human adventure. None of us wants that, but some of us are acting as if we are willing to risk it.

As I said in *Conversations with God - Book 1*, we must change from the everyone-for-themselves model. We need to deeply explore an alternative way of living together on the earth. Jack Reed did exactly that. He met with a small group of people for three years and explored with them, in detail, what it would look like for a Community and for an entire society to live together in a Highest Good For All model, and how that model, along with the necessary consciousness, would inspire others to both strive for the consciousness, as well as transform the whole economic/political/social/environmental model.

I am impressed with Jack Reed's work. I may not agree with every conclusion to which he and his group have come. I may not concur with every suggestion they have made. But I appreciate at the depth of my being their willingness to examine the question, to explore the issues, and to develop a model to place on the table for discussion by the whole of humanity.

Let us then use this model, let us then take advantage of this sterling work, let us then receive this gift from Jack Reed and his companions on the journey of life, who have given us one path that we might all take as we continue on our own journey. Let us see what there is to see about all of this. Let us use this model as a starting point for wider discussion.

As U. S. President John F. Kennedy said in the 1960s, we will not accomplish our goal in the first one hundred days, nor in the first one thousand days, but let us begin.

The human heart and the human mind cry out for an end to the killing, to the violence, to the conflict, and to the cruelty which has marked human interactions for so many thousands of years. The human soul calls out, "Who will be on humanity's team?"

I join Jack Reed in seeking a newer world, and I applaud his dedication, commitment, and high intention to produce a plan of action that we might investigate and discuss with real seriousness and with a genuine opportunity to, at last, alter the human experience.

There must be a way for people to live together in peace, and there is. It is not true that people are naturally aggressive, that power over rather than power with is the natural order of things, and that "survival of the fittest" and the "law of the jungle" are the natural mandates of human civilization.

These are primitive concepts that do not, in fact, ensure our survival, but mitigate against it. These are elementary ideas that hold in place elementary behaviors that keep the human race at elementary levels of evolution, even as the process of evolution itself urges us beyond them.

For some ideas that are definitely not elementary ideas, but could lead to the advancement of the human species to levels of collective experience more wonderful than any of us might heretofore have imagined, read this book from cover to cover. And do not agree with every word of it any more than I did. Question, question, question everything in it. Use it as the beginning, not the end, of a discussion that could change the world.

And if changing the world is something that you feel up to, accept my personal invitation, as well, to join Humanity's Team, a world-wide outreach which has been created to—as Jack Reed has done here—open the door for people to find a way to live together in peace at last. For more information on this initiative, go to www.HumanitysTeam.com.

We live in a time when every initiative must be taken, every attempt must be made, every opportunity must be embraced to bring about the kind of shift, the kind of raising of our collective consciousness, and the kind of change in our most basic beliefs, that would produce the world of which we have dreamt from the beginning, and that we are all capable of co-creating

Let us begin this work together. And thank you, Jack, for your contribution to that effort..

Neale Donald Walsch

Ashland, Oregon

April 2003

ACKNOWLEDGEMENTS

My gratitude and thanks to: Vicki Miller, Michael Feeney, Andrew Baillie, and Robert Ross for their vision, dedication, intuition, and creativity that created the Community Planet description upon which this book is based. Also, thanks to the Peace Theological Seminary for sponsoring the Community Planet class, to Linda Macfarlane, Craig Farnham, and Connie Stomper for their inspiration and support, to Emerson Holmes for his vision, to Carol Jones and Connie for their work with me on consensus, to Thomas Slagle for the Community drawings, to Audrey Simmons, whose ideas made this book better, to Bonnie and David Paul, Michael Mogitz, Pamela London, John Cawley, Tom Land, David Sand, Clea Rose, and Sandra Jewell for all the computer help, also to John for his wordsmithmanship, to Aly Roth and Ian Dietz for the cartoon, to Ellen Reid for her book shepherding, and to Ted Drake for his vision and the Bucky connection.

Have you ever wondered what you would do with your life if you had all the resources you needed and if you didn't have to be concerned with the impact your choice would make on anyone else? Man, I know exactly what I'd do. I'm really kind of a beach bum by nature. If I didn't have a passionate commitment to making this world a better place for all people, I would have long since retired to some tropical beach where I could spend my days in the ocean enjoying an endless procession of perfect waves, take walks on the beach, and sip coconuts while listening to the wind rustling the palms. I'd also have an organic garden, and a great stereo system for classic rock and reggae, and I'd invite my friends to come and stay with me for long periods of time.

Sounds good, doesn't it? I actually have the resources to do this, and every once in a while I realize that I could do it right now. But, just as quickly, I think of all the challenges that the planet, the people of the world, and future generations are facing—challenges that threaten the very survival of humanity. So, because I can see a very workable solution, I feel that it would be selfish for me to isolate myself in my idea of paradise without participating in creating the solution. Alas, I have always cared about all the peoples of the world, and, since I was 15, I've been thinking about the big picture of how to make the world truly work for everyone.

This book, then, is a description of the solution that I see. This solution would rather naturally bring about the greatest revolution in living since people first began the current way that we live and interact with each other. Because I, myself, like to read ideas and descriptions that are concise and not drawn out, I have attempted to be concise. However, you will see that I also reiterate ideas that are important because we currently are living and relating with each other and the planet in a thousands-of-years-old paradigm that is no longer viable if we want to have high-quality life in the next century. We need, therefore, to step out of the box and challenge some old assumptions. To that end, I have chosen to continually challenge you to look anew at how we as people live together.

Jack Reed

Chapter 1

T H E   B I G   Q U E S T I O N

As we look at our cities, our country, and our planet, we know what the challenges are. They are the problem buzzwords of our time: poverty, hunger, the economy, pollution, healthcare, crime, war, and the increasing destruction of our environment. Most of us are aware of the doom-and-gloom scenarios about what will happen by, say, the year 2020—when the population has grown to 8.2 billion or more, there isn't enough food to feed everyone, and we have altered and polluted the planet to such an extent that the environmental issues, such as global warming, have become by far the most significant issues of this millennia as they threaten all life on the planet.

Serious problems, right? But now ask yourself this: Since there are enough resources and manpower on this planet for ALL OF US to live not only abundantly but also in balance with nature, the big question is: WHAT THEN IS THE PROBLEM? Why are two of every five people in the world living in poverty? Why are there people who cannot get proper nutrition, sanitation, and medical care? Let's repeat the startling and simple truth that is the cornerstone for finding a solution:

IF WE CHOOSE TO MAKE LIFE WORK FOR EVERYONE, THERE ARE ENOUGH RESOURCES AND MANPOWER ON THIS PLANET FOR *ALL OF US* TO LIVE ABUNDANTLY!

Just now close your eyes and ponder that for a minute. Let it really sink in. Ask yourself why it isn't happening. Then, you may well ask yourself, "What can we do about it?" The forces at work that are causing the imbalances seem to be beyond our control.

There are too many environmental, economic, political, and social causes and situations to correct that it's simply overwhelmingly impossible. At best, most solutions are a Band-Aid approach since everything is interconnected. For example, we can't address starvation in a given geographical area by simply providing food because there are usually political, economic, and environmental causal factors that are quite complex.

Part of the problem is the pervasive, long-standing attitude of againstness that we hold towards each other and towards others. This againstness probably stems from our need/addiction to control our lives. This often happens at the expense of another, and it permeates most of the interactions between one power broker and another, between one interested party and another, and even between one family member and another. This againstness along with the unwillingness to go for a creative approach to collectively make our planetary situation truly work for everyone are roadblocks we must overcome. Given all the imbalances on the planet and the destruction of our environment, the sands are rapidly running through the hourglass for life as we know it on Earth. There is an answer, but it means that we must start making the planet work for all life on the planet. Stated simply:

IF WE'RE GOING TO CONTINUE TO HAVE A WORLD,
WE'RE GOING TO HAVE TO START MAKING IT WORK
FOR EVERYONE.

Given the connectedness of all things, we must go after the one thing that can address and include everything else, and that is HOW WE AS PEOPLE LIVE TOGETHER. Currently we live in what can best be described as an everyone-for-themselves world. That may look like every country for themselves or every family or every whatever grouping, but it all boils down to the everyone-for-themselves model. We do not have a "what would work for all of us" mentality and approach to life. The everyone-for-themselves approach to living and survival is so ingrained through thousands of years of practice that most people have never even conceived of an alternative approach—especially one that would include our entire planet. The piecemeal way our lives are set up, the way our cities are designed, and the way our economy runs all have the end result of isolating and separating us. They are set up for us to try to survive and get ahead on our own and to continue to intrude upon and disrupt our environment.

Therefore we need to move away from this individualistic model to one that really works for all of us and for all life. We have to start acting like one family where the needs of the one are the concern of everyone. This does not mean taking care of those who are thought of as not contributing, but it does mean setting up how we live together in a way that truly works for everyone. This is a total systems-approach—the systems-approach tells us that *all* things are interconnected and that to change a part, i.e. poverty or our ecology, we therefore need to change the entire system in order to really create effective changes. At this point in our history, nothing less is called for and nothing less will work for all of us. This new model has to be that we live on this planet in a way that is *for* THE HIGHEST GOOD OF ALL LIFE so that *we all* can experience more abundance, health, nurturing, loving, and fun.

Think about it, it's very simple to see the solution. In fact, it's so simple that that's why it's hard, because, in our fragmented approach to trying to understand and solve things, we're looking for something complicated to get us out of our present Earth predicament. We have so many thousands of years of programming in our power-based, everyone-for-themselves paradigm to overcome that it's difficult to perceive workable solutions for the planet as a whole. We have an endless history of againstness and conflict that get our minds focused and locked onto looking at life as a struggle for survival on our own as opposed to looking at life as a cooperative adventure that can work for all mankind and for all life on the planet.

We need to create a new model. All the "isms"—capitalism, communism, socialism, nationalism, racism, sexism, etc.—are not working for us, so we have no large-scale model of change to look at. However, CHANGE ON THE SCALE THAT IS NEEDED CAN ONLY BE BROUGHT ABOUT WHEN PEOPLE SEE AND EXPERIENCE A BETTER WAY.

"Since the everyone-for-themselves approach isn't working for the planet, why do we continue to do it?"

"Because we just do life that way, that's the way life is."

"But, why, when it really isn't working for individuals and for the well-being of the entire planet, do we continue rather than seeking a more workable alternative?"

"Because we've done it this way for thousands of years. It must, then, either be the best way or the only way."

"But why haven't we considered other alternatives?"

"We don't know. It's all we know. It's the way things are."

cartoon by Aly Roth and Ian Dietz

"HELP, I'M IN PRISON. I WANT OUT OF HERE!"

We are only limited by our assumptions. The assumption that we must continue doing the everyone-for-themselves model has us and our world in prison.

Fortunately, the best way to show this is also the easiest for a group of people to bring to pass. The way we live together and relate together in Community is the basic building block that is needed to transform the planet. If we design Communities based on a Highest Good For Everyone model, we can live very, very abundant lifestyles that would appeal to almost everyone while simultaneously restoring our environment. This book, then, is about how we can live in Community for The Highest Good Of *All Life* and about the ultimate transformation of the planet, which will be caused by making life work for all of us.

As you continue reading, you'll keep hearing some form of this term, "For The Highest Good," over and over again. [I apologize if that term doesn't just roll off the tongue, but I don't know of any other term that fully encompasses the concept of making the world work for everyone and for the planet.] It includes both creating the outer form to work for all life and the consciousness which that choice requires, and it permeates every aspect of how we choose to live together on this planet. It's an internal commitment to all life on this earth, to wanting the best for all life on the planet, and it's putting that into action by fundamentally changing the form and consciousness of how we live together. It is the antithesis of the short-sighted everyone-for-themselves paradigm that has wrecked havoc on the earth and resulted in the physical, mental, emotional, and spiritual hardships and lack that touch all our lives in varying degrees.

Again, the simple truth—there are enough resources and manpower on this planet for all of us to live very abundantly and in harmony with ourselves, each other, and the environment if we change our model of living and our consciousness from everyone-for-themselves to a Highest Good For Everyone model. Drink this in, for this must be *Our Next Evolution.*

As you look at this idea, I invite you to expand your consciousness to include the welfare of the entire planet. Imagine that you are *all* people in *all* countries and in *all* situations. In many cases you would currently have basic human needs that are not being met, and you would be living on the very edge of survival.

FROM NEALE DONALD WALSH'S
CONVERSATIONS WITH GOD: book 2

GOD: *"In terms of geopolitics, why not work together as a world to meet the most basic needs of everyone?"*
AUTHOR: *"We're doing that or trying."*
GOD: *"After all these thousands of years of human history, that's the most you can say?*

"The fact is, you have barely evolved at all. You still operate in a primitive 'every person for himself' mentality.

"You plunder the Earth, rape her of her resources, exploit her people, and systematically disenfranchise those who disagree with you for doing all of this, calling them the 'radicals.'

"You do this for your own selfish purposes because you've developed a lifestyle that you cannot maintain any other way.

"You must cut down the millions of acres of trees each year or you won't be able to have your Sunday paper. You must destroy miles of the protective ozone which covers your planet or you cannot have your hair spray. You must pollute your rivers and streams beyond repair or you cannot have your industries to give you Bigger, Better, and More. And you must exploit the least among you—the least advantaged, the least educated, the least aware—or you cannot live at the top of the human scale in unheard of [and unnecessary] luxury. Finally, you must deny that you are doing this, or you cannot live with yourself.

"You cannot find it in your heart to 'live simply, so that others may simply live.' That bumper sticker wisdom is too simple for you. It is too much to ask. Too much to give. After all, you've worked so hard for what you've got! You ain't giving up none of it! And if the rest of the human race—to say nothing of your own children's children—have to suffer for it, tough bananas, right? You did what you had to do to survive, to 'make it'—they can do the same! After all, it is every man for himself, is it not?"
AUTHOR: *"Is there any way out of this mess?"*
GOD: *"Yes. Shall I say it again? A shift of consciousness.*

"You cannot solve the problems which plague humankind through governmental action or political means. You have been trying that for thousands of years.

"The change must be made, can be made only in the hearts of man."

—*Neale Donald Walsch,* Conversations With God book 2, *Hampton Roads Publishing Co., Inc., 1997, Charlottesville, VA, pages 172-173.*

However, the solution is so simple that it has escaped us: let's make the planet work for everyone; let's choose to live *for* THE HIGHEST GOOD OF ALL LIFE.

As you continue reading, I invite you to toss out your reference points and to step outside the box of how you think life has to be. So hold onto your hat as I first point out the obvious in terms of current conditions on the planet, and then I offer a practical solution for not only saving the planet, but also making this Earth a more enjoyable place to hang out for *all* people and for *all* life.

Chapter 2
NEEDS OF THE PLANET
SEEDS OF CHANGE

As a starting point (for looking at the imbalances on the planet that need to be addressed), let's briefly take a look at the situation we, as people on planet Earth, find ourselves in at the beginning of the 21st century. Since you are probably well aware of many of our problems, I don't want to go into great depth on these issues. However, I do want to touch on them so that we can see later in this book how our proposed Highest Good model relates to resolving these problems.

I would also like to point out that, while this needs assessment is being done by sections, all the sections are in fact interrelated, and thus my examination by section is purely for the purpose of simplicity. This is by no means a complete list of the challenges we face, just an across-the-board sampler. As you read this chapter, please also keep in mind that this is not a doomsday scenario because we will be presenting a workable solution for not only surviving but even improving the quality of life for all life on the planet.

THE ENVIRONMENT

All of us living in the latter half of the 20th century have lived with the threat of a nuclear holocaust hanging over us. Surprisingly, though, as that threat has subsided, it has revealed to us that the real apocalypse is the ongoing destruction of our environment that now threatens the survival of life on our planet. It's ironic that the ultimate threat to our way of life was never really war, but rather our way of life itself, with our patterns of consumption, pollution, environmental destruction, and the effects of the unequal distribution of wealth.

The disastrous results of our way of life have been much more insidious than war because the effects have been building more slowly. It's not unlike the strange phenomena that biologists call "the boiled frog syndrome." If you put a frog in a pot of water on the fire and slowly increase the heat, the frog just sits there. Finally, at 100° C., the water boils, and the frog dies. Like the frog, most people continue to be unaware of the seriousness of our environmental degradation. Nobody seems to either know what to do about this impending disaster or be willing to truly own the problems and take a whole different course of action in order to resolve them. Our environmental plunge is tied into how the whole game of life has been played on this planet for thousands of years, so we may well have to take a fresh look at our assumptions about life to come up with some solutions on how to save the planet. In fact, as many authorities have warned, unless we take drastic measures soon and change how we are interacting with our environment, we may well experience an ecological collapse sometime within the next couple of decades.

In early 1992, the U. S. National Academy of Sciences and England's Royal Society of London issued a joint report warning, "If current predictions of population growth prove accurate and patterns of human activity on this planet remain unchanged, science and technology may not be able to prevent either irrevocable degradation of the environment or continued poverty for much of the world."[1]

Later that year, 1,600 scientists, including 102 Nobel laureates issued a "warning to humanity" which was even less optimistic: "No more than one or two decades remain before the chance to avert the threats we now confront will be lost and the prospects for humanity immeasurably diminished." They noted that the continuation of our destructive way of life "may so alter the living world that it will be unable to sustain life in the manner that we know. ... A great change in our stewardship of the earth and the life on it is required if vast human misery is to be avoided and our global home on this planet is not to be irretrievably mutilated. A new ethic is required (which) must motivate a great movement, convincing reluctant leaders and reluctant governments and reluctant peoples themselves to effect the needed changes."[2]

"There is strong evidence from the world's scientific community that humanity is very, very close to crossing certain ecological thresholds for the support of life on Earth. The Earth's ozone layer, our only protection from the harmful rays of the sun is being depleted. Massive erosion is causing a rapid loss in the fertile soil of our planet and with it a potentially drastic drop in the ability to produce food for our world's people. Vast destruction of the world's forests is contributing to the spread of the world's deserts, increasing the loss of biodiversity and hampering the ability of the Earth's atmosphere to cleanse itself. The planet's vast oceans are losing their animal life at a staggering rate and are fast reaching the limit of their ability to absorb humanity's waste. The land, animals and plants of our planet are experiencing a rate of extinction unseen on Earth since the time of the dinosaurs; extinctions brought on not by cataclysmic events of nature but by the impact of a single species: Homo sapiens. The increasing pollution of air, water and land by hazardous and toxic waste is causing wide-spread health problems that are only now beginning to be understood. All of these problems are being intensified by the explosive growth in the sheer numbers of human beings in the last half of the 20th century.

"For the first time in history, humanity must face the risk of unintentionally destroying the foundations of life on Earth. The global scientific consensus is that if the current levels of environmental deterioration continue, the delicate life-sustaining qualities of this planet will collapse. It is a stark and frightening potential. To prevent such a collapse is an awesome challenge for the global community."[3]

—From AGENDA 21, *the agreement adopted by all participatin nations at the United Nation's 1992 Earth Summit in Rio de Janeiro*

Also in 1992, Donella Meadows, Dennis Meadows, and Jorgen Randers wrote in their book, *Beyond The Limits*, that we have "overshot" the carrying capacity[4] of the planet. Their research shows that we are now "mining" fuels, minerals, topsoil, ground water, forests, and fisheries much faster than these resources are regenerating themselves. Processing the "throughput" from this mining is creating pollution, which has begun to overwhelm nature's capacity to detoxify it. On the basis of elaborate computer simulations of our current way of life, the Meadows group estimated that an economic and ecological collapse is almost inevitable within forty years.[5]

A shorter time frame has been given by the respected Nobel Prize recipient, Dr. Helen Caldicott, who emphasized in her book, *If You Love The Planet: A Plan To Heal This Earth*, that if we don't act now, by the year 2000 it may be too late to save most life systems on the planet.[6]

We could site scores more reports from reputable scientists that give us similar prognostications. Suffice it to say that there seems to be a consensus that our current way of living has led us into serious jeopardy. Also, there are plenty of great books where you can read about the gravity of our current environmental crisis, whereas this book is about transforming our way of life to make it work for all of us, and deliver us from these dire predictions.

Of course, we all are now aware of the global warming due to the greenhouse effect. Excessive carbon dioxide from the burning of fossil fuels and forests combined with the release of several manufactured gases is forming an atmospheric barrier that traps heat. Since the advent of the Industrial Revolution, manmade carbon dioxide being released into the atmosphere has increased by nearly 6000 percent. Global carbon emissions now stand at more than 6 billion tons annually while the maximum amount that the world's oceans can absorb is only one-sixth that amount. The remainder accumulates in the atmosphere where it, along with all our other emissions of heat-trapping waste industrial gases, continues to warm the atmosphere.[7] At the 1995 United Nations Conference on Global Warming, conference chairwoman Angelica

Merkel, Germany's environmental minister, declared in her opening address, "We have come to recognize that the greenhouse effect is capable of destroying humanity."[8]   Although predictions vary on the long-range effects of this greenhouse phenomena (such as the rise in sea level from the melting of the polar ice caps), potentially the most frightening would be the severe droughts and heatwaves causing a reduction of agricultural productivity.   The high temperatures and moisture reductions from climatic changes would severely impact crop yields.[9]   If these events happen as predicted, we may be on a course where the United States, the world's leading grain exporter, will not even be able to produce enough food to supply itself.

But of perhaps even greater concern is the destruction of the earth's ozone layer by manufactured chemicals.   The best known of these, chlorofluorocarbons (CFC's), carry chlorine to the ozone layer where one chlorine atom can destroy as many a hundred thousand ozone molecules.   Since CFC's take many years to rise up to the ozone layer, we won't even know exactly how much damage we've done for decades, and we continue to release more ozone destroying compounds as we seem unwilling to totally stop producing them.

In the worst case scenario the ozone layer could become so depleted that too much ultraviolet radiation would strike the earth's surface.   The Environmental Protection Agency (EPA), generally conservative, predicted that this will cause 80 million new skin cancer cases over the next 80 years.[10]   The U.N. reported that for each 1 percent of ozone lost, there are 100,000 additional cases of blindness caused by cataracts and a 3 percent increase in skin cancer worldwide.[11]   In Australia, melanoma has doubled in the past ten years.   However, that pales in comparison to what would happen if enough ultraviolet gets in to destroy the phyto-plankton on the surface of the oceans.   That would cause the break-down of the entire chain of life on our planet.[12]

Adding to the greenhouse effect and the rapidly increasing desertificaton of our lands is deforestation.   More than one-half of all the planet's trees and forests are gone.[13]   At the current rate of

"For humans to cause species to become extinct and to destroy the biological diversity of God's creation, for humans to degrade the integrity of the Earth by causing changes in its climate, stripping the Earth of its natural forests, or destroying its wetlands . . . for humans to contaminate the Earth's waters, its land, its air, and its life with poisonous substances—these are sins."[14]

—His Holiness Bartholomew I

"At the present rate of extinction—estimates range from 20,000 to over 100,000 every year—we may lose 20 percent of all the species on the planet within the next 20 to 40 years." [15]

—*Paul Hawkin,* The Ecology of Commerce

rainforest destruction (more than 125,000 square miles/year), the rest could vanish before 2025.[16] Yearly, forests decrease by an area larger than the size of Peru according to the Worldwatch Institute.[17] This devastation is commonly blamed on Third World economics and overpopulation, but, in reality, most of the rainforests are destroyed for foreign cattle, mining and timber interests. Because far more land has been damaged by livestock than anything else, it is my personal opinion that more harm has been done to the planet up to this point through our fascination with beef consumption than any other single factor. But it's not only Third World rainforests that are disappearing—less than 7 percent of U.S. forests remain since the time of Columbus.[18]   In addition, acid rain from the burning of fossil fuels has seriously damaged about 15 percent of Europe's remaining forests as well as affecting the health of North American forests and contaminating our ground water.[19]

The forces that have fueled these crises are economically driven and, once put into motion, are difficult to stop. Therefore, the environment routinely gets sacrificed for the economy. It is precisely this kind of ill-advised economic philosophy that has led the United States to losing over 75 percent of what may be our most precious life-giving resource—its topsoil.[20] Two hundred years ago most of the U.S. had at least 21 inches of topsoil. With the rate of loss continuing to accelerate (we lose an inch every 16 years[21]), it's now less than 6 inches.[22] Historically, topsoil depletion has caused the demise of many of the world's great civilizations,[23] and the U.S. Soil Conservation Service reports that the U.S. loses cropland to soil erosion at an annual rate equal to the size of Connecticut.[24] The U.N., in its resolution on topsoil, noted that the world loses 24 billion tons of topsoil annually; there is only an average of 6 to 8 inches of topsoil left on Earth; that many regions have surpassed the carrying capacity of the land; and that it takes anywhere from 100 years to 60 million years to produce just one inch of topsoil. They further stated that "We may have only a ten year window of opportunity to turn around this catastrophic destruction of ecosystems, watersheds, organic matter and topsoil."[25]   The U.N. Environmental Program also said that 35

UNITED NATIONS RESOLUTION ON TOPSOIL
PRODUCTION AND REPLENISHMENT

Whereas topsoil is absolutely essential for the nourishment and sustenance of plant life so vital to the preservation of Earth's ecosystems that provide our food, shelter, clothing and health; and

Bearing in mind the value of topsoil for the protection of the flora and fauna including soil biota and the bio-diversity of species in nature and man-made conditions, as well as for water quality and water retention, for afforestation and reforestation, for sustainable food production, and subsequently for reduction in greenhouse gases affecting the ozone layer; and

Noting that topsoil loss is over 23 billion tons annually; and realizing that there exists only an average of 6 - 8 inches (15 - 20 cm) of topsoil left on Earth today; and realizing that in each Nation many regions have surpassed the carrying capacity of the land; and

Whereas at current depletion rates we may have only a ten year window of opportunity to turn around this catastrophic destruction of ecosystems (above and below ground), watersheds, organic matter and topsoil; and realizing that our current dependence on geologic evolution produces only one inch (2.5 cm) of topsoil during a period ranging from 100 years to 60 million years; and

Noting that there are only limited conservation and replenishment efforts being undertaken currently in any one Nation; and

Noting that processes exist to produce 1 - 100 tons per day per site of fertile humus through topsoil production centers; therefore

Calls upon all Governments to place as a high priority the preservation and replenishment of the vital topsoil layer;

And further calls upon all Governments to continue efforts in topsoil evaluation and monitoring topsoil loss, conservation, and production; and also

Calls upon all Governments to establish topsoil production centers in farm lands, resource recovery centers, school yards, neighborhoods, villages, wildlife preservations, cities, and industrial sites; and

Encourages all Governments to establish topsoil production centers to promote educational information and training programs; and

Calls upon the United Nations, especially the pertinent agencies of the United Nations' system, to promote, develop and set aside funds for the purpose of supporting topsoil conservation, topsoil production and training programs; and

Calls upon Non-Government Organizations, educational institutions, women and youth networks, citizen groups and individuals to support Government efforts, as well as to mobilize their own human and other resources in production efforts and activities to strengthen the political will for urgently needed action in this area.

The U.S. Department of Agriculture reported that the productivity of our croplands was down 70 percent with much of it on the brink of becoming wasteland. They admitted that soil erosion was a huge disaster, but claimed that, "… halting soil erosion and soil degradation would be prohibitively expensive."[26] I wonder how expensive that is. I guess that it's considered more expensive than mass starvation. This is the madness of our everyone-for-themselves economic paradigm when the reality is that we have the resources and manpower to change this.

percent of the world's land surface is threatened by desertifica-
tion.[27]   That's more than one-third of all land on the planet! Add
to that the increasing world population and the devastating effects
of global warming on agriculture and we may see people leaving
this planet like never before. (Hang in there though, remember
that we're going to get to a workable solution.)

In terms of food resources, the planet has already peaked in the
amount of grain and fish per person that we can produce, and our
output is now declining.[28]   That, combined with an exploding
world population means that the world's food production per
capita has dropped steadily since 1984[29] and that the rate of decline
will increase considerably as the population continues to rise, our
soil continues to deteriorate, our water supplies decrease, and
global warming impacts our crop yields. With the declining grain
harvests, our grain reserve, the world's food safety net, is now the
lowest on record.[30]   Though our Midwest supplies much of that
grain, its water supply, the Ogallala Aquifer (the largest store of
ground-water in the world), is being used 10,000 times faster than
it is being replenished.[31]   The aquifer took almost a half-million
years to form, and it will be depleted within 15 to 40 years.[32] This
is a starvation event waiting to happen soon right here!

The Worldwatch Institute's *State of the World 1994* reported that
human demands are now "approaching the limits of oceanic
fisheries to supply fish (worldwide fish harvests are now
decreasing due to over fishing and the effects of pollution), of
range lands to support cattle, and, in many countries, of the hydro-
logical cycle to produce fresh water."[33] Even now *60 million* people
starve to death every year, *40,000 children on this planet starve to
death every day.*[34]   Imagine if you were watching—one child
starving to death every two seconds. Today that problem may be
viewed by some people as being "over there" in some foreign
place, but in our tomorrows it will be here, unless we drastically
change our way of living on the planet.

Our brief treatise on the environment would not be complete
without a few conservative estimates from the EPA. According to
the EPA's "Toxic Release Inventory," the industrial releases of toxic

THE WIZARD OF ID By Brant Parker and Johnny Hart

Reprinted by permission of Johnny Hart and Creators Syndicate, Inc.

Unfortunately this cartoon is no joke—China's lifeline river is so over-used that it no longer reaches the ocean, no longer adequately irrigates China's main agricultural area and is so poisonous in places as to be unusable.[35]

materials into the U.S. environment—to waste water treatment
plants, landfills, and directly into our air, rivers, lakes, and
underground wells by just the top 50 products of the chemical
industries was 539 billion pounds per year.[36] The total from all
sources takes into account only the relatively few chemicals that
the EPA certifies as harmful, and even the EPA stressed that this
is a low estimate.[37] The Global Tomorrow Coalition estimated
that we annually produce more than a metric ton of hazardous
waste for every person in the country![38] Of that total, about 500
billion cubic meters is radioactive waste.[39]

The EPA also reported that 40 percent of the U.S. population lives
in areas where the air quality is unhealthy.[40] Worldwide, 70 percent
of all city dwellers—more than 1.5 billion people—breathe unhealthy
air.[41] In Russia, where environmental safety first became a casualty
of the conflict with the West and later of their economic chaos, Alexei
V. Yablokov, the father of Russia's environmental movement,
reported that between 14 percent and 15 percent of Russia's territory
is now so polluted that it is unsafe for habitation. However, 40
million people live in those areas anyway.[42]

So why, with our health and the survival of the planet on the
line, don't we change the way we're treating our environment?
With our lifestyles and economic choices already set in motion,
there are difficult tradeoffs in the decisions we make. Although we
know that certain chemicals are causing havoc to our environment
as well as creating health risks, the solutions are not easy because
there are billions and billions of dollars involved. Picking just one
of a myriad of examples, we have the methyl bromide situation.
Methyl bromide, one of the most widely used pesticides on Earth,
has increasingly become the pesticide of choice for many farmers.
One of the reasons for this is that several other pesticides have
been banned because they seep into and pollute the ground water
and are linked with cancer. However, methyl bromide goes the
opposite direction, rising into the atmosphere where it is responsible for as much as 10 percent of the yearly depletion of the ozone
layer. We have recently discovered that it destroys ozone 40 times
faster than CFC's. Weighed against that is the chemical industry's
$3 million argument that banning the pesticide would result in

"The edifice of civilization has become astonishingly complex, but as it grows ever more elaborate, we feel increasingly distant from our roots in the earth. In one sense, civilization itself has been on a journey from its foundations in the world of nature to an ever more contrived, controlled, and manufactured world of our own imitative and sometimes arrogant design. And in my view, the price has been high. At some point during this journey we lost our feeling of connectedness to the rest of nature. We now dare to wonder: Are we so unique and powerful as to be essentially separated from the earth?

"Many of us act—and think—as if the answer is yes. It is now all too easy to regard the earth as a collection of 'resources' having an intrinsic value no larger than their usefulness at the moment. Thanks in part to the scientific revolution, we organize our knowledge of the natural world into smaller and smaller segments and assume that the connections between these separate compartments aren't really important. In our fascination with parts of nature, we forget to see the whole."[43]

—From *Al Gore's*, Earth In The Balance

Here Al Gore acknowledges the Systems Theory— we must realize that all things are interconnected.

devastating worldwide crop loses and corresponding economic consequences. Consequently a U.S. Department of Agriculture official said that instead of banning the pesticide, we should move much more slowly because there's too much at stake.[44] Move more slowly? Too much at stake? This is absolute madness—it could already be too late for our ozone layer, yet we persist in trading our future for the crazy economic system we're enmeshed in.

Granted, with the way we're doing agriculture, industry, and our very lifestyles, there are no easy choices. Civilization has usually meant how far we can remove ourselves from nature, and that circumstance has led to our current ecological crisis. The situation is further complicated by economics and politics, as big money special interest groups seek to either maintain the status quo or change it in a way that they can still lock in their profits.

Because there are billions and billions at stake, there has been a well thought out corporate strategy to cast doubt on the urgency of our environmental problems. In her book, *The Global Spin: Corporate Assault on Environmentalism*, Sharon Beder writes, "Corporations have used think-tanks and a few dissident scientists to cast doubt on the existence and magnitude of various environmental problems, including global warming, ozone depletion and species extinction. The strategy is aimed at crippling the impetus for governmental action to solve these problems, actions which might adversely affect corporate profits."[45] As evidence of this strategy, Beder cited an author of a handbook on public relations, Phil Lesly, who advised corporations: "People generally do not favor action on a non-alarming situation when arguments seem to be balanced on both sides and there is a clear doubt. ... The weight of impressions on the public must be balanced so people will have doubts and lack motivation to take action. Accordingly, means are needed to get balancing information into the mainstream from sources that the public will find credible. There is no need for a clear-cut 'victory.' ... Nurturing public doubt by demonstrating that this is not a clear-cut situation in support of the opponents usually is all that is necessary."[46] Boy, do they ever have that figured right as to how to fool most of the people into doing nothing so they can keep earning their corporate profits for whatever time there is left before the planet falls apart for all of us. However, these people, in their selfishness, are not thinking about their grandchildren, let alone the millions who already suffer because of corporate abuses of the environment.

If you don't think corporations are doing this, think about what the tobacco industry got away with. For decades the link between smoking and disease was known, but the corporations were able to "blow just enough smoke" by presenting "balanced" reports about the health risks so that they confused the issue long enough to continue to earn billions. Finally the public outcry prevailed to place some limitations, but millions died and continue to die preventable and often painful deaths. Still, this government continues to condone and subsidize tobacco.

We simply have to find a better economic paradigm than our current model. If you are not already aware of the environmental crisis, please awaken. "The simple truth is that we are the last generation on Earth that can save the planet."[47] Every day we are discovering new and previously unknown evidence of environmental damage. One day, numbered among the thousands of species that die out every year due to man's destruction of their habitat, we may well find mankind itself. Our epitaph could read, "Amidst the prospects of plenty, we died together because of the way we chose to live together."

"The end of the human race will be that it will eventually die of civilization."

—*Ralph Waldo Emerson*

HEALTH

Is there a health cost for all these pollutants entering the environment? A growing number of experts believe that most of our killer diseases are a direct result of our industrialized society. Again, let's look at the conservative EPA for evidence. The EPA estimates that 100,000 American workers die each year from job-related diseases, including exposure to deadly chemicals.[48] Farmers who use herbicides run six times the risk of contracting certain kinds of cancer, and children in homes where pesticides are used have seven times the chance of contracting leukemia.[49] The average American household also uses 25 gallons of hazardous chemicals per year.[50] The EPA estimates that 400,000 Americans contract toxic related diseases every year from 400 different toxins in their bodies.[51] That is a very, very conservative estimate as we continue to discover more about the effects that toxic chemicals (and the insidious ways they combine together to do even greater damage) have on the health of human beings and all life forms.

A growing number of medical practitioners believe that many of our minor illnesses which look like colds or influenza are in fact largely caused by contaminants in our air, water, and food. Our daily exposure to toxins is incredible. The EPA reported that we ingest an average of four pounds of pesticides per year and have residues from 400 different toxins in our body fat.[52] Not only do most household products contain toxins, but, besides the more than 2000 registered pesticides in our food,[53] over 3,000 chemicals are intentionally added to our food[54] as well as more than 10,000 unintentional chemical compounds that find their way into our food.[55] Many of these, such as the sulfides sprayed on our produce, build up in our bodies and eventually can make us sick. In a random survey of 900 breast-feeding mothers across the U.S., there were poisonous chemicals significantly exceeding safe levels found in the mother's milk in 100 percent of the cases.[56] In fact, "Mothers milk would be banned by the food safety laws of industrialized nations if it were sold as a packaged good."[57] Imagine, the breast milk of almost every single industrialized country nursing mother—toxic! What on earth are we doing to ourselves?

We keep hearing about the link between cancer and toxins. In 1900, cancer was only the tenth leading cause of death, accounting for only 3 percent of the deaths in the U.S.. Today it is the second leading cause of death, and claims more Americans each year than we lost in World War II, Korea, and Vietnam combined.[58] "Many scientists now feel that the presence of toxic chemicals in our bodies is largely responsible for these (immune system) epidemics."[59] Remember the dream that science was going to deliver us from diseases like cancer? Well, instead, while some

"The most alarming of all man's assaults upon the environment is the contamination of air, earth, rivers and sea with dangerous and even lethal materials. This pollution is for the most part irrecoverable; the chain of evil it initiates not only in the world that must support life but in living tissues is for the most part irreversible. In this now universal contamination of the environment, chemicals are the sinister and little-recognized partners of radiation in changing the very nature of the world— the very nature of life."[60]

—*Rachel Carson*, Silent Spring

"The number of chemicals is increasing, with 70,000 chemicals now used regularly, and 500 to 1,000 new ones added each year. Much is understood about the damage caused by those chemicals, but the greatest harm of all may come from what we do not understand about them." [61]

—Citizen's Guide to Sustainable Development

research proceeds to that end, the results have been far outweighed by the scientists creating the disease-producing toxic chemicals. It's what happens when the economics are everyone-for-themselves, rather than working for The Highest Good Of All.

Yes, there is a cost to our unthinking pollution in our industrialized lives. Included in that industrialized lifestyle are huge farms where massive amounts of chemicals are used to grow our food. The destruction of the environment caused by modern agriculture is based on the philosophy of ignoring nature and trying to increase production in the short term. We're also finding that pesticides and chemical fertilizers are now so prevalent in the environment worldwide that they are causing many mammals, birds and fish to become sterile, and many species may be a generation away from extinction. The chemicals so widely used to kill insects and weeds and fertilize soil (as well as being in many off-the-shelf products) mimic estrogen and inhibit testosterone to the point where these species are unable to reproduce. Because the adult populations appear normal, this problem has largely gone unnoticed and is only recently coming into focus. However, it's quite alarming because the disorders are so widespread and we have no idea what effect the extinction of so many different species will have on our chain of life. The buildup of these chemicals in our bodies also may be the reason why the human male sperm count is dropping and why one-fourth of our college students are sterile compared to one-half of one percent forty years ago.[62] The toxins may also explain the sharp increases in prostate and testicular cancer as well as breast cancer and endometriosis in women.

In the last few years infectious diseases have risen significantly, now killing 16.5 million people each year.[63] In nature we are seeing the mass die-off of entire groups of mammals due to pollution weakening their immune systems and, consequently, their ability to fend off diseases that are normally not life-threatening. Our immune systems are virtually identical to those of other mammals, so whatever is happening to them can and will be happening to us.[64]

As an example, in the Canadian Arctic the Inuits continue to eat as they have for thousands of years, living on a staple of marine mammals and fish. But now, as a result of the chemical warfare we've been waging against the planet, the Inuits' immune systems are breaking down, causing them to be ravaged by disease. The most vulnerable are the breast-fed infants, who feed on some of the most contaminated milk on earth. The Inuit women's milk fat contained over one thousand parts per million of PCB's. Among many devastating results, one in four Inuit children has chronic hearing loss due to infections.[65]

While the effects of PCB's may be observable first in the Inuits, a 1979 Govrnment study found PCB's present in 100 percent of human sperm samples.[66]   PCB's are probably the most notorious of the toxic chemicals used on food—a few parts per billion can cause birth defects in lab animals.[67]   Just ask the Inuits what this pesticide can do when it gets into our waters. Three years after Monsanto, the manufacturer, began production of PCB's, the faces of 23 of their 24 plant workers became disfigured.[68]   I wonder if they gave their workers "balancing reports." Hello, we're killing ourselves, and it's about money—there are billions at stake.

We still use dioxin—which the EPA reported likely causes cancer and can damage human immune and reproductive systems, even in trace amounts.[69]   Dioxin is one of the most deadly chemicals we've ever created—just one ounce could kill 10 million people.[70]   Yet dioxin is still in use as a common bleach for pulp and paper products (so they can be nice and white—at the expense of the environment) and a number of other industrial processes, including herbicides, where its killing properties make it very effective. We have sprayed millions of pounds on our farmland.[71] It's a crazy world where people are allowed to do this for economic reasons while dioxin gets into our food chain and slowly kills us. Why is it still in use? Dow Chemical, Monsanto, BASF and other manufacturers have done everything they can to hide the dangers.[72]   In this case though, it's not just about profits. Because dioxin was the lethal component of Agent Orange, the corporations also do their disinformation and misinformation to protect themselves from the veterans' lawsuits that would result if the truth were known.[73]

"Destroying the Balance of Nature"
by Marla Cone, Los Angeles Times

"Canadian biologist, Peter Ross was studying harbor seals in Nova Scotia when he heard the stunning news that a viral plague had claimed six of ten seals (20,000 harbor seals—more than half of Europe's harbor seals) in the North Sea. Why, Ross wondered, were the seals he was seeing in eastern Canada healthy and thriving? Tests of their antibodies showed that they had been exposed to the (same) distemper virus that had devastated the European seals. But, for some reason, the Canadian seals fended off the disease.

"Marine biologists suspected immune suppression, but they had no proof. What they needed were measurements of seals' immunity under real-life conditions. But, unlike the usual test animals such as mice and rats, seals live in the wild, not in a laboratory. Such an experiment had never been tried under natural conditions.

"Three years later, under the auspices of the Dutch government, Ross moved to Holland and embarked on a landmark study that culminated in the most compelling evidence that environmental pollution is severely suppressing marine animals' ability to fight disease.

"Seal pups were caught in the relatively clean waters off Scotland and divided into two groups kept in separate pens. One group was fed herring from the heavily contaminated Baltic Sea, while the other ate herring from the cleaner Atlantic. The difference in PCBs (polychlorinated biphenyls—a manmade chemical) intake was tenfold.

"After two years, Ross and his colleagues compared the groups' immune cells. The differences, reported in 1995, were far greater than anyone had predicted. Seals fed the Baltic fish developed 25 percent fewer "natural killer" cells—the first line of defense against viruses—and 35 percent fewer T-cells, the white blood cells essential to clearing infections and ordering production of antibodies. Such a severe loss of immunity is comparable to what is seen in some AIDS patients. But the scientists, for ethical reasons, did not take the logical next step and expose their subjects to disease. The seals, Ross suspects, all would have died.

"In wild seals, the immune damage is probably even worse than what Ross found. The captive seals were fed Baltic herring for only two years, while wild ones live 30 to 40 years. The captives' blubber contained 17 parts per million of PCBs, compared with hundreds, sometimes thousands, of parts per million found in wild seals and dolphins that died from distemper. And they were born in fairly clean waters, so their mothers did not pass chemicals to the womb during the fragile stage of immune system development.

"The most disturbing implications reach even further. The fish the seals ate had come from Holland's commercial markets. The same Baltic Sea herring is served at the dinner tables of most Dutch households.

"'The harbor seal is the canary in the gold mine,' Ross said. 'When 60 percent of a population dies, it means there is something wrong. Some people say, 'Who cares about cute, cuddly seals?' But what it indicates is the state of the world's oceans, and the commercial fisheries too.'"

"'What's going to hurt a marine mammal is probably going to hurt us too." —David Ferrick, Univ. of California at Davis immunologist.'

"'Disease is an expression of an environment out of balance,' said Milton Friend, director of the National Wildlife Center, the federal laboratory that investigates animal epidemics. 'And nothing is natural out there anymore.'"[74]

Another life-threatening concern is polluted water. Daily, at least 15,000 of our world's people die from drinking unsafe water.[75] Even in the U.S., the EPA has identified 495 waterways—10 percent of our rivers, streams, and bays—as being heavily contaminated by toxins.[76] Forty-two million Americans drink water dangerously high in lead,[77] not to mention other unsafe chemicals found in almost all tap drinking water. The National Resources Defense Council's estimate, from a study of the data from over 100 water utilities in the U.S., was even higher. Their 1995 study reported that over 100 million Americans were drinking contaminated water.[78] In some cases the water is even more harmful to shower in and breathe than it is to drink.[79]

America also annually dumps five trillion gallons of industrial waste directly into coastal waters along with 2.3 trillion gallons of sewage.[80] Because, as you remember, I'd much rather be body surfing in the ocean than writing this book, these facts especially affect me as Los Angeles' Santa Monica Bay, for example, is so polluted that one of the lifeguard supervisors advised me that the water in the Bay was unsafe to swim in. But these are small problems compared to the two billion people in the world who have no sanitation service at all and the 1.8 billion who lack access to safe drinking water.[81]

Contaminated water, food, and air is affecting all life on the planet. The insidious manmade chemical toxins are believed to be in the tissues of every living thing on earth. Says Steve Holladay, an immunotoxicologist at Virginia-Maryland College of Veterinary Medicine, "We're probably all—and I mean the whole doggone planet—immunosuppressed."[82] Much like what we're seeing happen with other species, our immune systems are being suppressed by toxins, and we are losing our ability to fight off infections. Eventually we could see mass epidemics from common diseases that our human bodies were once healthy enough to fend off. Now that scientific studies are making us more aware of the damaging effects of pollutants on life forms, we will, in the next decade, see an abundance of really scary results of the legacy of our unthinking pollution. Think about it, if Libya or Iraq were waging this kind of chemical warfare against us, we would

"The EPA ordered a freeze-out of [Dow Corporation's pesticide ingredient] DBCP on food and later banned all pesticides containing the substance. The action came after DBCP contaminated ground water in an area of thousands of square miles in the central valley in California and made agricultural workers who were exposed to it sterile. Aware of the pesticide's devastating effects, Dow sold much of its stockpile of DBCP to the Dole Corporation which used it on banana plantations in Costa Rica." [83]

—*Ross Brockley*, Multinational Monitor

PESTICIDE POISONING : [84]

• *48 die each minute, 25 million per year.*

• *In some third world countries, pesticides kill more than major diseases.*

—C. *Matthiessen*

Dear Dow, Monsanto, et al:

I realize that your decisions are based on your financial concerns and thus are just business decisions within the framework of our everyone-for-themselves world. However, I invite you to continue to read on so you may realize that there is a way that we can make the world work for everyone.

Love and Light,
Jack Reed

absolutely, without hesitation, bomb them into submission. But, instead it's us—our industries and our consumer choices—doing it to us slowly, but surely, as we allow the unconscionable slow poisoning of all life on the planet.

There are over 70,000 chemicals we use regularly, and 20 new chemical compounds enter the marketplace untested every day. Although we know a lot about the harm from some of these chemicals, we have complete data on only 2 percent and almost no data on 79 percent.[85]   We're treating nature and our bodies like a chemistry experiment gone bad. We mix in one toxic substance with other chemicals, some also toxic, and then wonder if we can get away with the resulting chemical reactions. The trouble with our experiments is that they have gone on far too long without proper monitoring and the results have often been insidiously subtle—like the poisoning of the Inuits. Then finally, when we see the results, we seem helpless to rectify the situation because of the economics involved.

The Livestock Connection:

Most of our farmland is used to produce food for the livestock that supply meat and dairy (the over-consumption of which is directly responsible for the very high rate of heart disease in the U.S.[86]). These animals have no way to eliminate the pesticides they ingest from feed and the growth hormones they're given. So when we consume non-organic animal protein, we also get a very concentrated dose of those poisons.

But perhaps the most damaging aspect of our fascination with meat and dairy relates in a way to one of the world's really serious health problems: malnutrition and starvation. According to the United Nations' Food and Agricultural Organization, two in five of the world's population are malnourished and nearly one in six people suffer from acute and chronic hunger.[87]

In the U.S., the number of people suffering from hunger rose from 20 to 30 million between 1985 and 1992, according to Tufts University School of Nutrition.[88]   About 60 million people in the world starve to death yearly.[89]   Some people make global correlations of those numbers with our meat and dairy consumption to

Scientists "astonished" by finding on harmful effects of pesticides

Researchers say chemicals that have minimal health impacts by themselves may be far more potent when combined in the environment

By Paul Recer
ASSOCIATED PRESS

WASHIINGTON — Pesticides that by themselves have been linked to breast cancer and male birth defects are up to 1,000 times more potent when combined, according to a study.

A federal environmental official called the finding "astonishing" and said if it is confirmed in other labs, it could force a revolution in the way that the environmental effects of chemicals are measured.

The study centered on endosulfan, dieldrin, toxaphene, and chlordane, all pesticides that are known to turn on a gene that makes estrogen in animals. Estrogen is a hormone that controls formation of female organs. A surplus of the hormone has been linked to breast cancer and to malformation of male sex organs.

By themselves, the pesticides have only a very weak effect on the estrogen gene, said John McLachlin of Tulane University, leader of a team that tested the chemicals.

"If you test them individually, you could almost conclude that they were non-estrogenic, almost inconsequential," he said. "But when we put them in combination, their potency jumped up 500 to 1,000-fold.

The study is to be published today in the journal *Science.*

"These findings are astonishing," said Dr. Lynn Goldman, chief of the Environmental Protection Agency's Office of Prevention, Pesticides and Toxic Substances. "The policy implications are enormous about how we screen environmental chemicals for estrogen effects."

The EPA monitors testing of environmental chemicals one at a time, said Goldman, and the agency now must consider how to test for effects of chemicals that might combine in the environment.

In recent years, many researchers have detected signs that certain industrial and pesticide chemicals released into the environment and absorbed by animals and humans may be able to disrupt hormones, perhaps causing cancer or birth defects.

Some of the chemical molecules, such as those tested by the McLaughlin group, act on the gene that makes estrogen. This can cause cells to produce a surplus of the hormone. Some researchers suggest that in male embryos, this added estrogen may affect formation of the sex organs. Estrogen surplus also has been linked to breast cancer, testicular cancer and lower sperm counts.

Researchers in Florida have found that at a lake where there was a pesticide spill more than half of the male alligators have smaller than normal penises and hormone levels near that of female alligators. In the Columbia River Basin, researchers found that young otters whose livers have absorbed insecticides have penises and testicles half their normal size.[90]

"The coastal zone may be the single most important portion of our planet. The loss of its biodiversity may have repercussions far beyond our worst fears."[91]

—G. Carleton Ray, University of Virginia

"There's no mystery to marine pollution. The worst problem today is the huge quantity of raw sewage and industrial effluent spewed into the sea, with no thought to consequences, from coastal cities all over the world."[92]

—Stjepan Keckes, United Nations Environment Program

"Of all environmental ills, contaminated water is the most devastating in consequences. Each year 10 million deaths are directly attributable to waterborne intestinal diseases. One-third of humanity labors in a perpetual state of illness or debility as a result of impure water, another third is threatened by the release into water of chemical substances whose long-term effects are unknown."[93]

—Phillip Quigg, Water: The Essential Resource

"Our planet is shrouded in water, and yet 8 million children under the age of five will die this year from lack of safe water. ... Two-thirds of the world's rural poor have no access to safe drinking water."[94]

—United Nations Environment Program

"The Environmental Protection Agency showed that more than 17,000, or 10 percent of the nation's rivers, streams, and bays are significantly polluted."[95]

—Citizen's Guide to Sustainable Development

point out that if Americans cut back their meat consumption by even 10 percent, we could adequately feed 100 million more people per year.[96]

Did you know that the production of meat, dairy, and eggs uses one-third of the total raw materials used by all sources in the U.S.,[97] that 70 percent of America's grain, 50 percent of all our water, and half our energy consumption goes for livestock production, and that *every pound* of grain-fed beef costs us 35 pounds of topsoil?[98] Because we import much of our meat from Central and South America, we could also help the rainforest situation, since much of the forests are being destroyed to raise cattle for export. The Rainforest Action Network reports that "each pound of Central American beef permanently destroys over 200 square feet of rainforest," and that, in just 20 years, Costa Rica, for example, destroyed 80 percent of its tropical rainforests for cattle production.[99]

Before globalization, most Third World countries were self-sufficient in their food production. Now, most of the Third World not only has to import food, but 75 percent of those imports are for corn, grain, and sorghum that are fed, not to people, but to livestock.[100] Then the livestock are either exported to the U. S. and other First World countries or consumed by the affluent few in the poor countries. Because less and less farmland is available to grow staples for the masses, the poor suffer. As the Worldwatch Institute reported, "In the economic competition for grain fields, the upper classes usually win."[101]

"In country after country, the demand for meat among the rich squeezing out staple production for the poor."[102]

—*John Robbins*

In addiction, by reducing our meat consumption we could conserve our diminishing water resources. It takes about 100 gallons of water to produce just one pat of butter.[103] Producing just one pound of meat takes 2500 gallons—the amount of water a typical American household uses for an entire month![104] We could float a destroyer with the water it takes to produce just one thousand-pound steer.[105] As former U.S. Senator Paul Simon warned, "It is no exaggeration to say that the conflict between humanity's growing

Vegetarian Baseball Team

A Japanese baseball team climbed from the cellar to first place by switching to a macrobiotic diet.

Beginning in October 1981, when he took overr as manager of the Seibu Lions, Tatsuro Hirooka prescribed a dietary change for his players, who had finished in last place the previous season. Hirooka limited their meat intake and banned polished rice and sugar altogether. Instead, he said, his players would eat unpol-ished rice, tofu, fish, and soybean milk. The following Spring, he ordered them into a vegetable and soy diet.

Hirooka told his men that meats and other "animal foods" increase an athlete's susceptibility to injuries. Natural foods, on the other hand, protect the body from sprains and dislocations and keep the mind clear.

The Lions took a lot of ribbing during the 1982 season. The manager of the Nippon-Ham Fighters—a team sponsored by a major meat company—called the Lions "the goat team" and sneered, "They are only eating weeds." But the Lions edged out the Ham Fighters for the Pacific League championship in what sports-writers called the "Vegetable vs. Meat War," then went on to beat the Chunichi Dragons in the Japan Series. Seibu again won the Pacific League championship and the Japan Series in 1983. Food for thought, isn't it?

"Significa" from Parade Magazine, *April 1984 by Irving Wallace, David Wallechinsky, Amy Wallace. Reprinted with permission from* Parade, *copyright © 1984*

Denmark's "Macrobiotic Experiment"

During the First World War, Denmark was blockaded, and widespread food short-ages and malnutrition were a very real threat. Mikkel Hinhede, superintendent of the Danish State Institute Food Research was appointed food advisor to the Danish government. Hinhede not only solved the problem—he achieved a complete reversal of the situation.

In the years before the war, Denmark imported inexpensive grain. Danish farmers bred pigs, cattle, and poultry, and sent eggs and butter to England. The Danes themselves were big eaters of meat and eggs. After the blockade, however, their grain supply was cut off, and there were over 5,000,000 grain-eating domestic animals and 3,500,000 to feed.

Immediately, Hinhede ordered that four-fifths of the pigs and one-fifth of the cattle be killed, so that more grain would be available for human consumption. In addition, consumption of pork and other meats was reduced or eliminated altogether. Hinhede also limited the production of alcoholic beverages, knowing that the grain used to make them could be better used to make a special whole meal bread called Kleiebrot. The Danes began to eat more porridge, more fresh greens, vegetables, peas, beans, and fruits, and lesser amounts of milk and butter.

From October, 1917, to October, 1918, the most trying period of the war, Denmark became the healthiest nation in Europe. In one year on a diet similar to the macrobi-otic diet, the cancer rate dropped by 60 percent and the death rate fell more than 40 percent. After the war, the Danes adopted their former diet and the mortality rate quickly returned to prewar levels.

From Mikkel Hinhede, "The Effects of Food Restriction During War on Mortality in Copenhagen," Journal of the American Medical Association 74 *(1920): 381-382.*

thirst and the projected supply of usable, potable water could result in the most devastating natural disaster since history has been recorded accurately, unless something happens to stop it."[106] A truly free market could solve this—if the cost of water to produce beef was not subsidized, the cost to produce the cheapest cut of hamburger would cost us $35 a pound.[107]

> *"Nothing will benefit human health and increase the chances for survival of life on Earth as much as the evolution to a vegetarian diet."*
>
> *—Albert Einstein*

Diminishing Health Care:

An estimated 1.8 billion people have no access to basic health care.[108] Even in the U.S., health care is in crisis. With skyrocketing prices, many who need it can't get it. When I worked for a rehabilitation agency, I had several clients with debilitating physical ailments, who slipped through the cracks in terms of treatment. One woman was virtually immobilized for years by constantly painful dental cavities. I tried for months to help her, only to find that, unless her ailment was life-threatening, no medical coverage was available. Try functioning daily with that much pain in your head.

Our health care is becoming more and more a program for the wealthy where the poor don't get served. In the 1980's the cost of health care increased 25 percent per year. This trend has caused company-sponsored health care plans to rapidly diminish. Since the government cannot seem to agree on what we can do about this, soon only those who can afford the rapidly increasing out-of-pocket expenses may have coverage. As government subsidies to health care on state and federal levels are reduced, hospitals are forced to take some patients at a loss. However, the costs are passed on to insurance companies and those who can afford to pay more, and that's driving up the costs. Now Medicare and Medicaid benefits are being cut too. But, even if we eventually go to socialized medicine, that would have to depend on tax dollars and no one has wanted to pay it. And, even if we go that route, many needed services will not be available to the middle class, let alone the poor.

NEEDS OF THE PLANET SEEDS OF CHANGE 37

Reprinted by permission of Johnny Hart and Creators Syndicate, Inc.

HERMAN By Jim Unger

"At these prices, I've got about 20 seconds
to recover and get out the main gate."

Herman® is reprinted with permission from Laughing Stock
Licensing, Inc., Ottawa, Canada. All rights reserved.

*"MY DOCTOR GAVE ME SIX MONTHS TO LIVE, BUT, WHEN I
COULDN'T PAY THE BILL, HE GAVE ME SIX MONTHS MORE."*
—WALTER MATTHAU

I knew a working woman who found herself feeling overly tired. When she went to her HMO doctors over the course of two years, they gave her the 10 minutes per visit that they felt that they had available and told her that her condition was stress and that she was just run down. Without ever taking a blood sample, the doctors eventually had her on three different antibiotics. Finally, she felt so bad that she went to a hospital emergency room on a Sunday. They did blood work and found that she had leukemia. She died on Tuesday. Her fate is a chilling example of the current state of our health care. Grotesquely, the managed-care system itself was successful—they kept their costs down.

THE ECONOMY

In the developing world today there are three billion people living in poverty.[109]   Of those, 1.3 billion live in absolute poverty.[110]We're not talking about what is defined as poverty in the U.S., we're talking about absolute, abject poverty where people can't meet the basic needs of food, safe drinking water, and shelter and where daily survival is the task at hand. Imagine, more than one out of every five in our brother/sisterhood of man exists in that condition!

While few of those people are Americans, we are not without our own crisis. Even with what is defined as poverty in the U.S. (which is rich compared to much of the world's population), over 15 percent of the people live in poverty.[111] That includes more than 20 percent of American children, among whom 5 million go hungry every day.[112]   Also, the average American worker is working longer hours for less money[113]—28.6 percent earned poverty-level wages in 1997, according to census data, up over 5 percent from 1973.[114] Millions more who hover above the line are likely to go below it if any crisis happens within the family. This is especially true because many low-end jobs have health risks, and limited or no health coverage. In fact, because most Americans have no savings, over 50 percent of the U.S. population is two paychecks or less away from potentially being homeless.[115]

But while the number of U.S. poor is growing, some of us are doing well. In the last 20 years, the after-tax incomes of the

"Those at the bottom of the economic heap have to contend with meager or unpredictable income despite long hours of backbreaking work, insufficient amounts of food and poor diets, lack of access to safe drinking water, susceptibility to preventable diseases, housing that provides few comforts and scant shelter, and the absence of social services that the better-off take for granted.

"Rich-poor disparities are about much more than just the access to modern conveniences or the inability to accumulate material wealth: they are often a matter of life and death."[116]

—*Michael Renner*, State of the World 1997

wealthiest one percent doubled, while 80 percent of the families saw their incomes remain the same or decline.[117]   The highest-earning four percent now make more than the bottom 90 percent![118] (It is possible that, if we factor in unreported, untraceable incomes, the incomes of the wealthiest 1,000 Americans might exceed the combined incomes of all the rest of us.)   Also, the richest one percent own more than the bottom 51 percent or, put another way, the richest one million families own more than the rest of us combined.[119]   Since 1968, the middle class has lost about 10 percent of its share of income to the wealthy.[120]   The bottom line is that the rich are getting richer, the poor poorer, and the middle class is shrinking.[121]

Given this trend, maybe our nation will begin to resemble the type of rich-poor gap that we see in much of the rest of the world. According to the Worldwatch Institute, in 1960 the wealthiest 20 percent of the world's people accounted for 70 percent of the global income.[122] The United Nations Development Program reported that by 1993 their share had increased to 85 percent! Meanwhile, the poorest one billion accounted for less than two percent of the global income.[123] While our situation is getting worse, the rich-poor gap in the rest of the world is still more than ten times that of ours, and the poor try to survive on less than 50 cents a day.[124]

How many Americans are really doing well? Just as the Senate tightened up the bankruptcy law in 2001, credit card debt at the end of the year 2000 had jumped 13 percent from the previous year to $2.9 trillion.[125]   In 1996 Standard & Poors reported that the average U.S. household had credit card debt of $3,400, more than double the $1,600 from a decade earlier.[126] By 1999 the *average* credit card debt carried by households not able to pay off their monthly bills rose to over $7500.[127]   Meanwhile, only 38 percent of Americans have any savings at all, and, of those that do, their savings average only $1,000.[128]   For people in their late fifties, their median savings, as they approach retirement, is only $10,000.[129]

Much of the blame for our economic woes had been placed on the deficit problem. Since the creation of the Federal Reserve in

1913 (illegally I might add—it was never ratified by two-thirds of the states in its final form), the national debt has grown to close to $5.7 trillion by the end of 2000. We'll see if the government can repay the debt (without continuing to borrow from social security), but meanwhile the interest alone is over $4 billion per week and there is over 13 times more debt than there is money in circulation to pay for it.

Our government creates money for itself through inflation—it borrows money at "x" level and pays it back after inflation has taken its toll with cheaper and cheaper dollars. Most victimized by this are the people with the lowest incomes because an ever-increasing percentage of their incomes must go to the basic survival expenses of food and shelter. However, this pattern is now also true of the middle class as more of their income must go to just covering the basics and more and more debt is accumulated.

It's a downward cycle that is lowering the quality of life for most of us. Politically the candidates often pledge more jobs as being the answer. However, with the wealth-poverty gap both in the U.S. and abroad, this creates a dilemma, because the ability of an increasing number of people to buy anything but necessities diminishes. Moreover, the other dilemma with increasing jobs is even more serious because it affects the sustainability of the planet. In our economic system, the idea is that we must keep creating jobs and manufacturing items for consumption. As we have seen, this has led to using up our planetary resources and creating pollution on a scale which is threatening all life on the planet. The Worldwatch Institute reported that "As a result of our population size, consumption patterns, and technology choices, we have surpassed the planet's carrying capacity."[130] In fact, at the standard of living now enjoyed by the industrialized nations, the world would only support two billion people[131]—about one-third of the planet's current population. The U.S. has 6 percent of the world population. If our levels of capitalism and technology could be expanded to the rest of the planet, there would only be enough for 18 percent of the people, and the other 82 percent would have nothing at all.[132]

Speaking of the rest of the planet, that brings us to the foreign debt predicament. While the World Bank and the IMF loan money to Third World countries in an effort to improve their economies (and create more markets for our products), most of it goes to the top wealthy few. As a result, the countries still are unable to repay their foreign debts and the burden falls on the poor as inflation rises. As an example, Russia has defaulted on billions as their government has colluded with siphoning money to a few while the masses suffer. Because the borrowing countries can't afford to pay even the interest on their debts, the IMF and World Bank have to keep loaning money to prevent them from defaulting.[133] This means that an even greater percentage of the assets in many of our banks are virtually worthless. Even in the U.S., banks are allowed to loan money on a fraction of their assets. For example, if a bank has $7 billion in assets, the government would allow them to loan $100 billion—$93 billion more than the bank has. This is money created out of nothing. What holds the system together is a confidence game. However, if there was ever a mass run on the banks, they would fold because the money isn't there. Also, if any of the major debtor countries were to default, this could not only cause a crisis with our banks but also would endanger the international banking system.[134]

So, if the U.S. has a compounding national debt it may not be able to pay and if many other countries have debts they can't possibly pay, the logical question is: who's got the money? The Japanese was once a popular answer, but let's look at what their situation was even before their late 1990's economic woes. Even in 1990 the average price of a home in Tokyo was over $430,000 (U.S. dollars) and the average size of that home was 674 square feet.[135] At those prices most workers in Japan could not afford to buy a home. In addition most Tokyo workers have to travel more than two hours to and from work and 20 percent travel more than four hours each day and that traveling is done in standing-room-only transportation systems with people packed in like sardines.[136] With their economic situation worsening, Japan's youth are bearing the brunt of corporate restructuring/downsiz-ing, and record numbers of Japanese college graduates are now failing to get jobs.[137]   But among the people with jobs, the six day work week is still common and many public services we take for granted—i.e. sewers—are sometimes still not available.   Maybe the Japanese didn't have the money after all. So who's got the money?

Well, as most us are aware, whoever controls the money usually gets to make the decisions in most countries. Previously we gave statistics that the income of the wealthiest one million families in the U.S. was greater than that of the rest of us combined. But again, that's based solely on what people report. In the complex web of who controls corporations including multinationals, people have traced the real control of the world's wealth to a few people who can largely pull the strings to make happen what they want to happen, when they want it to happen, and how they want it to happen. For example, Unilever Corp., having over 3,000 companies in 96 countries with sales larger than the economies of many countries, is one such transnational.[138] A few hundred of these transnationals control entire sectors of the global economy. They have grown beyond the reaches of governments and serve only themselves. They pretty much can do as they please according to their Golden Rule: he who has the gold, rules.

But even if you discount that degree of consolidation of power, we are well aware of the economic influence on politics. This happens both at the election level, through large financial contributions, and at the decision level, through lobbying and other economic pressures. This can happen at any level from local to national and even in the media. For example, the John Robbins Institute produced a one-hour television program that presented the destructive health and environmental realities of our excessive meat and dairy consumption. However, because the meat and dairy industries in their many forms do a lot of TV advertising, they were able to use their influence to block this show from being seen on network television.   The show was thus relegated to Public Broadcasting, which does not have sponsors. As a result of the limited exposure, most people are still unaware of the serious health and environmental issues involved in our excessive consumption of animal proteins. The messages and information we are exposed to in the media are largely controlled by big money interests.

POLITICAL

Supposedly our First Amendment guarantees free speech, but we, as the previous example shows, have limited free speech in this country. The intention of the Bill of Rights was to prevent domination of public thought and discourse by the few.[139] But, because big money interests control the media, they can usually buy getting out their message to the vast majority of the people versus anyone else who has something to say to the contrary. Thus, these big corporations can continue their assault on the environment. Because they invoke their First Amendment privilege to protect their saying whatever they want—true or not— they can get out their message and drown out the opposition.[140]

The power of media-spent money in shaping our lives is remarkable. The average American adult sees 21,000 commercials per year, and 75 percent of them are from the largest 100 corporations. In fact, corporations spend more money on advertising than is spent on all secondary education in the U.S.[141] So, let's do the math: the largest 1000 companies in America account for over 60 percent of the GNP (leaving the balance to 11 million small businesses) and 40 percent of the nation's wealth.[142] Also, one percent of Americans own fully 60 percent of corporate equities. For most people, the information and choices they are aware of are basically being controlled by a relatively few people.

More directly, in the political arena, these few people exert even more influence over our lives. As Paul Hawkin wrote, "Corporations have created a multi-billion dollar industry of lobbyists, public relations firms, scholarly papers prepared by conservative think tanks, artificially generated 'people's' campaigns, 'expert' witnesses at public hearings who work for, or are paid by, corporate interests and lawyers based in Washington, D.C., whose sole purpose is to influence lawmakers and regulators in their offices, in four-star restaurants, at lavish receptions, on overseas junkets. Where do congressmen go to bone up on issues? To Palm Springs to play golf, to Bermuda to snorkel, to Snowbird to ski, to Las Vegas to gamble. During the 1989-90 legislative session, members of the House of Representatives took

"We have devolved from a representative democracy to a corporate democracy. We do not have a system of one person, one vote. This is a system of 1 million dollars, a million votes."[143]

—Senator Russell D. Feingold

"Human rights, labor rights, and environmental rights are being completely subordinated to the right to make a profit."

—Julie Light, Managing Editor of Corporate Watch

4,000 privately funded trips, almost ten per member. About three-quarters of their junkets were paid by the corporations."[144]

The point is that the average person has very little say in our "democracy." Our freedom of speech, as was envisioned by our founding fathers, is not being protected. This was supposed to be a government by the people and for the people, and it no longer is that, and possibly never will be again as long as we cling to the everyone-for-themselves model.

We, the people of the United States of America, supposedly live in a "democracy." We therefore look to the political system to make changes for us. But, while our "democracy" may be better than most, there are so many things wrong with politics both here and abroad that it is easy to blame politicians for our current environmental, health, economic, and social predicaments. However, for the purposes of looking at solutions to the world's imbalances, I'm only going to look at a couple of issues related to politics.

The first issue is that we as a nation have become a collection of minority groups—by ideals, values, regions, age, economics, as well as by race. In this political system, hardly anyone feels that his or her needs are being met. As a result, in the election process we generally vote *against* someone or some issue and *for* what we see as the lesser of evils. Politicians know this and therefore run ads during elections where the opposition is routinely vilified. They do it because it's effective—we don't trust anyone, we know no one is really going to represent us, and thus we're looking for the best reason to vote against someone or something.

An article in the *Los Angeles Times* carried the subhead: "Polls and interviews show voters are angry at politicians, bewildered by the issues and disgusted with the choices. At stake may be democracy itself."[145] Just before Colin Powell announced in 1995 that he was not a candidate for President of the United States, the *Times* also ran an article titled "GOP Candidates Start Anti-Powell Research" and subheaded: "Politics: Information is being gathered on general's public record, private life. Dole, Buchanan camps are said to be leading the most aggressive drives."[146] This

GOP Candidates Start Anti-Powell Research

■ **Politics:** Information is being gathered on general's public record, private life. Dole, Buchanan camps are said to be leading the most aggressive drives.

By JOHN M. BRODER
TIMES STAFF WRITER

Copyright, 1995, *Los Angeles Times*. Reprinted with permission.

FEIFFER

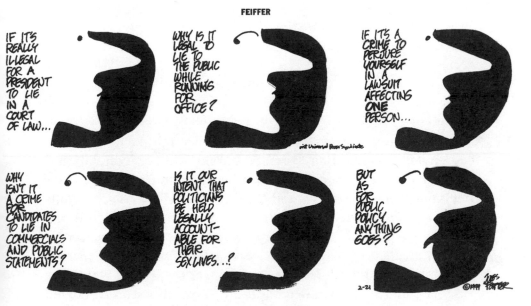

is a time of againstness, as we, as a people and as individuals, see the American dream slipping away.

One of the basic tenets of democracy was that the people would be responsible voters. But that is now almost impossible. To find out who the candidates really are, which special interest groups they are economically responsible to, how much integrity they have, and what the propositions you're voting on really mean, would require a staff of investigators and analysts working full time for you.

When the constitution was written, few had the right to vote, and they probably knew something about the men and the more simple issues of the time that they were voting on. As the population increased, government expanded, the territory of the U.S. grew, the Industrial Revolution produced drastic lifestyle changes, and people accumulated vast fortunes and economic/political influence, this all resulted in our knowing less and less about the people and issues we were voting on. As more and more decisions were reached over time which alienated first one group of people in certain life circumstances and then another group, eventually almost everyone in this collection of minority groups has been left feeling under-represented and with their needs unmet. I think that most of us consider ourselves minorities lacking in power and with little respect for our decision makers who have so much control over our lives by virtue of laws, taxes, services, etc.

I've already touched on the second issue I'd like to explore— the economic connection to politics. Why can't we, on national, state, and often local levels, clean up the environment and make decisions that are in our overall best interests? The answer usually is that economic interests exert a powerful influence on all levels. As Bill Bradley said, "I believe money is eating away at the core of democracy like acid eating away at cloth, and it's time to do something about it."[147]

A few of the more horrifying examples of this economic influence concern how big money interests have dictated the way we produce energy. First, Nicola Tesla, whose genius and electronic inventions dwarfed those of Thomas Edison at the turn of the century, invented and demonstrated a way to send electricity in waves through the ground without wires. That electricity could then power a light, a motor, and even a city in virtually limitless supply. From his proposed power station at Niagara Falls, he could have cleanly powered the entire planet. But, despite his credibility—earned from his hundreds of inventions that built the Edison and Westinghouse corporations and are the foundation for our electronic age—he could get no financing. He was told that this free and virtually limitless source of energy would undermine the economic interests of these corporations and the very rich, powerful individuals who owned and controlled them. Tesla therefore set out to build a power station with his own money to give free and clean energy to all the people of the planet. When his station was almost completed (and his own money almost all spent), it was burned down and destroyed. What a different life we would be living on this planet if the economic interests had not stopped Tesla. There would have been no threat to the earth from the burning of fossil fuels. Interestingly, Nicola Tesla—perhaps the greatest inventor of all time—remains virtually unknown to most Americans, overshadowed by his contemporary, Edison, although it was Tesla who really ushered in the electronic age.

Another clean source of fuel can be obtained from the hemp plant. The fuel burns cleanly and the plant also helps regenerate the soil. Farmers in this country used to grow a lot of hemp, which they could convert to fuel for their farm equipment while also producing a multitude of products—even clothing. However, hemp is also a cheap source of paper, and this caused its demise. As Hugh Downs reported in his commentary for *ABC News*, William Randolph Hearst, the newspaper mogul, owned timber interests and paper mills and consequently had a huge economic interest in using trees, not hemp, for paper.[148] Therefore, through his newspapers and other economic controls, he ran a campaign to illegalize hemp. He called it by the Spanish name "marijuana" and focused solely on the narcotic property of the plant's flowers. As a result, he succeeded in legally banning hemp from being grown. However, during World War Two when the U.S. needed fuel, it again paid farmers to grow hemp. A 1942 U.S. Dept. of Agriculture film, "Hemp for Victory," promoted the value of hemp and urged that farmers plant hundreds of thousands of acres. However, after the war Hearst triumphed. Otherwise we could be using clean-burning fuel and safely produced paper without the deadly dioxins from the bleaching of wood pulp, which have ravaged our ground water and waterways and the life forms dependent on them. Downs pointed out that hemp can be used to produce over 25,000 environmentally friendly products and that *Popular Mechanics* ran a 1938 article about hemp called, "New Billion Dollar Crop."[149] Of course, the key to whether something gets produced is: billions to whom? If powerful forces stand to lose, they would rather sacrifice our health and the environment. That doesn't necessarily make them evil, it's just that our everyone-for-themselves paradigm has long fostered these kinds of results.

HEMP THROUGH HISTORY[150]

- *The first Guttenburg Bible was printed on hemp paper.*
- *Christopher Columbus' sails and ropes were made from hemp.*
- *The first drafts of the Declaration of Independence were printed on hemp paper.*
- *Benjamin Franklin owned a mill that made hemp paper.*
- *The first American flag was made out of hemp.*
- *George Washington and Thomas Jefferson grew it. In 1794 Washington said, "Make the most out of hemp seed. Sow it everywhere."*
- *Henry Ford, who wanted to build and fuel cars using farm products, tested a car body made of hemp and other bio-based materials, and it ran off ethanol.*
- *The first Levi's jeans were made from hemp.*

Even without hemp, the technology existed to make non-polluting cars years ago. However, there have been a multitude of inventions that were either bought by the auto and energy industries, then put on the shelf or else the inventors have been harassed or forced out of business. Still, as in the time of Tesla, the big money interests that control the energy business also control our transportation and thus the quality of our environment. The government could clean up the environment by mandating that all pollutants be eliminated within three to five years. That would create the time to produce the changes, but it won't happen because certain huge economic interests would have too much to lose—which would be good for almost everyone, but bad for them. But we will probably see some good things happen, i.e. solar recharging stations for electric cars, as soon as the oil industry figures out a way they can make money on a changeover to solar-electric.

One of my personal pet peeves is the fluoridation of our water supplies. Fluoride is a poison that must be removed from fertilizer for plants and is known to be linked to all sorts of damage to our bodies from bone disease to genetic damage to cancer.[151] It is even more toxic than lead! It kills mice, rats, and humans the same way it kills bacteria in the mouth—it poisons them. However, we have been sold on the idea that it reduces tooth decay to the point that it's hard to find toothpaste without it. Yet all the responsible studies have shown that fluoride has no effect on slowing tooth decay,[152] and even the union that represents all the scientists and professionals at the Environmental Protection Agency were so convinced about the dangers of fluoride that they unanimously voted in July 1997 to take a stand against water fluoridation. Check out the required warning on your fluoride toothpaste: "WARNING: Keep out of the reach of children under 6 years of age. If you accidentally swallow more than used for brushing, seek professional help or contact a poison control center immediately."

So why, when Japan and nearly all of Europe have rejected fluoridation, is fluoride still used in the U. S.? Again, follow the money. Industries stuck with disposing of their fluoride (it's classified as a toxic waste—only slightly less toxic than arsenic) originally promoted it as a means of reducing tooth decay. Commercial interests, such as the phosphate fertilizer industry and aluminum manufacturers get to sell their hazardous waste product to municipalities for a profit, rather than having to pay the $7,000 per 5,000 gallon tanker expense of disposal for the fluoride toxic waste.[153] Now, even though toothpaste manufacturing companies know the truth about fluoride, they are afraid to tell us that they have been mistaken all these years, again because of the toxic disposal costs as well as exposure to lawsuits. So more and more cities fluoridate their water, and more and more people continue to die and suffer as a result of these financial wheels that have been set into motion. However, through grassroots citizen's movements and class-action lawsuits, I believe that the truth will eventually come out on fluoridation, and, when it does, both the government and some major corporations will be liable for billions in damages. For more information about fluoridation, refer to www.fluoridealert.org, www.fluoride-journal.com, or www.saveteeth.org. But I digress, as this book is not about againstness—it's about showing a way that we can all live together for The Highest Good Of All.

Politically one needs money to have power in this country. One also needs money to be heard. As a consequence, the poorer and uneducated people, for the most part, lack the power, the voice, and the money to change the social/economic/educational systems to truly meet our needs. Therefore, we have generation after generation of people in a lowly socio-economic position. This has an impact on everyone, not just on this group, as we have to finance welfare and the cost of crime driven by the desperation of poverty. Many of the generational poor who resort to crime feel that they don't have anything to lose because, if people don't have any hope of improving or getting by, then laws and prisons are no deterrent. So the political system is inadequate to meet the needs of the poor, those with no money or influence. As a result, society as a whole not only has to suffer the direct consequences of crime but also has to spend money for the legal system, for jails and prisons and supervision—money that could be spent on education, housing, and opportunities to improve those peoples' lives and give them hope.

SOCIAL

Some crimes, as I've said, grow out of economic desperation. When I was a state rehabilitation counselor, I had the unique opportunity to look at drugs through the eyes of some of the users and street pushers. Society has the attitude that we must put these "bad guys" into prison. But, when I got to know them and their backgrounds, they were people who felt trapped by their depressed living situations and economic opportunities. Selling drugs offered a way out, a chance for the good life. As I worked to help them get back on their feet after either incarceration or drug treatment programs, I found them easy to love and to empathize with. They, in turn, really responded to love and understanding, given without judgment. I also worked with many others who didn't sell, but used drugs and alcohol as an escape from their lives. Again, I empathized with their pain, and the sense of isolation and alienation that drove them to try to escape, and, again, love and understanding helped.

Incidentally, it's no mystery why Third World farmers would grow plants for drugs. Multinational corporations have gone into countries and bought up resources at the lowest possible price, then manufactured goods and sold them back at the highest possible prices. With few or no economic options, the farmers have been forced to grow the most lucrative cash crops to sell to drug dealers to try to survive. Interestingly, the multinationals' rape of the Third World then cycles back into the industrialized nations in the form of illegal drugs. The same is true of pesticides which were banned here because they were dangerous. They get sold to Third World countries and cycle back to us in the food we buy from them.

Another Third World issue we hear a lot about is overpopulation. The population is now about 6.2 billion at the turn of the century and projected to approach 11 billion by 2050. If people indeed survive, most of that growth will be in the already impoverished Third World, and, with the capacity of the world to grow food already waning—due to topsoil loss and generations of agriculture abuses to the land—the least productive areas will be these same countries. So, throughout the world, we will undoubtedly see ever-increasing starvation tragedies, like those we have already seen in poor countries.

Grandmother, 71, Arrested; Did Despair Lead to Crime?

■ Stress: As money woes and illness dogged longtime foster mother, she allegedly attempted an armed robbery.

By ABIGAIL GOLDMAN
TIMES STAFF WRITER

The district attorney's office is considering charging 71-year-old Mary Ruth Blanco with attempted armed robbery. Her family in West Covina is considering the way mounting financial trouble can drive good people to do bad things.

After a lifetime of taking care of others—53 years as a wife, 41 years as a mother and 35 years as a foster parent to scores of needy children, police said—Blanco was on the verge of losing everything because of something she never cared much about: money

Last week, she and her 75-year-old husband, Raymond, received notice that the IRS was going to garnish half of his pension check—$750—for eight months. A few days later, their mortgage company threatened to foreclose over $900 in unpaid property taxes.

Increasingly ill with diabetes. the grandmother who helped care for her daughter, son-in-law and 2½-week-old granddaughter was becoming desperate. Saturday night, authorities say, she snapped.

Blanco took a relative's vintage 32-caliber Colt automatic handgun, drove her red pickup to a nearby Unocal self-serve station on Pacific Avenue and demanded that a clerk empty the register, police said. Safe behind bulletproof glass.

Please see GRANDMOTHER, A23

But let's get back to the issue of the isolation and alienation which I believe is the crux of many of our societal problems. We've already looked at the desperation of poverty, lack of opportunity, and the crowding of people into inner cities (all of which keep getting worse in our current economic times), but let's look at another inhumane practice that goes on all the time. The largest, least represented and most disenfranchised minority group in this country is people who are elderly. I dislike using that label *"the* elderly" because it's stereotyping and dehumanizing. People are people first, and should not be lumped into groups like *"the* handicapped," *"the* Blacks" or *"the* foreigners." What we often do with older people in this country, especially those with few financial resources (which is the situation for most people over 65), is to lump them together in old age homes to die. We see many of them as mentally incapacitated and often they are treated as children. But how did those behaviors come about?

I think that isolation and alienation may, in fact, be the biggest problem of all the problems we've looked at. We are a society of every-person-(or, if we're lucky, family)-for-themselves. With that system, many people feel like they don't have the power and connections to really participate in life.

We must also realize that, unlike most of you who are reading this, many people really have no idea how to get in touch with and share feelings. They don't know how to get and give nurturing in their lives, how to express their needs and get them met, and how to love and be loved. They therefore have no idea how to form real friendships or to make any real connection with others and even with themselves. Thus, as people grow older, many are really on their own, alone inside and alone outside. We may eventually label them as being mentally ill or senile. But what if they had had the opportunity to really form friendships and a support system spanning all age groups? Maybe then those same people would be leading vibrant, healthy lives. It's interesting that our educational system doesn't teach us the essence of communicating and how to really share ourselves and get our needs met, when this has more to do with success in life on all levels than anything else we could be taught.

HIGHLIGHTS

The Senate sent a fiscal 1997 spending bill to President Clinton on Monday The measure covers nine Cabinet level departments and other agencies for the new fiscal year, which begins today The measure includes:

● $1 billion for the Drug Enforcement Administration, more than Clinton requested or the House and Senate approved initially.

● $396 million to build federal prisons, $100 million higher than Clinton's request

● $588 million for Commerce Department high technology programs, $238 million less than Clinton's request.

● $352 million for international peacekeeping, $73 million less than Clinton's request.

● $385 million for overseas family planning organizations, but delays its expenditure until March at the earliest.

● $800 million for work on two attack submarines.

Reprinted with permission of the *Santa Barbara News Press*.[155]

$385 million for overseas family planning and over twice that amount for TWO attack subs! Which priority is the greater threat to our planet?

Did you know that, according to Surgeon General David Satcher's 1999 report on mental health, during any given year one in five Americans suffer from some form of mental illness?[156] Indeed, the isolation/alienation factor has been increasing for all ages and situations. According to a 1990 survey, the "Youth Risk Surveillance Report" published by the U.S. Dept. of Health and Human Services, Centers for Disease Control and Prevention, for grades 9-12, in 1950 the suicide rate was 2.2 per 100,000. In 1990 the rate was 11.3. But more than that, 27.3 percent of the 9-12 graders had thought seriously of suicide, 16.3 percent had devised a specific suicide plan, and 8.3 percent had tried to kill themselves.[157] The Centers' 1995 reconfirmed these numbers.[158]

What is happening that is causing over a quarter of our population about to enter adulthood to think seriously about killing themselves? We've already touched on the economic deprivation and the growing number of poor, but this problem pervades the entire economic range. I suggest that again the cause is the isolation and alienation that people feel. We've had a breakdown of the family system where single parents or parents both working is the norm. We have families relocating away from their extended families and friends due to job locations and the economics of finding affordable housing. In short, many people have lost their support systems, and they feel alone and powerless to make the meaningful, nurturing connections that all of us need to have in our lives on a daily basis.

For some people, their support system and meaning in their lives is derived from their employment. But most workers also look forward to retirement and to get that retirement income. In most companies one can retire at 55 or 60 or 63, but the real financial rewards are to retire at age 65. From California's Department of Rehabilitation's stress management training, I learned that, according to insurance statistics, most people who work until age 65 live an average of one more year.[158] One year! That's one reason why the financial rewards are much greater for retirement at 65— it costs the financial institutions much less. As people leave work, meager as that support system may have been, they move into the separation of lives devoid of a support system, and they don't

by Jim Unger

"Let's face it, Stella, we've grown apart.
We need two televisions!"

Herman® is reprinted with permission from Laughing Stock
Licensing, Inc., Ottawa, Canada. All rights reserved.

know how to get in touch with their own needs, let alone how to get those needs met.

So the lives of most people at all ages are being fragmented. This happens through the economics of work and living locations, the isolation of our lives (both in terms of our diminishing support systems and the corresponding increasing difficulty in getting our needs met), and our growing alienation from others—including the bureaucracies and decision makers that control much of our lives—and especially from ourselves. Most of us feel like we don't have the time or energy to examine what we really want to do and how we really want to live. We live our lives with traffic and commutes where everything is spread out—we live here, work there, shop somewhere else, and, if we have time left over, exercise and do our recreation somewhere else, and so on, ad nauseam.

In addition, our lives are permeated with responsibilities and worrying about the pressures of paying bills, and taxes, trying to make ends meet, how to invest, what to buy, who to call, and everything else that must be done to keep afloat in life. At the same time, hanging over our heads is the constant reality of what would happen to us if we didn't handle these pressuring matters. I think that's what's so great about the vacations where we really get away. We are so trapped in our frenetic schedules, in our world of clocks, computers, and correspondence that we look to vacations, if we can afford them, to get away from all the responsibilities and live "in the now" for a brief time. According to a 1990 Harris Poll, Americans had one-third the leisure time that they had in 1973.[160] According to the Labor Department, nationwide, we are now working the highest number of hours since 1947, our overtime hours are the highest since the weapons producing years of World War II, and more people than ever are holding down multiple jobs.[161] Yet most people continue to experience a gradually eroding standard of living.

We need to be able to relax and to have real, meaningful, and nurturing connections with others and especially to get centered within ourselves. But because we usually spend so much time with work and economic concerns and we often live in such diverse places (even within the same city) from our support systems, most of us get together with good friends infrequently. Others have so little time and energy or skill to even culture such friendships that they have few real connections with people. Also, we typically have little time for exercise and little opportunity for fun recreation with others. It's so much easier to just be entertained by television.

One of the end results of the fragmentation of society and of the feelings of separation and powerlessness is what I call the element of "theyness." As we increasingly lead our lives in an every-person-for-her/himself fashion, we see others as "them," not as one of us, not as one of our family. We've become very impersonal in our dealings with others. However, our choices and actions will affect someone or some people we don't even know. Yet, as a rule, most of us don't see or care about that impact and don't understand that the effect of our actions eventually comes back on us.

As long as it's not me or someone close to me being affected, who cares? For example, when we're out and about (or even at home or work), it seems innocuous for us to just toss out our trash and litter because "they" will pick it up. It's too much of an inconvenience to carry it around and even more inconvenient to recycle it. So we just send things "away" for "them" to pick up and take to landfills without a thought about the effect that our choice is having on the environment, on economics, and on the people we pay to be "them."

Another of the "them" groups that plays a part in our daily lives is the farm workers. We see them bent over in the fields, working for very little and living in usually squalid conditions. The field pickers usually have no health insurance and end up with painful chronic back problems as well as lung, skin and other diseases from handling and breathing toxic pesticides and fertilizers. But, as long as we have relatively low-cost food on the table, most of us never think about "them." If we did, we might drive up the price of food, so it s better to just isolate ourselves from any thoughts of "them."

But "theyness" involves more than throwing things away for "them" to handle and minorities such as farm workers and people who are homeless or elderly. In our isolated and alienated lives, almost everything we do, like using products that either inhibit the sustainability of the planet and/or pollute the planet, has an element of "theyness" in it. However, the cumulative effect of all our "they" and "away" actions is that it all comes back on us in the form of taxes, health risks, and the regimentation and authority of society that cramps and preoccupies our lives.

Chapter 3
FOR THE HIGHEST GOOD
OF ALL LIFE

So, enough with the problems we're facing on so many different levels. Although you may have a different viewpoint on some of these problems, I think we can all agree that we must not benumb ourselves to the apparent overwhelming nature of our planetary plight, and that we must do something to make the planet work better for all of us. Because physical change initially comes about from a change in consciousness, the first step in that process must be moving into the consciousness that we, out of a heartfelt response, really want to make the planet work for all life. For all the reasons I gave in the first chapter, I call that consciousness "The Highest Good Of All." I now issue you a challenge to drop your reference points and assumptions about how we have set up life to work on this planet and to look at the world very differently than you may have up to this point. Then, with the consciousness of making it work for all of us, we'll start to look at how we can physically make the world work for The Highest Good Of All.

Let's start again with the basic truth: *there is enough on the planet for all of us—there are enough resources and manpower for all of us to live not only abundantly but also in balance with nature.* In fact, given an ideal utilization of those resources and manpower, we could create a model where everyone could essentially live like responsible millionaires on a pollution-free planet. Yet, in the midst of this potential for plenty, we constantly read that a lack of money is being used as the excuse for not doing—for not providing needed healthcare, for not cleaning up and taking better care of the environment, for not enabling retired people to live a more abundant life, for not providing better education, and so on.

A SUMMARY OF THE WORLD

If we could shrink the Earth's population into a village of precisely 100 people—with all existing human ratios remaining the same, it would look like this:

• *There would be 57 Asians, 21 Europeans, 14 from the Western Hemisphere [North and South], and 8 Africans.*

• *51 would be female, 49 would be male. 70 would be nonwhite, 30 white.*

• *70 would be non-Christian, 30 Christian.*

• *50 percent of the entire world's wealth would be in the hands of only 6 people and all 6 would be citizens of the United States.*

• *80 would be in substandard housing.*

• *70 would be unable to read.*

• *50 would suffer from malnutrition.*

• *Only one would have a college education. No one would own a computer.*

IN A TYPICAL DAY ON THE PLANET:[1]

• *250,000 people are added to the world's population.*

• *140 species are doomed to extinction.*

• *144,000 new vehicles are made.*

• *12,000 barrels of crude are spilled into the ocean.*

• *Forests covering one-half the size of Los Angeles are destroyed.*

HOW DID WE GET TO THIS PLACE?

As a starting point for looking at where we are now and what we can do about it, let's first journey back and look at where we've come from. In the ancient world, people would trade products such as grain for sheep or cows. Eventually, to avoid hauling around real sheep or real sacks of grain to make the deals, they started using tokens to represent the products. This trading system mutually benefited groups because it could improve their lifestyles over what they each could have alone.

This system continued to evolve through the centuries— sometimes peacefully and other times violently, as some groups would want more than just what they could obtain through barter. Several of these aggressive groups were the Western European Francs, Goths, Anglos and Saxons. These peoples, the descendants of barbarians whose histories were rooted in violence and centuries of fighting, would become the first people in history to spread their civilization across the entire planet. What they had in common was that they became the heirs of the Holy Roman Empire and came to believe themselves to be a chosen people.

But how was it that such small-scale countries and economics could end up dominating the world several hundred years later? India and China had all the inventions and many times the people. The answer is that the concept of individualism came out of the Western European countries. The West opted for individual (as opposed to collective) rights, the private ownership of property, and a free market economy. The ideas of individualism along with the world view that these people believed themselves to be the chosen people who could do what they wanted in the world, in the hands of the limited democracies—run by the property owners and the movers of money—were the basis of the phenomenal success and spread of the West through their conquests of others.

1492 marked the beginning of the systematic war waged against the native peoples of the world by Western arms, religion, and ideology. The conquest was accompanied by a genocide unparalleled in history. In the next century over two-thirds of the native population of the Americas died through violence or

disease.   Columbus wrote to Queen Isabella of Spain, "Our
European civilization will bring Light to the natives in their
darkness, but for ourselves we will gain gold and with gold we
will be able to do what we want in the world."[2] By this time gold
was the token of choice for trading, and the West forcibly took it
from the New World in exchange for death and religion. A strong
case can be made that in pre-Columbian times, the lives of the
natives of the Americas were better than they are now. Imagine
the arrogance of the explorers who came to lands where people
had no concept of private property. They simply planted flags and
claimed lands—reaching far beyond where they could even see—
for their monarchs. It didn't matter that there were already
millions of people there who had lived there for thousands of
years, people who viewed the land as sacred and not something
that could be owned. This audacity came from the consciousness
of superiority, and, thus, they viewed the natives as God-forsaken
heathens.   This action by the explorers, colonists and various
financial exploiters was as presumptuous and audacious as people
coming here in their spaceships from another planet, viewing us as
inferior, and claiming whatever land they chose for their planet.

Yet, it was only in relatively recent times, during the enclosure
movement in 15th century England, when common rights to land
were abolished and individual title to land was established. As
usual, power and the concentration of wealth in the hands of a few
were the motives as 15,000 peasants were cleared off 794,000 acres
in Scotland to create just 29 farms with 131,000 sheep. Each farm
had only a single family and imported servants. This institution-
alized ownership of land was deemed necessary to launch the
wool industry, and, from that time on, land became something that
could be bought and sold for whatever the market could bring and
could be passed on from one generation to the next. It also spelled
the end to the concept held by many cultures that the land was
God's land, and it was inconceivable that it could be bought or
sold. Individual ownership of land further set the stage for the
exploitation of the peoples of the planet and the environment.

Starting in the 17th century, people given to exploitation to
further their own ends misinterpreted the teachings of Francis

For some reason Columbus Day is a U.S. holiday. Perhaps it's because Columbus nakedly typifies the every-person-for-himself approach to life—even at the huge expense of others—that characterizes our heritage. In his book, A People's History of the United States, *Howard Zinn recounts Columbus's first new world contact:*

"When Columbus and his sailors came ashore, carrying swords, speaking oddly, the Arawaks ran to greet them, brought them food, water, gifts. He [Columbus] later wrote of them in his log:

"'They...brought us parrots and balls of cotton and spears and many other things which they exchanged for the glass beads and hawks' bells. They willingly traded everything they owned....They do not bear arms, and do not know them, for I showed them a sword, they took it by the edge and cut themselves out of ignorance. They have no iron. Their spears are made of cane...With 50 men we could subjugate them all and make them do whatever we want.'

"These Arawaks of the Bahama Islands were much like the Indians on the mainland who were remarkable (European observers were to say again and again) for their hospitality, their belief in sharing. These traits did not stand out in the Europe of the Renaissance, dominated as it was by the religion of the popes, the government of kings, the frenzy for money that marked Western civilization and its first messenger to the Americas, Christopher Columbus.

"Columbus wrote:
'As soon as I arrived in the Indies, on the first Island which I found, I took some of the natives by force in order that they might learn and might give me information of whatever there is in these parts.'

"The information that Columbus wanted most was: Where is the gold?"²

Bacon, the founding father of modern science, and came up with the concept that we could detach ourselves from nature and manipulate it to advance our own human interests.   Ignoring Bacon's warning—that nature, to be commanded, must be obeyed—from that point in time, the environment then became looked upon as something to be exploited for our own agenda. This misinterpretation of Bacon's philosophy and scientific method gave the expansion-minded Western civilizations the world view that it was their right to manipulate the environment in order to further their short-term goals and material interests on a scale never before imaginable.

Then, in the mid-18th century, the Industrial Revolution, born and developed in northwest Europe, changed the world economy forever. Western consumerism was born from mass production, and with it the expectation that it was a God-given right for them to have more of everything, and, after that, more again. So the money players kept their mass production going night and day, and scoured their environment for the resources they felt they had a scientific and moral right to take. But could it go on? Wouldn't they eventually run out of raw materials?

With the Industrial Revolution, the countries of northwest Europe had taken over the world's trade. The reason their manufacturing capitalism was able to continue was through the exploitation of the Third World. Other parts of the world had what the Westerners needed, so they colonized the Third World to get their hands on the raw materials to sustain the Industrial Revolution and consumerism. The Europeans had the means through military strength and steam power to make their wishes felt across the entire planet. Steam power allowed the Europeans to build railroads from the ports to the mines and plantations and to bring in all the equipment to secure the resources. However, they did not build railroads to anywhere else or train the locals to be managers. The net result was to wipe out the local economies and to install their own local administrations and transportation systems to suit their own businesses and to shape the countries to their needs. In almost every case that meant developing nothing else. We created copper republics, banana and tin republics, etc.

These countries which were once self-sustaining then became dependent for survival on exporting one or two products and the success of these products in the Western marketplace.

Eventually the colonies gained independence, but they were anything but independent. While they imported from the West, they still could only export the raw resources, now hooked into world prices. The more well-to-do who controlled the countries also wanted Western products. But since the countries themselves had little money, they had to get loans from the West, which was willing as long as the Third World was willing to continually rip up their countries to continue to supply Western consumerism. By 1994, the Third World was $1.2 trillion in debt, with the interest alone being $50 billion/year. During the past decade the poorest countries paid $1.5 trillion to the richest countries and still their debt doubled. Because they can't even afford to pay the interest, the only thing they can do is to continually sell off their countries—i.e., the rain forests for cattle and crops that soon destroy the fragile topsoil, leaving the land useless for further growing—just to pay the interest on their debts.

A WORLD TRAPPED IN AN ECONOMIC BOX

Eventually there won't be enough left to sell off to pay the debts, and the Third World will become poorer and poorer in relationship to the wealthier countries. As an example, Mexico, a major exporter of food to the U.S., now is importing over five billion dollars in food crops—mostly for the wealthy who can afford it. Thirty years ago Mexico was self-sufficient in food. Now, though, most Mexicans fall well below the poverty line and earn less than a living wage. While exporting agriculture into the world market was supposed to build Mexico's economy, now most of the Mexican people really can't afford the food that Mexico grows. They are casualties of being hooked into the world economy, and this pattern is being replicated all across the planet. In a world in which the farmers still grow an abundance of food, the farmers go broke and millons go hungry.

Even within the U.S., as we stated earlier in the economics section, the gap between the rich and poor is growing, and more and more people are falling below the poverty line. At the same time, remember that the national debt, with its compound interest, is also growing rapidly. It's like being in a casino poker game where the dealer averages taking 10 percent of every deal. Eventually he has almost all the money, and the whole system breaks down because not enough people can play. Therefore the dealer creates more money a little at a time, loans it out at interest, and continues to have the world more and more in debt to him. The dealers have been the power elite and money brokers within the wealthy countries. There is unbelievable wealth concentrated in the hands of just a few people. Remember earlier when I asked who's got the money. Well, if our national debt of over 5.7 trillion is over 13 times greater than there is money in circulation to pay for it, then the only way we can keep operating is to keep borrowing from those that have accumulated the money. But even the dealers may have now lost control of the system because there may eventually not be enough people in the world who can afford to participate in consumerism, and, at that point, the factories and services close for lack of a market.

Most people have looked at what's happening in the economy as if we're in a stable post-Industrial Revolution system with some minor ups and downs, but we're not. Manufacturing capitalism was based on the exploitation of the Third World. However, the population explosions, environmental damage, and the creation of a massive debt system are causing the system to lapse into chaos while the system plays out to its conclusion. Historically, the current problems are the same as they were thousands of years ago. We still have archaic political institutions in which the few dominate the many, unequal distribution of the fruits of the earth between rich and poor, and grossly wasteful consumption of those resources by the rich. While most people viewed the shakeup of Eastern Europe as a triumph for freedom, we viewed it as primarily economically driven, and that situation continues. The Western countries may be a few years behind as the situation is played out to its logical conclusion—the Third World first, then the poorer developed countries, then us. All this is happening against a backdrop of pollution and environmental destruction that is threatening the continuation of life on the planet.

"Our economic system has impoverished the planet at the expense of most of its inhabitants. But, instead of reigning it in, we're imposing it everywhere on Earth."[3]

—David Suzuki, Author and Professor of Biology,

University of British Columbia

"There is something fundamentally wrong in treating the Earth as if it were a business in liquidation."[4]

—Herman Daly, Economist, World Bank

"... economics has always regarded the environment and the resources it represents as a separate external thing that provides free goods. ... It never considered that we depend on that natural world to actually survive. It seems to me that there's no genius involved in saying that a system growing [from 1950 to 1990 the world economy quadrupled in size] within a larger system that is fixed in size [the environment] ultimately results in a total collapse of the two."[5]

—Bill Rees, Resource Ecologist at the University
of British Columbia

"A friend recently said that running a business with a conscience is like driving with the brakes on. ... Sooner or later we must realize that, despite the protestations of industry, it [industry] is completely lacking in ecological principles, and that what is good for business is almost always bad for nature."[6]

—Paul Hawkin, Economist

STUCK IN AN UNSUSTAINABLE ECONOMIC SYSTEM

Our economic system is based on a fantasy, the fantasy of unlimited resources and thus the potential for unlimited production. As we continue to alienate ourselves from nature by seeing it as a resource to use and abuse, we are now rapidly using up those resources in our non-sustainable economies. We are nearing the time when we have to face the reality that our economic system is doomed.

Since our plight was excellently stated in the Canadian Broadcasting Corporation's program, *Trading Futures, Living in the Global Economy*, I will quote from that show:

"All life on earth survives in the same way—making a living out of what that planet provides, and we are no exception. Everything that's vital to our survival comes from nature—air, water, soil, minerals—but the supply is finite, and somehow we've forgotten that. Yet, we believe that our economy can keep on growing forever, far beyond the limits of the natural world. We have come to think of nature as raw material—fuel for our industrial machine. The economic perspective sees nature as a resource for us to extract and use, instead of as the foundation for all life on Earth. That's what's carving up the world and denying us a sustainable future. We're stuck in an unsustainable economic system, and we're hitting the limits."[7]

Hey, but if our GNP keeps increasing, how can we possibly be heading for economic disaster? Again, let me quote from *Trading Futures, Living in the Global Economy*:

"It [the GNP] records production, but it doesn't record depletion of resources or the damage we cause to air, water, and soil. Like governments around the world, we cook our books, excluding the real costs of our economy. With this type of bookkeeping, a country could exhaust its minerals, cut down its forests, erode its soils, pollute its aquifers, and hunt its fish to extinction, all without showing a drop in its GNP.

"This type of accounting turns negative costs into pluses. Cigarettes kill 35,000 Canadians each year, but the medical costs help keep the GNP healthy. The Exxon Valdez oil spill created jobs, sales, and demand for services. The cleanup was perversely a two billion dollar shot in the arm for Alaska's economy.

"Economists so far haven't found a way to put environmental costs on the balance sheet. This accounting system supports conventional economic analysis: when global resource depletion and environmental damage aren't counted, things look good."[8]

But things don't look so good to Herman Daly, Senior Economist for the World Bank, who noted in the same program that, "We've moved from an era of economic growth into an era that we might call anti-economic growth. That means that expansion of the physical scale of the human economy now increases environmental costs faster than it increases production benefits. So, at the margin we're increasing costs faster than increasing benefits, this is making us poorer, not richer. ... I think in many ways it's not an exaggeration to say that we're living by an ideology of death. We're pushing into the capacity of the biosphere to support life."[9]

Daly also notes the fallacy of the GNP as a measure of our financial status. Because the GNP does not indicate whether we are living off income or capital, interest or principle, it is misleading when we are using up our resources. This is because the depletion of resources is not considered any different than sustainable yield production, which is the only true income.[10] But there is a substantial difference between the way economists look at GNP and that true income, for "... the value of a sawmill is zero without forests; the value of fishing boats is zero without fish ..."[11]

Since the time of the Industrial Revolution, we have been using up the resources that support all life on the planet. It's so insidious because it's happening slowly enough that we don't see the day-to-day effects of our folly, and, because most of the decision makers can still buy almost anything they want, they don't see that *we're living by an ideology of death.*

THE SORCERER'S APPRENTICE

The good news is that it's good news that the current economic system is in jeopardy. It's good news not only because we may be forced to do something about the threat to the environment but

"I think that we are blinded by a number of basic beliefs that we have. We believe, for example, that we somehow—because we have television, computers, and all that stuff—that we're not like other creatures, we're special, we essentially live outside of the rest of nature. And we've forgotten that, however sophisticated we are, we still breathe the same air that every other creature on the planet breathes, that air doesn't exist in a little bubble around our heads or around the United States of America. What happens here affects the rest of the world. When Chernobyl broke out, radioactive isotopes spread across the North, the Arctic, Canada. Why? Because air is a single system. If you use air as a garbage can, you're damn sure that garbage is going to end up in your body. And it's the same with water, water isn't infinite, it's finite. Water cartwheels across the entire planet. What happens in Brazil in the rainforest is ultimately going to be reflected by the water that we get here. So we live in a single system as fundamentally animals. And we've forgotten that. We think we're so special, that we lie outside nature, and that's been a deadly oversight on our part."

—David Suzuki, Author and Professor of Biology,
University of British Columbia

"We have tremendous freedom to choose our own lifestyles, and we have trouble accepting the responsibility for that freedom and of seeing ourselves not as the pinnacle of evolution or as those God gave the rest of the system to do as we like for our own purposes, but to develop some humility and wisdom as part of nature...

"We've been trying to force ourselves into the mechanical model socially. So, we've tried to build societies in which impersonal institutions form the parts of the whole, and we're all plugged in like cogs in wheels, and it isn't working. Our economic theories don't work because we haven't taken into account that we're a living system, drawing from nature and giving back to it. We've only looked at what we do with our raw materials for human purposes...It's our own fault that we've gotten into this global crisis, but now it's our opportunity to pull out of that crisis, to reorganize ourselves as a living system."

—Elizabeth Sahtouris, Biologist and Author

Above quotes from The Unfolding Story[12]

"We need to recapture that sense of being embedded in nature, being in a condition of reciprocity with nature that you do find in traditional forms of healing. You cannot simply take and take and take from nature without giving. So, the proper relationship between human beings and the natural world is one of reciprocity."
          —*Theodore Roszak, Professor of History and Author*

"Basically, the Enlightenment left us with a mechanistic, and individualistic and also a dualistic view of things, and all of those are now doing much more harm than good. The United States was founded within the Enlightenment, and the leaders were all thinkers who were shaped by the Enlightenment. So, to be an American, is to be a child of the Enlightenment. This is very, very deeply part of who we are, and there are many things about this that most of us would not want to give up; there are real gains. On the other hand, the Enlightenment was bound up with certain ways of thinking that are now doing more harm than good. One of them is . . . the individualism of the Enlightenment, and one problem is that, if your theory says that we are purely individual, increasingly we act as if that theory were true—that is, we can be socialized by community to not acknowledge the importance of community.

"Working only on individual problems isn't going to work. We have to fundamentally reorient ourselves and understand how we embedded in this whole natural process in the whole natural world and rethink our lives in that way."
          —*John B. Cobb, Jr., Educator and Theologian*

"What's unrealistic is to pretend that we live on top of nature as an industrial society that's invincible, whereas we actually are so embedded in the processes, that denying that is just folly."
          —*Charlene Spretnak, Ecologist and Author*

Above quotes from The Unfolding Story[13]

also because the system already is not working for growing numbers of people. At the risk of repetition, let me hammer the point once more—*there are enough resources and manpower on this planet for all of us to live very abundantly.* Given this reality, looking at what we are doing to ourselves, to others, and to the environment makes what we are doing seem really, really crazy!

Using money as the excuse for not providing basic human needs and needed services is REALLY CRAZY! *Money is an artificial construct.* You can't eat it or shelter yourself with it. It's basically an agreement. Even in the beginning, though, that concept was based on the "we-ness" and "they-ness" of groups of people and individuals within those groups, and that concept just doesn't make sense anymore in a world that now needs action taken to make the system work for the continuation of life on the planet.

As an example of the absurdity of our current economic model, a few days after the devastating 1994 earthquake in Kobe, Japan, the *Los Angeles Times* ran an article titled, "Major Rebuilding Effort Could Aid Economic Growth, Analysts Say."[14] The article began, "The killer earthquake that hit western Japan on Tuesday caused immense damage likely to run into billions of dollars, but the reconstruction effort should give a boost to economic growth, analysts said." A half century ago the onset of World War Two helped lift the world out of a depression. What's wrong with this picture? Why do we have to have disasters to assist our economies? If a disaster can spark economic growth, why can't we pick any disaster—like pollution, environmental damage, healthcare, billions of the world's people living on the edge of survival or the 40,000 children who starve to death every day—and do something about that? Is it just because we are numb to these daily disasters? If all those resources and manpower were there to be put into use, why can't we put them to use without a "disaster" and feed people who are starving, shelter people who are homeless, and restore the environment? Is the whole system we created to serve us, the everyone-for-themselves paradigm, now beyond anyone's control or was it just never designed to make the world work for everyone?

DEVASTATING JOLT IN JAPAN

Major Rebuilding Effort Could Aid Economic Growth, Analysts Say

By DAVID HOLLEY
TIMES STAFF WRITER

TOKYO—The killer earthquake that hit western Japan on Tuesday caused immense damage likely to run into tens of billions of dollars, but the reconstruction effort should give a boost to economic growth, analysts said.

"These sorts of things bring out the worst in economists, because a disaster is good for economic growth as long as someone is willing to pay for rebuilding," said Jesper Koll, head of economic and markets research for J.P. Morgan Securities Asia Ltd. "The Ministry of Finance and the politicians have made it clear they'll provide all possible help, and the Bank of Japan will keep interest rates low."

Houses, roads and bridges will need to be rebuilt, he noted, "and that adds jobs, that adds income."

What has happened to us with this old exchange system is like what happened to the Sorcerer's Apprentice in Disney's movie *Fantasia*. The apprentice, needing to fill a large container with water, picked up the wizard's cap and created a broom with arms to haul buckets of water for him. The apprentice, pleased that success was being achieved with minimal effort, then dosed off and dreamt of his new-found power to control the universe. Just as he was dreaming that he could direct the rise and fall of the waters, he was awakened by the rising water level from the now out-of-control broom. As he tried to control his creation, he only succeeded in creating a rapidly escalating dilemma. By not being able to stop the legions of water-carrying brooms he'd set into motion, the waters threatened to completely inundate him. Only the wizard's reappearance saved him

At first the broom carrying the buckets of water (the money exchange system) seemed to make trade easier, but, as more players got involved and people thirsted for power positions, the system eventually got out of control and took over. It became a monster with a life of its own, burying the individual needs of most people. With that monster (which is really an illusion, because money is an artificial construct) still in control, now everyone thinks that they're at the mercy of the illusion. Yet we have so bought into that illusion that we now believe ourselves as people to be at the mercy of money and/or the lack of it. With the survival of the planet in the balance, let me say again that this *really is crazy!* However, the wizard represents the consciousness of the Highest Good For All Concerned. We need that wizard consciousness now.

The wizard would tell us that, in truth, economics is a philosophy, not a science. Our Federal Reserve can put into or take out of our economy as much or as little money as they want, whenever they want. Nowadays, a lot of money is not even tangible—it's electronic—and the Fed can just create it and put it wherever they want, or make it disappear. If a philanthropic wizard could create, without the Fed knowing, billions of dollars to provide housing, healthcare, education, and sustainable, income-producing businesses for those in need, this would have a negligible effect on our economy—except for helping those people.

"Money–something we created as a medium of exchange. It stands for things: cars and shoes and cooking pots and all the things they're made from, like minerals and oil. But, the world's things are limited in supply, while there is no end to the amount of money we can print or accumulate. With this (printing sheets of money) we can pretend that growth and wealth are infinite. Funny money–once it stood for real value. More and more it stands just for itself in this strange world we've created where money breeds money without ever touching reality at all."[15]

   —*From* Trading Futures, Living in the Global Economy

Meanwhile, as was pointed out earlier, natural disasters become a boon to the economy. Again, this is crazy—we don't need these outside stimuli. We can do whatever we want—healthcare, education, restoring the environment—but, at this point, it's more politics than it is economics, and every one of the players has just agreed to play everyone-for-themselves economics the way we're doing it. Also, the U.S. and the big money interests can exert enough pressure on foreign countries to get them to play the same game. Therefore, it's only a political reason why we don't end suffering, hunger, and poverty. Again, *economics is a philosophy, not a science.* Why don't more of us question why we use "lack of money" as the excuse for not doing what is needed to save this planet.

As a result of our buying into the money illusion, the present economic, political, and social systems look like they were either created by a madman or maybe by just a few self-serving people around whom the rest of society has rotated since the days of the pharaohs, monarchs, and the landed wealthy and "nobility" from the feudal systems. In truth, capitalism eventually replaced feudalism, but control by the power/money elite has really usurped capitalism and democracy. Historically, we have just about always lived by the Golden Rule: he who has the gold, rules. This has resulted in our being so entrenched in thinking individualistically—trying to get by in this every-person-for-himself system—that we haven't stopped to think about what would really work for all of us and for the planet. We have been behaving like people in battle—we want to have more stuff and more power/control than the next person, even if it's at the expense of someone else. When we're not doing this individually, it's group against group or country against country with staggering amounts being spent on weaponry. Meanwhile, more than a billion people are undernourished and three billion in poverty—one-half of humanity excluded from the global marketplace due to the everyone-for-themselves economic system.

IT'S EVERY-PERSON-FOR-HIMSELF

I keep using the terminology "everyone-for-themselves." What does the term mean? Well, it literally means that everyone basically acts out of his or her own self interest. It means, therefore, that we don't get together and really explore how we can make a situation work for all of the parties involved. I mean *really* taking the time and care to thoroughly and creatively explore how we can *positively* make that situation work for everyone involved and everyone and everything that the solution would affect. Instead, the parties involved are generally preoccupied with what effect the outcome will have on their own positions. They are concerned that others do not get more or get a better deal than what they get, and they therefore are very watchful and suspicious of the others involved.

There's an interesting little exercise I use in the team-building work I do. The group pairs up and two people stand facing each other and grip hands shoulder high. I tell them that the object is to score as many points as possible in one minute and the way to score a point is to touch the other person's shoulder. It sort of looks like two people about to do standing arm wrestling. When I say go, that's exactly what most pairs proceed to do. At the end of one minute, some people have struggled mightily and have managed a standoff scoring no points. Other people have dominated their perceived opposition and earned a score of ten or whatever to their partner's zero. I never say to the group that the object is to defeat one's partner, yet, in our every-person-for-himself society, that's exactly what most people are predisposed to do. Others mildly cooperate and score a few points, and once in awhile I get a pair of people who get that they can accumulate the most number of points by really exercising their creativity in cooperating with one another. In a minute's time it is possible for those creatively cooperating pairs to score a combined 500 points. At the end of the exercise, those that entered into the everyone-for-themselves power struggle are tired and stressed, those that mildly cooperated are still experiencing some degree of isolation and being tuned out, and those who creatively cooperated feel elated and energized.

This exercise is a perfect metaphor for the everyone-for-themselves paradigm versus a Highest Good For All approach. The everyone-for-themselves paradigm has winners and losers vying for a perceived limited amount of resources, whereas the Highest Good approach has no such bounds, and we are limited only by our imaginations. In the above exercise, the power struggle produced small scores as compared to the cooperative approach producing scores several times higher. It's like when we use the lack of money as the excuse for not providing needed services for each other and for the planet. That's a very limiting approach. Of course we can provide adequate healthcare, nutrition, and an abundant standard of living for everyone while still protecting and healing the environment if we just choose to let go of this mass hypnosis that has gripped us for thousands of years. It's just like the exercise—in the competition based model, it isn't possible to do this, but we do not have to continue buying into this paradigm.

There has been a lot of brainwashing to convince us that cooperation on the scale of making life work for everyone is bad or won't work. We don't question the need for the everyone-for-themselves paradigm because, for thousands of years, variations of that system have been the only models presented for us to look at. More accurately, I should say that this is how history has been taught to us. Drawing on the work of the noted archeologist, Marija Gimbutas, Riane Eisler in her book, *The Chalice and the Blade*, gives us a remarkably different picture about peaceful and abundant cooperative societies that existed for thousands of years.[15] Pick it up, it's worth reading. Conveniently though, we were not taught much about these alternative cultures, which generally were far more successful and long-lasting than the power-based models that now are the norm.

Well, you might say that it has to be this way because even in the human species it's survival of the fittest—the weak don't survive and flourish. In Darwin's *Origin of the Species*, evolution was defined in terms of adaptation in the continuous struggle to survive. The theory was immediately embraced by the power brokers of the last century in order to justify the squalid conditions at the onset of industrialization. Mankind was seen as not being exempt from the domination by the fittest, and this, supposedly, was all a natural process. However, Darwin never talked about "survival of the fittest," a concept often credited to him, but rather, he described those who survived as *fittest for a specific ecological niche.*[17]

Yet, while Darwin's theory might explain some aspects of evolution, in it's nakedness it is a narrow approach. Cooperation has also played a huge role in creating our world. For example, flowers have evolved vivid colors and inviting scents to attract bees, which pollinate and, as a result, provide for the perpetuation of the species. In fact, the interdependence and cooperation among the species is the very backdrop of evolution. Among all the species, the choice is there for us, as humans, to fully embrace cooperation for the Highest Good rather than trying to dominate each other and the world's resources.

It's amazing that we unquestionably believe that competition and the survival of the fittest is how we have to do things in our capitalistic, democratic way of life. In his 1986 book, *No Contest,* sociologist Alfie Kohn analyzed hundreds of studies conducted over the last sixty years that compared cooperation with competition. His findings concluded that both, in business and in education, cooperation consistently outproduced competition.[18] In the next section I'll give you a very graphic example of the cooperative synergy that is available to lift a whole group of people.

The everyone-for-themselves struggle for survival ideology is also a doomed approach for humankind because it does not take into account that the Earth is a closed system with finite resources. We can't just take and take and take for personal gain, it has to be balanced for all of us. Otherwise, we will be just like all the species that have disappeared because their habitat became depleted and no longer capable of supporting life.

"Our economic system has turned the whole world into a marketplace where everything on Earth is up for grabs—even the future of the planet."

"The [financial/exchange] market tends to concentrate wealth. If you have money, it helps you to get more. If you don't, market forces work against you."

"Current economic theory says wealth will trickle down from the top, but it doesn't seem to be working. Everywhere, the rich are getting richer and the poor are getting poorer."[19]

—*Quotes from David Suzuki, narrating for* Trading Futures,
Living in a Global Economy

"We're all in this together; we're almost all of us losers, and, unless we act together, we will get exactly what we deserve, which is to say we will continue to be victimized by the forces of globalization and transnationalization."[20]

—*Susan George, author of* A Fate Worse Than Debt. *Quote from*
Trading Futures, Living in a Global Economy

"What is the use of having a nice house without a decent planet to put it on?"

—*Henry David Thoreau*

A REVOLUTION—OR DO WE HAVE TO KEEP DOING THE OLD SYSTEM?

What if enough of us decided to change the rules of the game and throw out the limitations so that we can make life work for all of us? If we changed to "It's all right for you to have every bit as much as me, including equal power," then all the energy and resources being spent trying to perpetuate our economic and political caste systems could be used to enable every one of us on this planet to live very abundantly. And I'm not talking only material wealth but also in terms of addressing and healing the isolation and alienation that most people feel to some degree. In Chinese medicine, illness is the concentration of or lack of energy in one place. Too much wealth concentrated in too few hands and not enough in others creates an economic illness through the lack of flow. In our everyone-for-themselves world, the wealth of the planet has now been concentrated into the hands of so few, while millions starve and billions live in poverty, that our planet is indeed ill—in spirit as well as ecology.

There is a new movement happening in this country right now where some people are attempting to bring more balance into their lives by trading off time spent pursuing income for time to be more nurturing towards themselves. While a 1995 nationwide poll commissioned by the Merck Family Fund found that 82 percent of the respondents agreed that "most of us buy and consume far more than we need, it's wasteful," 28 percent are doing something about it by cutting down on their consumption to create more time for themselves.[21] Of those, 90 percent are satisfied with the results.[22] This trend, called the voluntary simplicity movement, is growing so rapidly that it is becoming recognized as a movement. The *Washington Post* reported on January 9, 1996, that, "This (voluntary simplicity movement) is a grassroots reaction to the fractured American Dream…Some experts say the turn toward the simplified lifestyle nationwide is starting to reach proportions that foretell a fundamental shift in American society and its consumer culture."[23]

Joe Dominguez, a former Wall Street broker, and Vicki Robin in their book, *Your Money Or Your Life*, took it a step further.[24] They

"Why should we live with such hurry and waste of life. ... When we are unhurried and wise, we perceive that only great and worthy things have any permanent and absolute existence, that petty fears and petty pleasures are but the shadow of reality."

—Henry David Thoreau

"There is more to life than increasing its speed."

—Gandhi

"The world is too much with us. Getting and spending, we lay waste our powers."

—Wordsworth

"The mass of men lead lives of quiet desperation."

— Gandhi

outline a way to basically earn enough to invest and then live cooperatively in small units very cheaply off the income from the investments. Their book is aptly named as they have reclaimed their lives by not buying into the old system and now help others to do the same.

While the simplicity movement is certainly a step in the right direction in terms of people leading fuller, more balanced lives and alleviating some of the pressure on nature through reduced consumption, it still is not the revolution that is needed to rescue the entire planet. These people have admirably chosen to make a small difference, but the system as a whole needs to be changed to effectively rescue the planet from the monumental challenges that we face.

As an example of how a larger group of people can share and work together for The Highest Good Of All, the story of the Mondragon region in the Basque region of Spain comes to mind. This difficult area to live in was devastated by the Spanish Civil War and years of subsequent government persecution under Franco. Out of the ruins, Don Jose Maria Arizmendianieta, a Catholic priest who rejected *laissez faire* capitalism and the State collectivism of Karl Marx, guided five professional men in the village of Mondragon into starting their own manufacturing firm. They organized their firm as a cooperative in which the highest paid worker never earned more than three times what the lowest paid workers earned and where all workers owned one share of the co-op, earned an equal share of the profits, and could elect and be elected to the board of directors. (This income spread is a bit different than our system, where the average CEO in 1995 made 187 times the wage of the average factory worker, which was an increase from 1960 when the spread was 41 to 1.[25])

The cooperative started in 1956 in the village of Mondragon, manufacturing two products with 24 workers. By 1959 they had jobs for one hundred people. Their firm was modeled after the successful 1844 Rochdale cooperative in England which flourished until it opened itself to more capital participants who outvoted the

"Those at the top are rewarding themselves ever more handsomely as they are cutting wages at the bottom, and that's a new story...

"The problem is that we now have two Americas. We have the America of the top 20 percent that is doing quite well and even better, and we're having the America of the bottom 80 percent, what we used to call much of the middle class included in that, and that's an America that is increasingly looking at the top 20 percent moving further and further away."

—Harley Shaken, *Labor History Professor at University of California at Berkeley*

"In 1980 the average CEO made $625,000. That's 42 times more than his employees averaged. Eleven years later [1991] that CEO was making $2.5 million—104 times more than his employees. And last year [1995] the average CEO earned $3.7 million. The salary chasm between the CEO and employee is now 141 to 1."

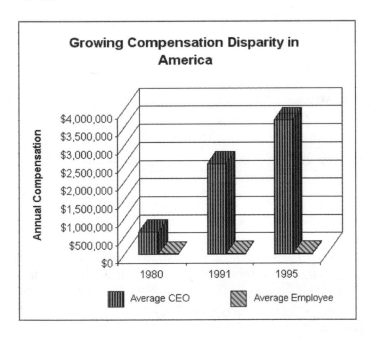

The above quotes are from the CBS Reports *television show aired August 8, 1996 entitled* "Who's Getting Rich And Why Aren't You?"[26]

original group and took control. Within three years the Rochdale company then became an ordinary capitalist firm.

However, the Mondragon co-op model proved to be so successful that, in less than 30 years, it grew from one cooperative with 25 workers to more than 100 worker cooperatives with 19,500 workers in the region.[27] This was made possible by starting cooperative banks which mobilized small reserves enabling the local co-ops to be financed. Because the goal was for *everyone* to succeed, the banks would meet with prospective new co-ops and help them succeed. They would help find land, supplies, a market for the products, personnel, training, etc. They would also do feasibility studies, monitor progress, and make up one-third of the coop's board of directors. The system proved so successful that only 3 of the 103 worker cooperatives created between 1956 and 1986 were shut down.[28] Compare that with what we know about starting businesses in the everyone-for-themselves paradigm. Since only 20 percent of our new businesses survive even five years, Mondragon's survival rate of more than 97 percent across three decades indeed commands attention.[29]

Since the cooperatives were worker owned, the Spanish government would not help with welfare, medical care, etc. No problem. The co-ops created their own co-op social security and healthcare. They even built a co-op hospital and a co-op university where the students also worked and produced products and owned the co-op. Many of the supermarkets and schools also became cooperatives. Because housing was expensive, they also built co-op housing owned by the tenants.

How successful are these worker-owned cooperatives? The productivity of the Mondragon co-op workers is the highest in Spain, higher than the most successful capitalist firms, and the net profit on sales is twice as high as the most profitable capitalist firms. Also, the Basque region never received nor had to depend on outside investment capital to get started or to expand their businesses.

The reason for the success of the now prosperous Mondragon region is that the people decided to pool their resources and make

Mondragón in the 1980s

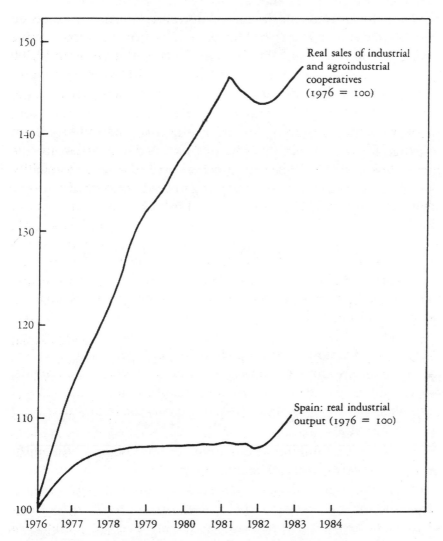

Real sales of industrial
and agroindustrial
cooperatives
(1976 = 100)

Spain: real industrial
output (1976 = 100)

SOURCE: Keith Bradley and Alan Gelb, "Cooperative Labour Relations: Mondragón's Response to
Recession," *British Journal of Industrial Relations* 25 (1987): 85.

INDUSTRIAL OUTPUT AND SALES (1976-83): Mondragon and Spain[30]
Copyright © Blackwell Publishers. Reprinted with permission.

it work for everyone. Because managers and workers both knew that they served each other's interests, they could move ahead boldly with an unusual degree of agreement. Also, since they lived in the same villages, no differences were perceived between managers and workers. They also limited the co-ops to 500 members (beyond which they split up and formed a new co-op) because they found that co-ops couldn't operate beyond that number. This also helped maintain a family feeling. The now prosperous Mondragon region is an example of people working together for the mutual benefit of all. Had the everyone-for-themselves paradigm been in effect instead, the result probably would have been that a few people gathered most of the money while the majority of the people would still be living in poverty in the region.

LET'S MAKE LIFE WORK FOR ALL OF US

What if we thought of ourselves as one family where the needs of one, whether it be a person, a group or a country, are the concern of everyone. Granted that to do this we would have to rein in our egos and sacrifice our selfishness, but what could we gain? What do we really want more of in our lives? Some immediate thoughts are more leisure time, more play, quality time with good friends, opportunities for creative expression, beauty in nature, etc. We'd all probably also opt for less stress, more peace, less pollution, and more healthiness.

So, again, in thinking of ourselves as one cooperative family, let's plan how we all could be living very abundantly on all levels. Let's let go of our notions of this everyone-for-themselves social, economic, political system. Let's start from scratch in terms of what we think has to happen to accomplish our goal, and let's just say that the environment and all life forms must be taken care of in the best way possible. These are the only requirements. Theoretically, let's also toss out all jobs and then start creating and, if necessary, putting back only those things that support our goal.

If we are truly cooperating as one family and we are taking care of all life, we find that we need only about 20 percent of the

"In the economic world money markets rule, even though they don't produce a dime of real value."[31]

—*From* Trading Futures, Living in the Global Economy

"The strength of the idea of private enterprise lies in its terrifying simplicity. It suggests that the totality of life can be reduced to one aspect—profits. ... Private enterprise is not concerned with what it produces but only with what it gains from production." (Which is why we use up so much of our time and resources producing so many unnecessary nonsense products.)[32]

—*E.F. Schumacher,* Small Is Beautiful: Economics as if People Mattered

"Human rights, labor rights and environmental rights are being completely subordinated to the right to make a profit."

—*Julie Light, Managing Editor of* Corporate Watch

current jobs. Only 20 percent, and probably less, of the current jobs are essential! The other 80 percent plus are either there to protect and perpetuate our everyone-for-themselves economic caste system or they are what I call "nonsense jobs" which are created solely for the sake of providing a person or some people with money to survive in the current system. Falling into that category are an incredible number of products that are created, again, solely for peoples' incomes in our non-cooperative economic model. Just drive down any city street and see how many establishments wouldn't have to be there if the idea was for the system to really work for everyone.

As an example of the waste of mind power and creativity in our capitalistic system, I know of two very bright men who wanted to make big money with as little effort as possible. What they came up with was providing a bunch of cheap products for promotions, thus using manpower and resources for products that will soon take other jobs to haul them to diminishing landfill sites. They are making a lot of money, but it would be nice to put creative people to work doing something useful and not needlessly consuming our planet's resources. Many lawyers are very sharp too, but, in a cooperative society, few if any of them and the host of other jobs they support would need to exist.

All the jobs involved in the game of making money from money would also be gone. That means the banks, investment houses, and speculators. Dealing with the stock market is really like going to Las Vegas. There are the slots and the dealers who take the house share of the money. Meanwhile, some of the players win, some lose, and a bunch of non-essential and nonsense jobs are created. The interest game was also one of our system's really horrible ideas. Who invented this system-from-hell which basically enslaves individuals and paralyzes whole countries, while a few money brokers do very well? Jobs were created to make money off of money, and, now, as I related earlier, the whole economic system has grown into a monster-out-of-control that really is not working well for most people on the planet. If something needs to be done, we need to have a system where we can just bring our manpower and resources to bear on correcting

Bond Traders' Power Again Riles Markets

By TOM PETRUNO
TIMES STAFF WRITER

In the course of a few hours on Friday, some Americans' home-buying plans were upended, many businesses and cities suddenly faced higher borrowing costs and the stock market lost a stunning $190 billion in value.

All because the U.S. economy put more people to work in February, many of them in low-paying, temporary positions that probably aren't anyone's idea of a dream job.

WHAT'S WRONG WITH THIS PICTURE?

the problems and just DO IT, and do it in a way that's in harmony with nature! Then we can start saving the planet.

The current economic system is one of consumerism, which aims towards more jobs, more production, a bigger GNP, and less sustainability. If we can create a system that will work for all of us while also eliminating those 80-plus percent of the jobs and the nonsense and unessential products and their accompanying manufacturing plants, storage facilities, and stores, then we could cut way back on our work week hours, do more leisure and creative activities, have more time communing with nature, and use the manpower to start restoring the planet. We could also use that manpower to start creating a better lifestyle for all of us.

Again, there are enough resources and manpower for every being on the planet to live abundantly. Not providing services and a good living environment for all life because there is "not enough money" is an illusion based on our lack of cooperation and creativity. But, what is not an illusion in our consumerist society is that the damage done to our environment has become the major issue of our time. Adding to this, our skyrocketing world population coupled with our rapidly decreasing ability to produce food with our ecological damage means that the quality of life in our everyone-for-themselves economic system will continue to decline. In fact, a Cornell University Team concluded in a 1994 study that the world can support only two billion people at the standard of living now enjoyed by industrialized nations.[34]

We are at almost 6 billion now with 8 billion forecast for the year 2019. The National Resources Defense Council said that the 55 million people that will be born in the industrialized countries during the 1990's will pollute the planet more than the 895 million born in third world countries.[35] Remember that the Worldwatch Institute reported that "As a result of our population size, consumption patterns, and technology choices, we have surpassed the planet's carrying capacity."[36] That is RIGHT NOW! With our declining environment and a couple of billion more people, the situation will become much worse unless we choose to do something drastically different.

"Over time our relationship with money—earning it, spending it, investing it, owning it, protecting it, worrying about it—has taken over the major part of our lives."[37]

—Joe Dominguez and Vicki Robin

"Our...civilization engenders a multitude of wants that smother and harass the average American."[38]

—John Muir, quoted by David Shi

"Excessive consumption may be understood from a world view of estrangement from self, from land, from life, and from God. Consuming the fruits of the Earth unrestrained, we become consumed ourselves by avarice and greed. Excessive consumption leaves us emptied, out of touch with our deepest self."[39]

—His Holiness Bartholomew I

"Worldwide, whether in forests, mines, or fisheries, there is intense economic competition to garner hard currencies. Desperate for foreign trade, countries wind up producing too many products for the world markets at too low a price. It is a viscous cycle, the industrial equivalent of the tragedy of the commons. There are too many steel mills, too many car makers, too many oil seed producers, etc. While we are awash in cars, steel, and material goods, we are rapidly depleting the underlying resources at extraordinarily rapid rates, and the prices of products do not reflect diminished supply because there is an apparent but temporary surplus on world markets. In other words, the rate of extraction is increasing worldwide; the short-term intensification lowers prices while simultaneously increasing the damage to the environment. Our means of forestalling our feedback from our environment is to take over other environments (changing tropical forests into farms as an example) as a way to increase our drawdown of resources."[40]

—Paul Hawkin, Economist

Yet, amazingly, the multinationals are pushing for globalization to open up new markets. This is really crazy because it will only hasten the environmental decline of the planet. The physicist/ecologist Vandana Shiva excellently discussed this concept:

"Development, to me, is a word that basically has extremely benign beginnings, in the biological domain, where a seed of the oak tree develops into the oak tree. It's something built into the seed. It's something built into the structure of self-evolution, self-organization. Development really comes from that biological sphere—a child develops into a grown-up, stays himself or herself, but becomes different. And that capacity of inner-generated evolution is where the word "development" really began. But the way it came out of the World Bank—and it did come out of the World Bank—development became, not internally generated, but externally imposed. Development was not something that happens with your resources, your abilities, the abilities of a society, an organism, a person; development becomes that for which you have to take loans and credits, and get indebted; and get enslaved—just the opposite of what development should really be. ...

"The narrow concept of development—and not just the narrow concept...the perverse concept of development, as it has guided the relationships between the North and South over the last five decades—is definitely anti-ecological. It's anti-ecological because it tries to globalize a pattern of production and consumption that is globally impossible! It tries to universalize the consumption of materials at the scales in which the affluent industrialized West does. We know that twenty percent of that tiny population of the West consumes eighty percent of the planet's resources. So if the development project really had to be achieved, it would need literally five planets to meet its objectives. It is therefore against the very logic, ecological logic of this planet's resources. We don't have five planets! We just have one. ...

"'Maldevelopment' is basically a development paradigm that destroys; does not build. Maldevelopment is development that does not build on peoples' capacities, it does not build on the

"As countries became more and more indebted in the seventies and eighties, they were under pressure from banks, from some of the multilateral financial institutions and from their own internal elites to export more, to gain foreign exchange to service the debts. And what that means for most developing countries is increasing exports of primary products, because the international trading system is biased in a major degree against manufactured goods and against value-added products. So basically you're thrown back on sugar, timber, bananas, pineapples, etcetera; standard tropical products. Unfortunately, most other tropical countries produce the same products, so you get a massive infusion of these goods into the market and the price drops. But since your principle goal is to generate foreign exchange, instead of that resulting in less supply it results in even more, because you've got to produce even more to earn the same amount of foreign exchange. Now that commodity trap—that 'desperation production,' as they call it—quite often leads to massive deforestation of the countryside as poor people desperately try and scratch a living from the hillside in order to feed their families, usually growing crops that are totally unsuited for the terrain; usually with no inputs; usually with no technical assistance They're basically trying to survive. If enough people do that—and they've done it in many parts of the Third World—you can get environmental destruction on a really massive scale."[41]

—David Rumnalls, Senior Advisor to the President of the International Development Research Center and co-founder of the International Institute for Environment and Development

limits which ecosystems put on human activity. It disrupts cultures. It violates ecological boundaries, and it just imposes a very, very narrow model of what a preferred human existence is on the entire world. In fact, when development started...and it started absolutely around 1948, where the rest of the world, of the Third World, which had been left poor because of colonization, was declared 'underdeveloped.' Suddenly, we were 'underdeveloped.' And development was a yardstick in which the only measures were how much paper you can consume and how much cement you can consume, how many chemicals you can consume, how much petrol and fossil fuel you can consume. Now quite clearly, subsistence societies did not consume any of that! They were not involved in the ravaging of the planet. And maldevelopment basically sucked them in with loans from the World Bank and bilateral aid. And made them feel that unless they could shift from organic fertilizer into chemical fertilizer they were 'underdeveloped.' Unless they could shift from their bullock carts to tractors, they were 'underdeveloped.' Unless they could shift from the hundreds of diverse housing materials that are used across the world according to what is available, what is the climate, how will people protect themselves and give themselves shelter? That diversity of housing was devastated by concrete and steel."[42]

Indeed, we can have an abundant lifestyle for all the billions of people on the planet, but this cannot be achieved in an everyone-for-themselves paradigm based on the God of profit. It can only be done when we create a model where we can make the world work for all the people, and this means equitably sharing, conserving, and renewing resources. It also requires having the consciousness where we care enough to act for The Highest Good Of All.

Don't mess with Mother Nature! We're now finding out what happened to earlier societies that prospered and grew and then mysteriously abandoned their civilizations. With their farming practices along with their need for lumber, many cultures from Mesopotamia to the great pre-Columbian cultures of Central America ruined their environment to the point where it could no longer support them. Eerily we now are repeating this past mistake, only now it's on a worldwide scale, and, unlike previous

"LIVE SIMPLY, THAT OTHERS
MAY SIMPLY LIVE."

—*Mahatma Gandhi*

(This, however, doesn't mean that we have to live poorly. In fact, we can live much more abundantly than we do now. Although, to do this and preserve our planet means that we need to change the way we live together and how we share together.)

"Simple living is not about being deprived in any way. ... Simple living is about freedom, plain and simple. Freedom to choose the kind of life you want. Freedom to enjoy what is important to you."[43]

—*Janet Luhrs*

"The average North American needs, conservatively, ten to twelve acres of production land to support his or her consumer lifestyle. ... Extrapolating the present North American lifestyle to an anticipated world population of ten billion, using existing technologies, would require about 125 billion acres of ecologically productive land. Our planet has, however, only 22 billion acres of such land. To bring just the present world population of almost six billion up to North American standards, would require at least two additional Earths..."[44]

—*William E. Rees, Director of the School of Community and Regional Planning at the University of British Columbia*

"If you don't have an internal sense of your worth, you've got to be filled up by buying stuff."[45]

—*Rabbi Daniel Swartz*

civilizations, there is no new land to migrate to! When history looks back on us 50 years from now, the question will be asked, "Why didn't people of the 20th century see what they were doing and change it? This was madness."

We are now near the end of the line in our current way of relating with our environment. Those who don't believe that are still clinging to the attitude of subduing the environment to serve mankind's needs. In his book, *The Green Lifestyle Handbook,* Jeremy Rifkin described environmental relationships as being "similar to personal relationships. By attempting to subdue nature, by refusing to accept it on its own terms, by manipulating it to serve expedient short-term material ends, we have made our long-term relationship with the environment less secure and now face the prospect of a wholesale depreciation of the life-supporting processes of the planet."[46]

To take care of ourselves and all life, we need to move into sustainability, which means a way of living on this Earth so that each generation passes on the Earth's natural resources intact to its children. We are facing an emergency and must make decisions that will be not only for our Highest Good today but also for the Highest Good for generations to come. While changing the way we live in order to preserve ourselves and our planet may be a big change, it can be accomplished with a workable plan. I call that plan "The Next Evolution: making the planet work for everyone," and I'll get into the details of that plan in the next chapter.

NEW DEFINITIONS

To keep our resources intact, we need to eliminate as many non-essential jobs and products as possible, and, acting as one family, we need to share our wealth and resources. We need to redefine wealth as USE and ACCESS rather than as POSSESSIONS and POWER. The everyone-for-themselves paradigm has used up our planet's resources by producing more materialism—for some, *and only some,* people, but not for the vast majority of the people on the planet. The majority would have far more if wealth were redefined as "use and access" and if we all acted according to that definition.   We can live cooperatively with so much more abundance available to us. As a planet, we can no longer afford to have individual ownership of so many things when we can get by, and do even better, on much less when it is shared. For example, almost none of us have boats, but, with the Highest Good "use and access" approach, more people could enjoy boating and with far fewer boats (and thus the resources it takes to build and maintain them). In almost any marina, about 99 percent of the boats go unused most of the time. If we shared access, those boats would be in use rather than 99 percent docked. Just think of the possibilities if this were a "Use and Access" world—we would all have the freedom to do so much more.

Did you know that there are over 25,000 supermarket items, including two hundred kinds of cereal? There are also over 11,000 magazines, mostly filled with ads for more products.[47] There is such a tremendous amount of stuff in stores and warehouses with more being produced all the time (and eventually hauled off to landfills). In fact, there may be as much in storage as there is being used. Much of it is also the art of selling us what we don't really need. Such is the nature of capitalism. Also, in the spirit of sharing, we need to look at quality of life more in terms of intangibles such as fun, shared creative activities, nurturing, loving, etc.—things that money really can't buy. I have reserved the next chapter to describe more in detail what that might look like in a creative model of living that would work for all of us.

The idea of great wealth at the expense of great poverty doesn't make sense any more when we must now do no further damage to our environment. Molly Olsen, a member of President Clinton's Council on Sustainable Development, stated that "A society with a grossly disparate distribution of the fruits of development cannot possibly sustain itself in the long term."[48] Take deforestation for example. Because most industrialized countries have already destroyed most of their own forests, most deforestation is now occurring in Third World countries where people are living on the edge of survival and need either more farming land and/or fuel to survive even this generation. Along with that, their debt-ridden governments think they must sacrifice their forests and resources looking for short-term profits to pay off their debt interest. We

Which Comes First —Food or the Forest?

■ Mexico's lush Selva Lacandona is being ravaged by peasants who claim slash-and-burn agriculture is the only way to keep their families from going hungry.

By FRANK CLIFFORD
TIMES ENVIRONMENTAL WRITER

LAGUNA MIRAMAR, Mexico— From the air, the forest looks like a green serape tossed over a camp-fire. It is tattered, scorched and smoldering—slowly being burned to bits.

Less than a thousand miles from the U.S. border, Mexico's largest rain forest—the Selva Lacandona—may not survive beyond the

"One of the signal accomplishments of Rio (the 1992 Rio de Janeiro Earth Summit Conference) was the official linking of environment and development issues, including an explicit recognition that poverty itself is a driving force behind a large share of environmental degradation."[50]

The Earth Summit Agenda 21 document concludes with this statement:

"An environmental policy that focuses mainly on the conservation and protection of resources without consideration of the livelihoods of those who depend on the resources is unlikely to succeed."[51]

can't just ask Third World countries to stop cutting down their forests because the issue must be tied into improving the quality of their lives. We can't have people living in poverty trying to support a family because they will take from the environment what they have to in order just to survive.

But, as a reminder, the issues are not just environmental. We can't have people working at minimum wage trying to support and effectively raise a family. Put yourself in the place of those trapped by poverty, the lack of education and skills, and even the lack of positive role models. With that hopelessness it's easy to understand why people turn to drugs and crime.

So we must change the world on the level of how people live together. For this to happen, it requires a change of consciousness where we switch from the everyone-for-themselves paradigm and start acting for The Highest Good Of All. We must also consider the Earth as a partner in that change. Imagine the Earth as a living being—would we choose to continue to slowly poison it or choose to begin to heal it? To heal it, we have to start thinking about what we're doing every time we buy, use, or discard anything, and we need to creatively rethink how we can change the whole system that created our current patterns in the first place.

Unfortunately though, we haven't set up our lives so that we as a group can easily make Earth-healing choices. On the one hand, we have those trapped in poverty forced to use up the environment, and, on the other hand, we have consumerism producing unnecessary, and far too many, products with their accompanying packaging and disposal problems. Most of our cities' landfills are full and closed and are contaminating our ground water in addition to releasing methane gas into the atmosphere. We Americans have been throwing away enough "waste" each year to fill a convoy of ten ton garbage trucks that would reach over half way to the moon.[52] The packaging for our consumeristic lifestyles contributes the largest percentage of that "waste"—50 percent of all paper produced in the U.S. and 90 percent of all glass.[53] We Americans also have the highest level of consumption in the world. With 6 percent of the world's popula-

tion, we consume more than 30 percent of the planet's resources.[54] In addition, we use twice as much energy per person than any other country and are responsible for more than one-fourth of the carbon dioxide and CFC emissions.[55]

As a result of the Industrial Revolution and the resulting pollutants now being released into the environment, man now has the possibility to destroy the planet, even without a nuclear war. However, the fact that there may be no easy way out of the world economic dilemma, along with the now obvious environmental threat, may be a good thing. Ultimately it will push us in the direction of trying to act for The Highest Good Of All Concerned, of acting like one family, of taking care of each other in a more loving and nurturing way, and of addressing the quality of life for everyone on the planet.

WE NEED A WORKABLE NEW MODEL

So where do we start? There are so many imbalances, so many things that need to be corrected, and so many just causes that trying to do something about each little area of interest gets to be an overwhelming task. Save the dolphins, the whales, recycle, end political corruption, save the rain forests, do something about crime, reduce our drug use, eliminate domestic violence, etc., etc., etc. So much to do, and so little time left for the planet. Also, there's the problem that everything, as physics' Systems Theory tells us, is interrelated, so something like saving the rainforests is not as easy as it seems because it relates to so many factors including the quality of people's lives. Therefore, there must be a systems approach to rescue the planet, and it must include and address the quality of life for everyone on the planet. To do this requires two things: we need a different approach for how we as people live together, and share together and we need to move into the cooperative consciousness required to do this—the consciousness where we truly dedicate ourselves to living for The Highest Good Of All.

Because most of the people in the world would have no idea what it would look like if we chose to live together for The Highest Good Of All, the first step would be to create a MODEL

"We recognize that poverty, environmental degradation, and population growth are inextricably related and that none of these fundamental problems can be successfully addressed in isolation."[56]

—Making Common Cause, A Statement and Action Plan by U.S.-Based International Development, Environment, and Population NGO's

COMMUNITY, based on the concept of making life work for all of us, to show the world how life could be very, very different. While "intentional" egalitarian communities are certainly not a new idea, with many small ones currently existing, none have been created with the intention and on the scale that is needed to arouse worldwide interest. We need to see an approach that not only could heal the planet but will also show a different way of living with a daily quality of life that would be more uplifting for almost anyone living on the planet.

The way we live together and relate together in community is the basic building block that is needed to change the world. The creation of a model Community that demonstrates living for The Highest Good Of All will enable others to see how we can all cooperate and enjoy a higher and happier standard of living. With the successful demonstration and media coverage of this model, people from all over the world will be able to see and hear about a lifestyle that they too can enjoy and how we can start by setting up life to work for everyone, for The Highest Good Of All.

Again, there are enough resources and manpower for all of us, all life on the planet, to live together very abundantly. We just haven't set it up that way yet because of the legacy of our everyone-for-themselves socio-economic-political approach. It is now time, so I invite you to expand your consciousness and open your heart as we describe a model that could work for everyone, that would stave off the dire predictions of what otherwise is in store for us.

Chapter 4

LIVING FOR THE HIGHEST GOOD IN COMMUNITY

THE WAY WE LIVE TOGETHER AND RELATE TOGETHER
IN COMMUNITY IS THE BASIC BUILDING BLOCK
THAT IS NEEDED TO CHANGE THE WORLD.
—The Community Planet Foundation

Utilizing the concept of living For The Highest Good Of All
Life, how do we design our model living situation (Community)
so that it will work for all of us? We must not only meet the needs
of the planet by living sustainably, but we must also meet the
needs of the people involved by optimizing the quality of life for
ALL people. So the questions are:

(1) Does being ecological mean that we have to suffer? and

(2) Does sharing our resources mean that we all have less?

The answer to these questions is an emphatic NO! In fact,
living in harmony with each other and the planet can be more fun,
far more abundant, and much more satisfying than the lifestyles
most of us are currently living. Given the Western society's
penchant for consumption and indulgence, if we can't provide a
more satisfying model for living, we won't change how we live
until the decaying environment eventually forces us as a society to
change our consumption patterns. But we don't have to let it get
to that point because doing the best for the planet will also
optimize the quality of life for all of us if we choose to live together
in a way that can truly work for all of us. So open your mind and
your heart to the possibility of how we could be living, and, if

there's something that we may leave out of our description or that you may wish to alter somewhat, just put that in because you would be a part of this model too and your needs are important.

HOW HAVE WE DESIGNED OUR TOWNS AND CITIES?

As a starting point let's look at how traditional towns and communities get started. How did your town or city end up looking and operating as it does? Chances are that it started out with a single home or two—possibly even farms—located on some fairly flat land. Then there were probably more homes built as people moved into the area, and they were followed by some businesses. When the cluster grew big enough, government and service buildings were added until there was an unplanned and unintegrated hodgepodge of structures and streets. Also, because of the everyone-for-themselves economic model, most of the space under roofs and most of the concrete laid down to cover the earth ended up robbing people of their connection with each other and with nature, which eventually got pushed out of their lives.

With the advent of cars, we started paving streets, driveways, parking lots, walkways, and freeways until an astounding amount of land was covered with asphalt and concrete. Since it was easier to build on the lowlands and flatlands, we forced the farms further and further out from the cities and, with suburban sprawl, further out still—eventually even leading to the demise of the small farmer. Then, as the cities overcrowded, those who could moved away from the town centers dreaming of the good life with a home in suburbia. They moved into their large suburban homes, which now don't even reflect the current living/relationship patterns. But, with the need for the everyone-for-themselves income, we often have to jump back onto the freeways and spend a lot of time in congested rush hour travel. We also have to get back into our cars to go and do almost anything—shopping, recreation, errands, meetings with friends, etc.

So, before anyone ever stopped to do an environmental or sociological impact study, we created havoc for both our immediate environment and our lifestyles. We pushed out nature. We pushed out fresh food grown on the best farmland. We tied up our lives in traveling and depersonalization to the point that many of us now get minimal exercise (we are now a nation of overweight and obese people largely because of this factor), minimal playtime, and, most importantly, minimal quality time spent with good friends and family. Chances are, for many of us, the jobs we have to do to support ourselves take up—and sometimes become— most of our lives, and many of us spend 99+ percent of our time with concrete between us and the earth.

CAN WE DESIGN LIVING IN HARMONY?

But what if we could live in harmony with the environment, with each other, and with ourselves, and what if we could also enjoy really abundant, nurturing, creative, and fun lives? Imagine living in a Community of loving, nurturing friends who live and work together as one family. This Community has been meticulously designed and built so that we are living in harmony with all life. Because we have chosen to live in a way designed from the beginning to be for The Highest Good Of All Life, we are living integrated with nature rather than having to use the vast amount of building and concrete space inherent in the everyone-for-themselves model.

The Community produces all its own clean energy and, through cooperation and the use of positive technology, is as nonpolluting and sustainable as possible. Nature flourishes on hundreds of beautiful acres, and most of the organic food is grown through advanced techniques and nonobtrusive, edible landscaping. Since vehicles are parked at the outskirts of the community, and pavement is used minimally, it's a wonderful place to play outdoors or go for a walk and touch the land.

When residents are done working in supportive, nurturing jobs, the Community offers a full array of recreational, creative, and growth opportunities. Organized sports, games, music, movies, just hanging out with great people, and other fun and relaxing activities are freely available, and the residents enjoy them with friends who are within easy walking distance.

The population of the Community would be between 400 and 500. That size would be large enough so that the Community could have the kinds of amenities and opportunities for a variety of recreational and creative expressions, yet not so large that it would preclude each person from taking an active role in the decision-making process in the Community.   Cooperative communities have existed for years, but none based on the Highest Good For All model on the scale that would have more universal appeal such that people not living there would say, "Yeah, this Community's lifestyle is much better than my own. I'd like to live there!" Most are too small to have the amenities and the diversity that would appeal to people used to certain opportunities of urban living.

Critical to the design of the Community is what I call the fun factor. Communities have stagnated and ultimately failed because they weren't fun, and people lost interest. But, if people are having fun, others are drawn in. Thus, for the Community model to be viable, fun and pleasure must be interwoven into every facet of the Community. In fact, a Highest Good approach mandates that fun, joy and loving be the essences in our daily lives, because they are so essential to our individual and collective well-being. People need to know that we can have a society where we're really connecting with each other and having a lot of pleasure. Most people now have grown up thinking that fun is having control over others, being self-indulging, being greedy, being lustful, and competing with and having enjoyment at the expense of others. People need to rediscover in a deeper way what fun is for them, and a Community designed for The Highest Good Of All will provide the ideal stage for this rediscovery. The tremendous potential of the "use and access" principle I described earlier is an integral part of this.

SUGGESTING A MODEL

Not being an experienced writer, this chapter, describing how life could be in a cooperative Community on the scale I'm proposing, was the hardest chapter to write. What was the best way to paint a picture of how life could be? I considered a "day-in-the-life" type of approach, but that seemed a little trite to me. Instead, since presenting the vision of how life could be very different is the key factor to seeing how we can live together in harmony, I decided to go with a more detailed description of a possible Community designed for The Highest Good Of All.

As a way of introducing a description of what life would look like in a Community built on the principle of The Highest Good Of All, I'd like to share with you the introduction from the proposed model that I, along with a few members of the Community Planet Foundation, wrote a few years ago. We have been working with various models, so keep in mind that this is just one possible option we're considering and there are a lot of possibilities:

"Imagine looking out and seeing unspoiled nature with clean air and a stream running by with clean drinkable water. Imagine at the same time that you are in the middle of a Community where people are living and working together as one family. The residents here increase their abundance by sharing Community resources which allows everyone access to a full range of recreational, educational, and creative interests. A purpose of this Community is to support individuals in their growth so that they can make their dreams a reality. It is also the aim of its members to find peace and harmony within themselves, with others, and with nature, in hopes that this will assist in bringing peace to this earth.

"This is the vision shared by the members of the Community Planet Foundation, which is bringing forth a planned cooperative Community. We are designing an environment that enables us to live in greater harmony and balance with ourselves, each other, and our environment. In this Community it is necessary that our lifestyle not only has abundance and success but is also nurturing and fun. In creating such a model Community, others will be able to see how we can all cooperate and enjoy a higher standard of living. Others can learn from sharing our experiments and experience through publications, seminars, workshops, and temporary residence in the Community. Eventually we envision that the replication of our Community or similar models will have a transforming effect on individual and world peace and the prosperity of all mankind.

Conceptual community drawing by Thomas Slagle

"Our first challenge is to create that initial successful model. To do so we believe that the key area to focus on is how we live together. We consider issues such as how to incorporate the latest technology and how to live in harmony with nature to be very important. However, our primary concern is how we interact and relate with one another and how we make decisions that include and involve everyone. Without this we would be missing the essence of what a Community really can be—a loving and joyful support group for all its residents.

"To capture the essence of what we want in our Community, we created this affirmation:

"We are living in a Community, a home of peace and loving, dedicated to:

- Demonstrating harmony with all life;
- Nurturing and supporting each other;
- Sharing our wealth as one family;
- Listening to the truth within each other and responding with kindness, consideration, and loving honesty.

"At first our plan was to describe the Community through focusing on areas like economics, agriculture, education, recreation, etc.. Instead we chose to focus on more expansive questions involving how people live together:

1) How do we share our abundance?
2) How do we interact with our environment?
3) How do we reach consensus?
4) How do we beautify our environment?
5) How do we enjoy ourselves?
6) How do we enrich ourselves?
7) How do we coordinate what we live to do?
8) How do we nourish ourselves?
9) How do we vitalize ourselves.?
10) How do we communicate?
11) How do we bring forth inner wisdom?
12) How do we expand our Community?

"To see how much more expansive these twelve 'How do we ...' focus areas are, notice how the areas of health involves so much more when we consider, 'How do we vitalize ourselves?' Likewise with food production and preparation, when the question is 'How do we nourish ourselves?' it makes us think about all the aspects that are important in nourishing ourselves rather than just putting good food in our bodies. We see how the twelve focus areas are all interrelated, and we think it is important that, as we move into a new age of cooperation, that we begin to consider our lives as a whole rather than to compartmentalize them.

"As we explored the twelve focus areas, we intentionally tried to avoid making hard and fast rules; we wanted the individual to have as much freedom as possible. At the same time we realized that everyone in the Community would have to have a commitment to the Community's well-being and its mission for it to succeed.

"There are three parts in describing each of the twelve focus areas. The first is a short Overview. Next are Essence statements, which are the ideals we feel are the essences for that focus area. Last, we list the Guidelines, which are the standards we will observe and the explanation of how our community functions with respect to that focus area."

IT'S IMPORTANT WHAT QUESTIONS WE ASK

Not only is it important that we ask questions about how we live together, but it's important to ask the right questions. Any community is only going to be as good as the fundamental questions it asks and is willing to take on. The questions determine the outcomes, so it all starts with the questions. In 18th century America we once asked the question, "How can we live with more freedom, equality, and harmony?" It was, at the time, revolutionary in the world. Even today, everywhere in the world, people know of Washington, Jefferson, and Franklin. But we've stagnated and largely forgotten that noble question that was the foundation for our country, and it's now time to take freedom and equality to the next level. In fact, with what we've done to the planet, it's needed for our very survival.

Any good idea, or good question, is always subject to corruption if it is not constantly and creatively explored and energized. Right now it's obvious that the power brokers and money interests in our everyone-for-themselves paradigm have exploited the once noble question our founding fathers asked. The planet isn't going to survive in an everyone-for-themselves paradigm with the questions that the power-based system asks: "How can we get control and shape people's lives?"; "How can we gather for ourselves as much wealth as possible?"; and "How can we disempower and numb people out so they don't overthrow the system and we lose control?" While the last question may not be absolutely conscious, the big players absolutely have a huge stake in maintaining the status quo. Remember the Nicola Tesla story earlier, well that's just one of a million examples.

Because of the stagnation and narrowness in the questions we currently ask, that's why we, in our Community Planet Community description, decided we had to be really expansive in the questions we chose to ask about how we live together in Community. For example, the question we asked about how we govern ourselves—"How do we reach consensus?"—stands in stark contrast with the current ideology of how does everyone try to get their way and how do the power brokers manipulate and control the masses. If we were to ask "How do we reach consensus?" in all our decision-making, the question is so expansive and all encompassing that we would eventually come up with a decision-making system that includes The Highest Good For All. As part of that question, we would take on the more fundamental question I've posed, "Given that there are enough resources and manpower on the planet for all of us to live abundantly and in harmony with our environment, what is the problem?" As long as we have the imbalances on the planet that we currently have, we need to passionately keep asking that question and start acting upon it. Eventually we would end up with a model that would work for all life on the planet and for future generations.

Again, it all boils down to what questions we ask and are willing to take on, and I think most societies have been asking very limiting questions, at best. For example, the Puritan culture, which still has an influence on us today, asked very controlling questions: "How can we get people to behave out of fear?"; "How can we punish people to keep them in line?"; "How can we show that suffering is good?"; "How can we keep women in their place?"; and "How do we repress people and get them to keep their feelings to themselves?" At this time in history we need to ask very different questions, the kinds of questions that we asked in our Community description of how we would live together more successfully and more abundantly. Underlying all the questions is our foundational, fundamental question, *"HOW CAN WE LIVE TOGETHER FOR THE HIGHEST GOOD OF ALL CONCERNED?"*

HOW DO WE SHARE OUR ABUNDANCE?

One of the first questions a group of people living in any community needs to ask is how to define their financial interrelationships. This question gets answered by default in our current world economy because we just continue the old everyone-for-themselves paradigm without exploring other possibilities. Also, wealth is typically defined as a person's net worth. But isn't wealth so much more than that? An ailing and/or depressed billionaire would probably give all his or her material wealth in exchange for health and happiness. Recognizing that abundance in our lives means far more than material wealth, in our question concerning how we interrelate with respect to "wealth," we chose to ask how we can ALL live together abundantly. This planet could be a paradise for ALL of us to share. It's a very abundant place to live, if we would just make that choice.

As I stated in the previous chapter on the Highest Good, sharing resources has incredible advantages. We can have so much, much more when we pool our resources. We currently tie up so much of our wealth in individual possessions that we individually use. If we can redefine wealth as use and access rather than as possessions, then we can really cut down on our consumerism while at the same time having access to much, much more than we would individually have. We don't need to each own a lawnmower, a complete set of tools, laundry appliances, vacuum cleaners, etc.—we only need easy access to these things.

Although there is nothing comparable in scope to the model Communities we're proposing, the 60 members of the Twin Oaks community were living on only $250 per month each in 1986[1], and the 14 members of Alpha Farm in Oregon were living comfortably on $140 per month each.[2] Through sharing resources, we can not only have use and access of far more things than we normally would, but we would be using far less of our own financial resources, not to mention using far less of the planet's resources. We also don't need as many people laboring to produce the quantity of material goods that we consume.

In designing a model Community, one of the most challenging questions to consider is to what extent do we share our individual and group wealth. Even if we're eventually headed towards an egalitarian model, for our first model Community we may want to create a system where people with diverse economic backgrounds, choices, and lifestyles can still participate together as we transition from the old everyone-for-themselves model. In the transition period, we think it is important to provide for these individual choices while at the same time capitalizing on the tremendous economic and lifestyle benefits through living cooperatively. On the one hand, we want to take care of each other as a family. On the other hand, sharing everything equally might be asking too much of many people at first. That step would probably be further down the line when people can see how well it works to live cooperatively. With the dual purpose being to create an abundant Community that is a joy to live in and to provide a working proto- type to encourage other Communities to spring up around the planet, we know that we have to create an economic model that will make sense, and work, for almost everyone.

At first, because our planning group for the Community Planet Foundation's model was sharing oriented, we considered what would happen if we all shared equally. We felt that we, the planning group, could all do it and, through sharing resources, could all enjoy a very abundant lifestyle. However, we also knew that some people might be turned off to this—people who, at least at first, might individually want more than others. As we always worked with design situations where everyone can win, we came

"*Money is not required to buy one necessity of the soul.*"
                                        —*Henry David Thoreau*

"*Elimination of poverty, in the absence of growth
(which so far has failed to reduce poverty anyway), will
have to come from greater sharing, more population
control and [truly sustainable] development. The political difficulty of facing up to sharing, population
control, and qualitative development as the real cures to
poverty will sorely tempt politicians to resurrect the
impossible goal of growth—more for all with sacrifice
by none, for ever and ever, world without end, amen.*"[3]
                            —*Herman Daly, Professor, at the University*
                                of Maryland School of Public Affairs

up with a unique solution.

Because we see ourselves as one family, we decided that, "The land, structures, and communally-used or provided resources belong to and are the responsibility of all residents." As we look at the damage we've done to the planet, in retrospect it looks truly crazy that people have been able to do whatever they wanted to the environment regardless of The Highest Good Of All. When individual interests can do what they want with the land, water, and air as opposed to planning as a group with the welfare of generations to come taken into consideration from the start, then we have a recipe for the life-threatening environmental problems we now face. Instead, we need to design land usage to work for everyone; we need to again think of and act towards land and nature as being sacred. If we don't do this, housing and cities get stuffed together, nature and productive land upon which to grow food disappears, pollution becomes a major problem, and concrete spreads like a seal over the land while walking disappears. This is OUR WORLD, *IT BELONGS TO ALL OF US*, including future generations, and we need to plan and share it and its resources with ultimate care for all life in order to keep it intact for our children and our children's children.

In regards to housing, group ownership becomes a very freeing concept. As the system is now, people can become stuck in housing situations due to finances. Many have moved to suburbia with long commutes and the necessity of jumping into a car to do almost anything. We usually also have no idea who our neighbors are and no real connection to them as people. Because buying and selling is at the mercy of the ebb and flow of the market, people get trapped in locations, sometimes for years, while their lives get progressively more isolated. Then, because they need their 9-to-5 jobs to continue their lifestyle, they get trapped on the treadmill of life.

Our model Highest Good Community would provide basic human needs to all residents. These benefits include food, shelter, health needs, recreational and creative equipment and supplies,

A century and a half ago Thoreau wrote about situations where people get trapped by their housing. This description in Walden *could just as easily be about the entrapment many people feel today.*

"And when the farmer has got his house, he may not be the richer but the poorer for it, and it may be the house that has got him. ... I know one or two families, at least, in this town, who, for nearly a generation, have been wishing to sell their houses in the outskirts and move into the village, but have not been able to accomplish it, and only death will set them free."[4]

—*Thoreau, Henry David,* Walden

communication systems, educational opportunities, and transportation. However, if a person chose to work outside the Community and the person earned more than the average cost per resident cost of living, the resident would only be obligated to contribute ten percent of that excess amount to the Community. Likewise, residents working within the Community and making money outside (i.e. through outside investments) would contribute ten percent of their outside income. With the above system, we felt that all residents would have a baseline lifestyle at a very high level, and the people who want even more could not only still have that, but also their increased riches would benefit the whole Community as well.

As I wrote earlier in the "Highest Good" chapter, the now prosperous Mondragon area of Spain is an example of people working together for the benefit of all. Another example of the value of cooperation is the kibbutzim in Israel. With less than four percent of the population living on about 250 kibbutzim, they still produce forty percent of Israel's agriculture and seven percent of Israel's industrial exports.[5] At the same time, they provide all the food and housing for their members as well as the medical needs, education, and entertainment, and recreation.[6] With an entire Community planned from the beginning to be in harmony with all life, with the sharing of resources, and with our renewed sharing with nature and with each other, we can do even better in our model Community in terms of the abundance of our lives on all levels.

The Community Planet Foundation's overview description for "How Do We Share Our Abundance?" is as follows. Again, there are many possibilities, so this particular description is just our attempt at painting a possible picture based on the Highest Good For All. Because a friend of mine said that the "Guidelines" portion of the description read a little dry, I tried to spruce it up a bit by interjecting some non-italicized comments.

HOW DO WE SHARE OUR ABUNDANCE?

We in Community Planet operate under the premise that there is enough wealth on the planet for everyone to have a very abundant standard of living. Historically the problem in achieving this has been in

Out of Reach

The Gap Between Housing Cost and Income of Poor People in the United States

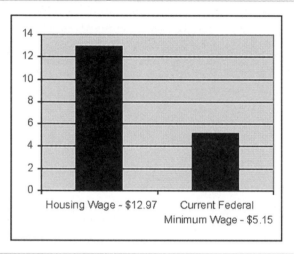

Housing Wage	Hourly wage, at 40 hours per week, needed to afford U.S. Median Fair Market Rent for a 2-bedroom unit. Currently $12.97
Current Federal Minimum Wage	Currently $5.15

• The number of poor, unassisted renters is at an all time high, and the number of housing units available to them is decreasing

• The housing wage one must earn to afford a one or two bedroom unit anywhere in the country exceeds the minimum wage, often by a factor of two or more.

• Low wage workers are faced with impossible demands on their ability to live in decent, affordable housing.

the distribution of wealth. With people tying up so many resources in the accumulation and protection of possessions, much of the planet's wealth goes unused. When we share a Community, we do not need tennis courts, swimming pools, and beautiful gardens of our own, we just need access to those facilities within the Community. Likewise, we do not need a car for every person, we just need enough cars so that everyone who needs to drive away from our Community has access to one. We can collectively save a huge sum of money by sharing our abundance on many levels. Possibly wealth in our times needs to be redefined as use and access rather than ownership.

We have also created a system in our Community where people with diverse economic backgrounds, choices, and lifestyles can still participate together. In Community Planet, we think it is important to provide for these individual choices while at the same time capitalizing on the tremendous economic and lifestyle benefits through living cooperatively.

<u>*ESSENCES:*</u> *How do we share our abundance?*

- *By supporting our growth through an attitude of dynamic openness.* (It's amazing the abundance that can come to us when we are open to the gifts that God has in store for us.)
- *By sharing our wealth as one family.* (We must eventually recognize that we are all sisters and brothers on this planet.)
- *By sharing out of our overflow.*
- *By sharing on the basis of need.* (When will we finally learn that the needs of the one are the concern of everyone?)
- *By being joyful givers on all levels.* (Giving joyfully and being of service are excellent ways to be abundant.)
- *By recognizing that the source of our abundance is in our inner qualities of love and joy.* (We need to realize that the quality of our lives has more to do with what is happening inwardly than what is happening externally.)

<u>*GUIDELINES:*</u>

- *The land, structures, and communally used or provided resources (i.e. vehicles, furniture, equipment, etc.) belong to and are the responsibility of all residents.* (We don't

The U.S. is among the wealthiest countries in the world, and yet it is filled with people, rich and poor, who are anxious about their future and who feel that they don't have enough.

"Our economic life is defined by scarcity. Adam Smith wrote of economics as the maximization of each individual's self interest within a context of scarcity. Each player must compete for the resources needed to sustain life or to increase comfort....

"But there have been other cultures, and still are, that have sufficiency and generosity as the foundational principles of their economic system and their way of life. Native Americans, for example, gained status thorough giving things away. Resources were to be used with care out of respect for the Earth and to ensure that future generations would have enough.

"In modern American culture as well, there is a yearning for a way of living not based on scarcity and greed. A survey commissioned by the Merck Family Fund shows that most Americans highly value family life, responsibility, and friendship— but believe that other Americans are more concerned with material prosperity. Approximately 28 percent of those surveyed had voluntarily made changes in their lives in the past five years which had resulted in lower earnings—and few regretted making the change. ...

"If we seek to fulfill our non-material needs with material purchases, to paraphrase Donella Meadows, we can never have enough. Our needs for family, friends, community, and a spiritual life get put off while we work hard to pay off the debt from purchasing all those things that were supposed to make us happier. The less time we have for meeting our real needs, the more needy we feel, and the vicious cycle continues."

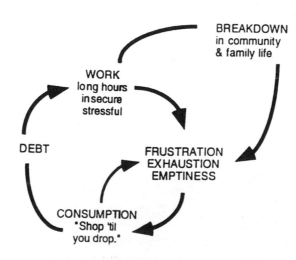

—*Sarah van Gelder, "Real Wealth, Redefining Abundance in an Era of Limits"* from YES! A Journal of Positive Futures / NO. ß1[7]

need the burden of so much stuff, it's ALL ours.)

- *Residents have ownership of their personal possessions,
  which may include furniture, equipment, vehicles, etc.,
  which the residents have individually purchased.*   (But you can
  still use my oldies cd's—I can't listen to all of them at once.)
- *The living structures belong to the Community and the
  residents may have lifetime tenancy.*   (Let's free ourselves
  up without losing any of the real advantages.)
- *The Community provides basic human needs to all
  residents at a fair and reasonable exchange rate. These
  benefits include food, shelter, health needs, recreational
  facilities and equipment, communication systems, and
  transportation. Every resident working in the Community
  will earn enough to provide for their living and personal
  expenses.*   (Until we truly take care of one another, it's still
  an everyone-for-themselves world.)
- *Residents working outside the Community contribute 10
  percent of their income over "x" amount/month to the
  Community general fund. ("x" = the average cost of
  living per resident.) They have the option of contributing more
  than 10 percent.*

  ** Residents working within the Community and also making
  money outside (i.e. through investments) contribute 10
  percent of their outside income.*

  * They have the option of contributing more than 10 percent.
  (I'll be sharing all of mine and getting so much more
  in return.)

  ** They do not receive the monthly income if their income is
  greater than the amount of the cost of living plus the
  monthly income.*
- *Requisitions are available for emergencies, trainings, education, etc.*
- *Excess Community income, by the process of consensus,
  can be put into the general fund, put into special projects,
  or used in any other way that the Community decides.*
  (This must be our decision, not the decision of special

interest groups.)

- *Incoming residents give a non-refundable entrance fee to the general fund of the Community. The guideline is that the fee is large enough to show commitment but not too large as to exclude people.*

- *When a person chooses to leave and get re-established outside the Community, the Community, to the best of its ability, will support that person to get re-established.*

Think of the impact that redefining wealth as use and access would have on crime. People currently don't know what to do about crime. We talk about harsher punishment and more enforcement, but creating a lifestyle with abundance, opportunity, nurturing, and loving based on a sharing model would reduce crime much more effectively. Because of the resource sharing in the Community, crimes of property become almost meaningless. What can a person really steal when they have access to virtually everything the Community has to offer?

Also, living abundantly has less to do with consumption and material goods than it does with the quality of our lives on all levels. I know of one family of four that was living in a cabin in California's Sierra Nevada mountains on less than $10,000 a year. The husband then got a job in the San Francisco Bay area that paid $200,000 a year. However, with all that this income could buy, the family came to the realization that the quality of their lives and their abundance was far greater when they were living in their cabin.

Interestingly, while our consumption has increased 45 percent since 1970, the Index of Social Health reports that, during this same time, the quality of our lives has dropped 51 percent.[9] Consumption and materialism do not equate with abundance and often are the antithesis of what abundance truly is. A 1995 Merck Family Fund survey indicated that Americans would be happier with lifestyles based on gratifying personal relationships rather than on consumption.[10] According to a *U.S News and World Report* poll, 51 percent "would rather have more free time, even if it means less money."[11]

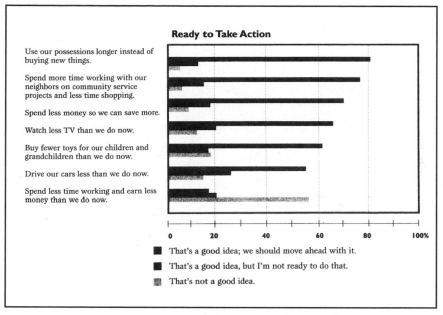

Reprinted with permission of the Merck Family Fund

—The Harwood Group, "Yearning for Balance," a 1995 study of citizen perspectives on the issue of consumption, commissioned by the Merck Family Fund

"Because we each need a lot less money to live on, we'e not chained to permanent 9-to-5 jobs that most people do just to survive, even when they dislike their work. We've created our own cooperative businesses or work at part-time jobs in town, jobs we enjoy and which reflect our values. Since we need to work less than full-time to support our simpler lifestyle, this leaves us more time to pursue our deeper interests: spiritual growth, service projects, travel, hobbies, and education. To us and to most community members, the major attraction of reducing our living expenses is having time for self-fulfillment and things that really matter. In addition, having fewer possessions means that fewer possessions 'possess' us and occupy our time and attention. So instead of focusing so much on things, we can focus on people and notice more of the beauty of the natural world around us."[12]

—Corrine Mclaughlin and Gordon Davidson, *describing their Sirius community in their book,* Builders of The Dawn

"At the present time we have a society based on having and owning: we need a society based on being and giving."

—*Mike Scott*

One downside of what we typically think of as wealth is that most of us get stuck on the treadmill of having to slave to perpetuate our lifestyles, and that really drains the life out of most people. We've been chasing a concept of freedom that we've thought of as having enough money to do what we want, when we want, to the extent that we want. The trouble is that in an everyone-for-themselves model this isn't possible for the vast majority of people. If there's not even enough money in circulation to pay the national debt, then there is a finite amount of what people think of as wealth, thus producing the haves and the have-nots. We've bought into having lots of possessions because we think they create freedom through security. However, freedom is anything but being stuck on the treadmill, and wealth is really so much more than money or material goods.

Part of the essence of freedom is having fun and pleasure, and living in our Community will be incredibly fun and rewarding on all levels as we heal the alienation and isolation that have characterized our civilization, and we move into being nurtured by nature and by each other. That really is our divine heritage.

HOW DO WE INTERACT WITH OUR ENVIRONMENT?

Remember that, since the time of Francis Bacon in the 17th century, the question that our culture has asked about our environment has been, "How can we detach ourselves from nature and manipulate it to advance our own human interests?" This question has led us to our current environmental crisis. Utilizing the concept of The Highest Good of All Life, the question we must ask is, "How do we design a physical situation that will work for *all* of us and *all* life on the planet?" We know that we must meet the needs of the planet by practicing sustainability. We must also meet the needs of the people involved by optimizing the standard of living for all people.

Let's imagine taking a piece of land for a Community. This could either be raw land or land where we could eventually replace any existing structures. The first thing we'd do is an environmental impact study in order to see how we can best protect and restore nature, what the population carrying capacity of the land is, where it's best to build and to grow food, etc. While the minimum amount of land needed would depend on each location, I would foresee at least 1,000 acres for a Community of up to 500 people. While some of you may think that's a lot, keep in mind that we don't have to live as packed in as we now do, especially as we start growing food within the Communities and as we begin to restore nature. In designing the Community as a whole, we can plan for its growth and limit its size to that which the area can naturally support.

Because of the cooperative nature of the Community, one of the immediate design improvements we can make would be to design it to be a pedestrian Community. We could bring walking back into our lives, and, when needed, use the Community solar rechargeable electric carts. Because most people would work within the Community, we could also cut way back on the use of cars (which would be parked on the outskirts of the Community). For a Community of 500 people, we may only need 50 or so cars, probably even less. With the amount of resources most of us tie up in our cars, just think of the savings we can have in transportation. Also many, if not all, of these cars could be run with non-polluting energy. In addition, just picture a living situation without fences and without all that concrete and space we use for roadways and parking areas.

According to the USDA, we're losing over 3 million acres per year of agricultural land to development.[13] That's almost three times the size of Delaware, much of it being put under concrete, every year! Almost all of this is due to the lack of cooperation in our current system. When we all finally start living For The Highest Good, there are machines that eat concrete and turn it into sand. Then we can reverse our current course and instead start eliminating millions of acres of concrete every year. In addition, the buildings would be designed from the beginning to be multi-use and multipurpose structures. In the current everyone-for-themselves paradigm, most private and even civic structures go unused a great portion of the time. In a cooperative Community, we would need to have fewer structures while, at the same time, having far more facilities for all of us to use.

Conceptual pedestrian Community by Thomas Slagle

Using existing technology, we can generate all of our own energy—through solar power and other options, depending on location. As examples, there are six thousand villages in India that are running on photovoltaic[14] and the story of the Gaviotas village in Colombia provides us with an incredible model of energy self-sufficiency in the most challenging of environments.[15] Also, when designing from scratch rather than trying to retrofit, we can save a huge amount of energy by designing and building in energy efficiency in the first place instead of coming along later and trying to correct past mistakes. It's interesting that ancient cultures even knew how to save energy in their designs, but we blindly build for convenience and try to muscle in, by use of fossil fuel, things like heating and cooling. Technologically, this Community would in many ways be like a Disney World Epcot Center built along the lines of sustainability. The Community would be a living demonstration of a future that is not grim, foreboding, and poverty stricken, but rather a future that is both sustainable and very desirable. Built with local, non-polluting building materials, the Community would also be a showcase for positive design, technology, and building materials.

Designing a Community to work for everyone will look different in different environments. However, in every environment, we can improve the quality of all life by designing and building cooperatively. For example, in areas with a lot of snow, we can build domes over the living and working areas, just like they put domes over stadiums. This will enable the residents to enjoy the winter while at the same time being able to walk around and play without the burden and expense that snow and ice and cold impose.

In many places water is now a problem. However, there are many ways to deal with water without resorting to dams and pumping water from great distances—practices that have had a devastating effect on our nation's waterways. For example, the California city of Arcata uses a two pond wetlands system where the sewage is naturally purified by plants. That water can be recycled for agriculture, etc. It is also possible to design structures that collect and store vast quantities of rainwater. Ancient cultures knew enough to do that. They didn't have the ability to use fossil fuels to build dams and pipe water hundreds of miles. If an area like Los Angeles had been designed effectively in the first place, we would not have to pump water long distances. We would also not be sending so much pollution into our bay, making it dangerous to swim in and contaminating the sea and the chain of life that it supports.

Because we can design a Community with recycling in mind, it will be easy to recycle our paper and just about all of our waste products. When we can't recycle, we can use our group purchasing power to buy products without all the wrappings that characterize today's commercialism, and we can buy products that are biodegradable. When we had to buy these more positive products individually, we may have thought them to be too expensive in our previous lifestyles. Remember too, that when we can share and recycle resources, we use far, far less of our planet's resources. For the survival of our planet, we obviously need to start using resources only at the rate that they can naturally renew themselves.

The promise of technology in our age was that it was supposed to improve our lives by lifting us above the whims of nature. While science and technology have largely delivered on that promise, it has often come at a price—the earth has been monumentally damaged, and there is now the threat of irreversible damage not only to the environment but also to the future quality of ALL life on the planet. Technology was meant to be our servant, not our master, and we are now left with the task of trying to figure out how to correct the damage that we've done. This task is made even more difficult because we don't want to sacrifice any of the Western consumerism to which we've become accustomed. Creating a positive model for future development is the key to returning technology to its role as a servant to humankind. Fortunately, we currently have the science and technology to rectify most of the problems facing us, especially given that we can change the way that we live together to make it work for all of us. However, it is obvious that we first need a revolution of consciousness. As Einstein said, "It has become appallingly clear that our technology has surpassed our humanity."

"*Our scientific power has outrun our spiritual power.
We have guided missiles and misguided men.*"

—*Dr. Martin Luther King, Jr.*

"*The most striking thing about modern industry is that
it requires so much and accomplishes so little. Modern
industry seems to be inefficient to a degree that surpasses
one's ordinary powers on imagination. Its inefficiency
therefore remains unnoticed.*"[16]

—*E. F. Schumacher, Economist*

From our Community Planet description:

HOW DO WE INTERACT WITH OUR ENVIRONMENT?

We are creating a Community that is in harmony and balance with nature. In designing a Community as a whole, we can plan for its growth and limit its size to that which the area can naturally support. Our design will include the recycling of resources and the fostering of a positive relationship with our environment. We will also make maximum use of the technologies that work in harmony with nature, while minimizing those technologies that pollute. Ours is a Community where people, nature, and technology work in unison to create an environment that works for the benefit of all.

ESSENCES: How do we interact with our environment?

- *By respecting and living in harmony with our environment.*
- *By keeping as natural an environment as possible.*
- *By utilizing innovations in technology to preserve our natural environment.*

GUIDELINES:

- *Limit the number of people in the Community to that which the area can naturally and sustainably support.* (We've gotten into our imbalances with nature by trying to concentrate too many people into areas that will not naturally support those numbers. There is enough land for all of us to live in balance with nature.)

- *Maintain as much natural surface area as possible and respect the flow of nature.*

    * *Minimize concrete surfaces. (Use natural pathways instead of roads.)*   (We have enough concrete already.)

    * *Encourage natural wildlife in harmony with space and nature.*

    * *Build on the basis of need.*

    * *Utilize multi-purpose buildings.* (So much of our space under roof goes unused in an everyone-for-themselves world, and this has caused a proliferation of buildings that

are not necessary if we truly cooperate.).

Require justification for individual housing space (square footage and number of rooms).   (If we are cooperating with each other and with nature, we don't need as much space under roof, we just need the flexibility to change the space we're living in.)

- *Keep pollutants from going into the environment.*   (With the current crisis in our immune systems, we've got to do this.)

Recycle waste materials.

Recycle water.

Use biodegradable products whenever possible.   (And it's almost always possible. If not, we need to start making more innovative choices so we don't pollute.)

Use natural pest control.   (Organic farmers do this now, but the huge growers are dependent on chemicals because of what they've done to the land. We need to return farming to smaller local operations.)

Minimize noise pollution (i.e., have noisy machinery underground).   (We have too much noise in our lives, and we don't have to live that way. In Cairo people are going deaf from the constant honking of car horns.)

Utilize unobtrusive indirect lighting for pathways.

- *Self-produce as much natural energy as possible by using the most efficient, non-pollutant energy systems available.*

Maximize solar heating and cooling.

Recycle energy (i.e., exchanges between heating and cooling systems, etc.)   (In the consumptive way we've designed things, this resource has gone untapped.)

HOW DO WE REACH CONSENSUS?

When we were meeting to generate the Community Planet description, we realized right away that perhaps the most important question to consider in designing a Community in harmony with the principle of The Highest Good of All is "How are we going to govern ourselves?" The age-old, supposedly politically correct model is democracy's "majority rules" system. Unfortunately, this is the very system that has swept across the planet, resulting in the mess in which we currently find ourselves. So what were the alternatives? Through the centuries, many groups like some of the Native American cultures and the Quakers have successfully used consensus decision-making. Right away we loved the idea because a Community of people living together really do need to be living in harmony with one another, while still providing for individual needs and considerations.

Popularly, consensus is thought of as decision via compromise in which everyone loses something. So you don't get confused with how politicians use the term, we described consensus as "differing with other forms of decision-making because it stresses the cooperative development of a decision with people working with each other rather than competing against each other. Everyone has a chance to be heard and come into harmony with the decision. Thus a decision is reached that is acceptable to all, a decision that everyone can say 'yes' to. There is no voting, and therefore no losing minority. Because the essence of consensus is creativity and accessing The Highest Good of All Concerned, there also isn't the need for compromise."[17]

So, in the spirit of The Highest Good of All, the question of how we not only govern ourselves but also do our decision-making in the Community became, "How do we reach consensus?' Meeting weekly for months, we brainstormed, explored, and sometimes argued about how we could do consensus decision-making in a Community of up to 500 people and still have it work. It was a monumental, yet fun endeavor which finally paid off in the very unique design which you will read about in the "Guidelines" section. Through the whole process, we, ourselves, adopted the consensus process, and every decision we made after that point was always done by the process of consensus.

When we ask "How do we reach consensus?," the question stands in stark contrast to the fundamental question that the governments run by the power brokers have asked through the centuries. Their question has basically been "How can we impose our will over the greatest number of people with the most efficiency and the least resistance in order to further our own self interests, and how can we get it past people so they either don't notice or don't object?" Make no mistake about it, this has been the basic agenda on the part of the forces that have controlled governments. Also, whether it's decision-making in businesses, organizations, or groups of all types, the most powerful and outspoken have always had a disproportionate influence over these decisions that affect our lives. The everyone-for-themselves approach has been characterized by a very definite lack of true consensus. It's time that we start asking how we can make decisions on all levels that work for and include everyone. To do that we need to consider the deeper questions we keep asking: "Given that there are enough resources and manpower for all of us to live abundantly, what is the problem?" And, "How can we live together for The Highest Good of *All* Life on the planet?" This takes creativity, it takes challenging our assumptions about how we have to live together, and it takes respecting and valuing each other and all life on the planet. We can do this, and we must.

A consensus decision-making system is only workable when there is the commitment and consciousness to go for The Highest Good of All. However, as I said before, if we're going to continue to have a world, we're going to have to start making it work for everyone. This first model Community will require that consciousness of committing to go for The Highest Good of All. Then, when people see how much more freedom and abundance they can have through cooperation, that will probably be the most significant thing the Community will contribute to changing the world. As McLaughlin and Davidson wrote in *Builders of the Dawn* about the Philadelphia Life Center (Movement For A New Society), "They see consensus as a concrete example of the real healing work that is needed in the world, the elimination of power relationships between people and the celebration of our mutual humanity. It teaches people to open up on a more spiritual level, on an interactive and intuitive level with others."[18]

Majority rule is a competitive, win/lose approach. You win when you get the most votes, and you lose when you don't. Because you're trying to prove that you're right and the opposition is wrong, there is often much divisive arguing. Also, people listen to the arguments not really out of concern for the needs of others but to try to develop counter arguments. Historically we've voted for so many issues and for so many people that have lost that none of us really feel that we are represented politically and that our needs are being met. The majority rules system has resulted in all of us, except the power brokers, feeling that we are a minority group. As a result we usually vote for the lesser of two evils; we vote against someone or something rather than voting for someone or something in an election. That's why most election commercials focus on trying to give us reasons to vote against the opposition because they're so terrible. They do this negative electioneering because it works. I'd be embarrassed as an adult to engage as a candidate in the typical election process of these rather immature power-based accusations. Yet that's what happens now more than a frank discussion of platforms and values. In our "democracy" we also see partisan politics every time any hi-profile issue comes up—the other party almost always takes the opposite side. They do this just to be against whatever decision is made, and they do it purely in an attempt to try to discredit the other side and try to win the "againstness" vote.

As we all have experienced, there is a hierarchy of power in majority rule groups where the opinions of leaders, money interests, and outspoken players carry a vastly disproportionate influence over the rest of the group. People outside of the power game who may be shy in speaking out or have difficulty putting their ideas into words may be ignored even though their ideas may be better. Also, because whoever the minority is in the moment can so easily be dispensed with by just outvoting them, the notion that everyone can participate in a democratic system is not really accurate.

With so many people and their input being left out of the process, the quality of majority rule decisions is also diminished. The process often boils down to voting between two positions

REAL LIFE ADVENTURES
By Wise and Aldrich

The political convention that
represents most of America.

FEIFFER

FEIFFER © JULES FEIFFER. Reprinted with permision
of UNIVERSAL PRESS SYNDICATE. All rights reserved.

This post-election cartoon captures the essence of political campaigning.

White House Seeks to Still Criticism of Mrs. Clinton

In an election year, anything can come under attack. Aren't public figures allowed to seek counsel or therapy just to enhance their lives?

■ **Counseling:** Psychotherapists defend first lady. She calls her consultations an 'intellectual exercise.'

By RICHARD T. COOPER
TIMES STAFF WRITER

WASHINGTON—Published reports that First Lady Hillary Rodham Clinton had consulted with Jean Houston, a psychological counselor, and had imaginary conversations with the late Eleanor Roosevelt have kindled new heartburn inside the White House.

White House officials expressed concern privately Monday that—coupled with Whitewater, the developing controversy over White House use of FBI files and other problems—the news might be used by critics to hold the Clintons up to ridicule.

They relied on two allies Monday: psychotherapists and the first

lady herself.

Mrs. Clinton opened her remarks at a Nashville, Tenn., conference on family issues by joking that she had just had an imaginary talk with First Lady Roosevelt, "and she thinks this is a terrific idea." The audience laughed.

In a statement issued Monday, Mrs. Clinton described the meetings with Houston and others as an "intellectual exercise." She said: "The bottom line is, I have no spiritual advisors or any other alternatives to my deeply held Methodist faith and traditions on which I have relied since childhood."

Psychologists and psychiatrists indicated Monday that Mrs. Clin-
Please see TALKS, A11

proposed by the main factions.   Innovative and creative approaches and solutions are often not considered, and systems-approach solutions are virtually never considered. Supposedly this is to expedite the process, but instead this causes monumental inefficiency as the sub-quality decisions negatively impact our lives. Those decisions then have to be redecided again and again through the years because they either don't work or are short-sighted in the long run. Also, because people are left out of the process, they may easily feel justified in feeling resentful and not supporting and/or sabotaging any given decision.

In true consensus decision-making, everyone has a chance to participate and be heard. The softer voices and the more unique approaches all have the opportunity to be responded to by the group. Also, not just logic but feelings and intuition are valued as well. As an example, when a group of us were meeting to create a description of how the Community would work, there were a few times when most of us would decide upon what we thought was a good logical approach to describe an aspect of the Community. However, our one more intuitively-oriented person would say, "It isn't right," and really stuck to that. When we'd ask her what wasn't right, she couldn't really give us a logical response. After some initial frustration, because we all needed to be in agreement on a decision, we eventually started sharing new ideas and brain-storming beyond what we felt was the obvious. In that process we then always came up with a new idea which we would get excited about and develop into a much better approach than our initial one. She would then say, "This is it." After awhile we began to trust the intuition and feelings of the group members. Sometimes those feelings were really our own individual issues, but the safety and loving support of the group allowed us to rapidly clear those concerns. It has been said that consensus has an advantage over majority rules because the best thinking of the entire group is included, but my experience is that the synergy of the group creates even more than the sum of the parts.

In *true* consensus decision-making, the process of creating a decision that works for everyone brings in the element of *creativity* as well as the qualities of caring and concern for others. We really

"I DO NOT BELIEVE IN THE DOCTRINE OF THE

GREATEST GOOD FOR THE GREATEST NUMBER.

IT MEANS IN ITS NAKEDNESS THAT IN ORDER

TO ACHIEVE THE SUPPOSED GOOD OF FIFTY-

ONE PERCENT, THE INTEREST OF FORTY-NINE

PERCENT MAY BE, OR RATHER SHOULD BE,

SACRIFICED. IT IS A HEARTLESS DOCTRINE

AND HAS DONE HARM TO HUMANITY! THE

ONLY REAL DIGNIFIED HUMAN DOCTRINE IS

THE GREATEST GOOD OF ALL."

—GANDHI

"Since we have all been conditioned by society to think mainly in terms of ourselves and how we can meet our own needs, it's a huge shift to have to think in terms of the whole community and the needs of everyone. It takes some careful re-education to be really considerate of others and to learn to trust that other people can also think about you and be aware of your needs. And at the same time, you have to maintain your individual integrity so that you don't get overwhelmed by an over-identification with the group or by too much dependency on it. ....

"In truth, the only individuality a person has to give up in community is the 'right' to take advantage of others, to be dishonest, or to attempt to obtain from others or from the community more than s/he is willing to give them."[20]
    —*Corrine McLaughlin and Gordon Davidson,*
        Builders of The Dawn

Reprinted with permission of The Center For Visionary Leadership.

"No one is born knowing how to function in a democracy, any more than we are born knowing how to drive a car. Co-ops need to train their members continually in the arts and skills of democracy, just as we always need to keep training new drivers how to drive a car."[21]
    —*Joel David Welty, "The Rochdale Principles of 1844 in Today's Cooperatives," from the 1990-91* Intentional Communities, A Guide to Cooperative Living Directory.

"Win-win is not adversarial, it's synergistic. It's not transactional, it's transformational."
    —*Stephan Covey,* First Things First

have to listen to and respond to the needs and concerns of others. In that process of going for The Highest Good of All, innovative, high-quality solutions are reached, and the support of the group in implementing those decisions is assured. While this may sound too good to be true, keep in mind that a prerequisite for living in this Community must be that a resident is committed to going for The Highest Good of All. This does not at all mean giving up individuality, but it does mean not imposing one's ego-position on the group and it means that all residents are committed to looking at their own personal issues, issues that may seem to have nothing to do with the issue being decided. The group supports this exploration by creating an atmosphere of safety within the group that allows people to relax and really tune in to their inner thoughts and feelings rather than having to defend themselves. Consensus is not "group consciousness," but rather it requires people to be honest and mature and to express what their needs are, where they're at, and what will work for them. While the final decision may not always be everyone's personal first choice, it will be one that serves The Highest Good of All Concerned, one that everyone feels that they can support. As opposed to the disempowerment in our current "democratic society," it will be exciting for people to become reinvolved with the decisions that affect our lives.

Quoting from the Community Planet Foundation's consensus training materials:

"CONSENSUS VS. OTHER MODELS: In consensus decision-making, each participant takes a leadership position by contributing 100 percent in sharing information, feelings, thoughts, intuition, loving, compassion, inspiration for going for the Highest Good, etc. In traditional decision-making models, many of the key decisions that affect our lives are made by others, and we then try to individually control our own little ten acres to fit within the rules. This has led to isolation and alienation within individuals and between people.

"These traditional models tend to be patriarchal, power-based systems with centralized decision-making. In consensus decision-making, there is empowerment of the individual. Each person is important, and each must stand forth in his/her integrity. But it is a new age of leadership, not me first or my needs first, but rather each of us must stand forth to recognize our inherent oneness and make it work for all of us. To do this, each person must not only be responsible for themselves, but also for the whole group.

"PARTICIPATING FULLY: True consensus requires full participation by all involved. That may look like a range of behavior from sharing your concerns and/or creativity to just being really present, listening and supporting and holding a positive focus while putting good energy into the room.

"INDIVIDUALITY VS. HIGHEST GOOD: We must balance the idea of individuality and responsibility for ourselves with going for The Highest Good of All Concerned. In consensus it is important to not use our individuality against the group, but rather for others. It is now time on our planet to drop the old consciousness of separation and make life work for all of us."

Because individuality and individual self-interest are so highly valued in our culture, it's time to clarify how individual needs interface with a Highest Good For All model of living. Does making life work for everyone mean that we have to sacrifice our self-expression and individual needs? Not at all, in fact, with more support and less stress and pressures from life, people will have much more of an opportunity for expression and for getting their needs met. Sure, people are responsible for their own self-interests, but, to have a quality life, what we must understand is that getting our needs met in a truly optimal way means having happy, healthy and abundant people and a healthy environment around us.

Getting individual needs met means considering the big picture, considering the whole context within which we live. Self indulgence at the expense of others ends up sabotaging the very self-interest we're after. The immediate wins that people go after are often really not in one's self-interest in the long run if those

"Such a process [consensus] can be seen as—and often is—a cumbersome, complicated, irritating, frustrating way of arriving at a decision. After all, does the wish of everyone have to be considered? And the silent answer of the group is that, yes, every person is of worth, every person's views and feelings have a right to be considered. When one observes this process at work, its awesome nature becomes increasingly apparent. The desires of every participant are taken into account, so that no one feels left out. Slowly, beautifully, painstakingly, a decision is crafted to take care of each person. A solution is reached by a process that considers each individual's contribution—respecting it, weighing it, and incorporating it into the final plan. The sagacity of the group is extraordinary.

"The process seems slow, and participants complain about 'the time we are wasting.' But the larger wisdom of the group recognizes the value of the process, since it is continually knitting together a community in which every soft voice, every subtle feeling has its respected place."[22]

—*Carl Rogers,* A Way of Being

[My note: in my experience it doesn't have to be painstaking, but it may be. With humor, fun and loving, it's possible to bypass frustration.]

"You must have a tremendous commitment to each other and to the work you are doing to use it [consensus]. I've watched people using this process grow tremendously from slumber, from spiritual slumber, personal slumber, disconnectedness from other human beings, to being excited about working together, about being fully equal participants in a group.

"The usual things that are done to keep women and blacks and others out of decision-making cannot be done with a consensus process, where everyone has equal opportunity to participate. Groups of people can't be voted out, shouted down, excluded.

"Consensus is a strong breaking away from the old cultural values of a dominating, aggressive society that is very patriarchal and closed off to spiritual values and to human interaction. Consensus is like learning to walk for the first time, or like being on another planet—it's that kind of difference. People come into a consensus workshop or group thinking it's just another decision-making process, before they become aware that it means changing your life. It means reaching out, opening up to others. You can't lie, and you can't hide. You can't be a power mogul. Consensus is based on openness and trust."[23]

—*Casey Capitolo of the Philadelphia Life Center, as quoted in* Builders of The Dawn.

wins come at the expense of the planet or any of its people. It is not a rich life with rich and happy surroundings when those around us have to struggle to try to get ahead and are stressed out and not having a lot of fun in their lives. It really limits our opportunities when our neighbors have no time or energy to share with us.

In a Highest Good approach to living together, we can create abundance for all. Then our self-interest is achieved with having happy people around us who can really share and appreciate our successes. We must expose the myth that cooperation means compromising our own self-interests. Remember that the Systems Theory tells us that all things are interconnected. We can either choose to continue to go for the immediate gratification, which later can work against all of us, or choose to lift everyone. We call this latter approach "enlightened self-interest" because it encompasses the fact that we are all interrelated and it is the only approach which will even work for us individually over time.

With everyone having input into the process, you might think that it may take too long to make decisions. While that may be true at times, the long-term benefit is that time is actually saved by making much higher quality decisions instead of having to continuously work to correct poor quality decisions that didn't include the needs of everyone and the environment. As people gain trust in and experience with consensus, the process gets faster and faster without loss of quality. Also, because of the participatory nature of consensus, it's difficult to work consensus with more than twelve people in a group. Therefore, for our Community to work consensus in a group of up to 500 residents required an innovative approach. Perhaps the best way to share that solution is to just quote our Community Planet description:

HOW DO WE REACH CONSENSUS?

Perhaps the most essential question for Community living is "How do we reach consensus?" We decided that in our Community we would all have a direct role in the ongoing decision-making. The key to doing this is that all residents belong to hubs of about a dozen people. In addition to being a support group, these resident hubs are where the key issues of guiding the Community are explored and decided. There are also twelve focus areas which deal with the work and planning of the twelve questions of how we live together. People working in the same focus area also form a second grouping of hubs called Focus Hubs. To prevent special interest groups and individual personalities from taking control, we have a set of checks and balances. With everyone belonging to both a resident hub and at least one Focus Hub, the Community has the benefit of many perspectives. Also, all the information about what is happening within the Community is available on Communit-linked computer so everyone can be informed about all Community proceedings and activities.

Since everyone who joined the Community has shared the vision and agreed to the guidelines of the Community, there is already a strong basis for consensus. However, when differences of opinion do occur, we value the importance of working to resolution so we can all move forward in cooperation and a greater oneness.

ESSENCES: How do we reach consensus?

- *By creating a positive atmosphere for people to communicate and participate.*
- *By involving everyone in the decision-making.*
- *By encouraging the natural leadership of each person.*
- *By making participation in decision-making creative, spontaneous and fun.*
- *By supporting and assisting individuals in reaching their personal goals.*
- *By making decisions that support the Community affirmation.*
- *By creating decisions where everyone wins.*
- *By keeping the guidelines dynamic, flexible, and simple.*
- *By listening to the truth within each other and responding with kindness, consideration, and loving honesty.*

  (While I'm editing this, in rereading these essences, I have nothing more to add—they stand for themselves.)

GUIDELINES:

THE DECISION-MAKING STRUCTURE: (This section may seem a little complex at first reading. Referring to the Community Planet Hub System chart on the nexp page would be helpful.)

- *Essence Hubs - Each resident belongs to a small decision making support group.*
- *Main Hub - one resident from each of the Essence Hubs participates in the Main Hub on a rotating basis.*
- *Focus Hubs - Each resident belongs to at least one of these hubs. There is at least one hub for each of the twelve focus areas. These Focus Hubs make up the entire working structure of the Community.*
- *Management Forum - Representatives from the twelve focus areas make up this group.*

ESSENCE HUBS:

- *Deal with Community essence issues and the generalities of the working of the Community.*
- *Consist of a suggested size of about twelve people maximum.*
- *Can consist of family members* (and/or friends—make it a fun group of people to hang out with, support one another and discuss and explore interesting issues) *who choose to be together.*
- *Must have representatives from at least "x" different Focus Hubs and may not consist of people all from one Focus Hub. ("x"=1/3 of the total number in the group.)* (The idea is to have a broad representation from the 12 working structures of the Community, both so that there is a broader base of information and experience available for exploration and creativity and so that we don't have highly polarized Essence Hub groups.)

FOCUS HUBS:

- *Deal with the specific details of how to implement the vision and direction of the Essence Hubs (through the Main Hub).*
- *Are support/coordination groups for accomplishing the work within the Community.* (Each job or section of work in the Community is in one of the 12 Focus Hubs—our 12 "How do we …?" questions/groups.)

THE DECISION-MAKING PROCESS:

- *Community decisions are coordinated at the Main Hub Essence Hubs.*

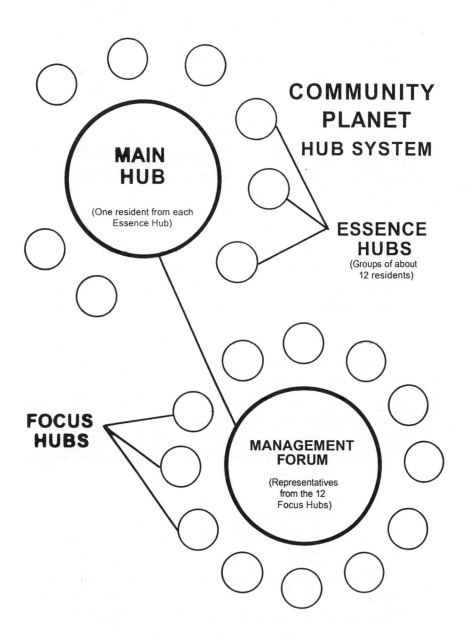

- *The ideas, questions, and suggestions the Community considers can be generated by either the Main Hub or the Essence Hubs. The information exchange and decision-making is therefore a two-way process.*   (As opposed to decisions coming down from the top.)

- *Community consensus is reached by unanimous agreement of the Main Hub members after those members have received the unanimous agreement of their own Essence Hubs.*   (That's our very definition of consensus.)

- *To aid the Community to come into consensus, a communication system is available which allows anyone in the Community to address the Main Hub while simultaneously the proceedings of the Main Hub can be shown to all the Essence Hubs. (See "How do we communicate" for details.)*   (When the Main Hub meets to make decisions that concern all residents, the Essence Hubs meet at the same time. Through the use of technology, each Essence Hub is able to communicate with their Main Hub representative, and each person also has the capability to address the whole Community, if needed. If we are to truly do consensus, it is necessary that everyone has the capability to be heard. In my experience with consensus, anyone could, at any moment, have the inspiration that changes everything and leads us to a far better decision.)

- *Main Hub has the final say on all decisions.*   (And, in consensus decision-making, that's still really all of us.)

- *Management Forum coordinates the efforts of the twelve Focus Hubs in implementing the Community plans and activities.*

- *Management Forum and the Focus Hubs work under the direction, guidelines, and budget passed by the Main Hub.* (So we're working under ourselves rather than some power structure.)

- *Main Hub decides upon an Annual Vision to establish a direction and budget for the year(s) to follow.*
   * *Management Forum proposes and presents an Annual*

Vision to the Main Hub.

* The Annual Vision can also come from the Essence Hubs. "Annual Vision Time" starts a week-long conference/event where everyone gives input through their hubs. (Sounds like fun, sort of like a party with a purpose.)

* The Management Forum works on the practicality of the Vision.

* The Main Hub may change the vision/budget at any time when the conditions warrant.

THE HUB GROUP MEETING FORMAT FOR SUPPORT:

- *To create a harmonious atmosphere at the start of each meeting by doing a centering process and having a time for personal sharing so each person is heard and supported.* (Because people bring their baggage from their lives into meetings, giving them a chance to be supported and to place any disturbances into the 'Light' brings people more fully present so the meetings are more productive.)

- *To give everyone the experience of being listened to and understood.* (In my experience, when meetings are not going well, there's almost always a safety issue—a person just not feeling safe inside, either with themselves or with the group—at the bottom of it, and taking the time to deal with that can move us quickly from a stuck, tense, or uninspired place. Often it just takes acknowledging the safety issue and sometimes sharing a little about it.)

CHECKS AND BALANCES:

- *Decisions are unanimous.* (True consensus, by its nature is the ultimate check and balance.)

- *Each resident is a member of both an Essence Hub and at least one Focus Hub so there is a duality of perspectives.* (We loved it when we came up with this. Since we each belong to at least two different Hubs with different perspectives, it's sort of an internal check and balance within each of us. In our society, we need to not be so attached to our own ideas, but instead have a greater flexibility and openness to all ideas and to build on all ideas to reach the best possible decisions.)

- *There is an Annual Vision and Budget with allocations to each focus area.*

- *The Management Forum reports to the Main Hub on a regular basis and a monthly financial statement goes out to everyone.*

- *All transactional and meeting notes are Community accessible on computer or other media.*

- *An accountant(s) (in the "Consensus" Hub) monitors the Community expenditures.*

- *Budgets may include one-time (one check, one item, and/or one payee) spending limits above which one must get approval from the Main Hub.*

  (Also, remember that leadership is rotated, giving everyone an opportunity so that we don't reproduce our society's modus operandi of having the same small group of people involved in leadership. Everyone has leadership potential. Styles may differ, but with support, people can blossom and be very effective and often add something special to the group.)

DISPUTE RESOLVING FORMAT:

- *Win/Win resolutions are encouraged.* (Since our group wrote this, I've had lots of experience with consensus, in many and diverse situations, and I've seen this outcome every time.)

- *Personal responsibility is encouraged by looking within first with the consciousness that we create, promote or allow everything that happens to us.* (Taking personal accountability for our lives.) *Then, if clarity is still needed between the parties involved, the disputes are settled by the following flexible options, always bringing in loving and creativity:*

  a. *Between the parties involved.*

  b. *With an agreed upon third party.*

c. Within the hub(s).

d. By the Main Hub.

This system is flexible with each situation, and the parties involved can choose the options. (And again, win/win decisions can be found with creativity and compassion. If we're going to have peace on earth, it all starts with the interactions in our own personal lives.)

EMERGENCY PROCEDURES:

•*1) Immediate situations (something requiring action within 24 hours, or until an emergency committee can be formed (whichever is less): The Main Hub chairperson calls the Management Forum chairperson, and they gather the expertise they need to deal with the situation.*

•*2) Other Emergencies:*

> * *Main Hub chairperson declares an emergency and:*

>> ** *Notifies residents of the situation.*

>> ** *Calls an emergency committee (rotating Main Hub representatives on a predetermined rotation basis).*

> * *Emergency committee then finds short term solution(s). Short-term solutions are actions to be taken, within a one-week period, necessary to maintain the health and welfare of the Community.*

>> ** *The committee recommends long-term solutions to the Main Hub.*

>> ** *The committee's authority ends upon resolution of the emergency by the Main Hub.*

> * *Main Hub or Management Forum may, by a simple majority, override the decision that there is an emergency.* (This is not an exception to the process of consensus, but rather it prevents immediate action on the part of a person(s) who has been acting without consensus in a perceived emergency.)

> * *There are designated successors in case people for either the "Immediate" or "other" emergencies are not available.*

> * *There are set maximums of money that can be spent for*

each type of emergency.
* The committee's authority extends to the short-term
solution, and they will make a full report of procedures,
expenses, etc. to the next Main Hub meeting.   (In this
Community, a person will not be able to make decisions for
the people that are not in the best interest of all the
residents. Contrast that to what our current governmental
leaders have been doing.)

As an epilogue to this consensus section, perhaps the biggest
export of our model Community will be this concept of going for
the Highest Good, and consensus decision-making will be a major
key ingredient in that. It is unreasonable to expect most people to
begin to work consensus right now. It really does require the
commitment to go for The Highest Good of All Concerned.
However, as people see and hear about the benefits of working
consensus in a Community setting, people will become interested
in getting training in how to work the consensus process.
Consensus can have a transformational effect on relationships at
every level.

In my experience as a trainer, I have seen marriages, families,
and businesses greatly improve by practicing consensus. In fact,
in one of my trainings, I saw a marriage start to disintegrate right
in front of me. Instead of panicking (like my co-facilitator), I
thought to myself, "How perfect," and I just took them through
their crisis by using the very principles of consensus. Since they
were committed to their own personal growth, I pointed out to
them how perfect it was that this holding onto positions was
happening because that's what happens in our lives all the time,
and that's what's been happening in our society, where we have
been at odds with one another for thousands of years. Without
making anyone wrong, I simply asked if we, all of us, could start
to make other choices, start to let go of our past hurts (often having
nothing to do with the current situation—like the hurts from our
family backgrounds), and start to make going for The Highest
Good of All Concerned bigger than all our stuck positions.
Magically, one reached out and then the other. We took a 15-

minute class break, they started talking, and now, four years later, they have a great relationship. My co-facilitator was impressed. Years of therapy may not have been able to save their marriage. Consensus is so powerful, I have seen many miracles like this.

I'd like to conclude this section that relates to how we govern ourselves by saying something about rules. I think that we'll find that the fewer rules we have, the better we'll function. A lot of rules reduce freedom and responsibility. I think we've noticed that the more we try to enforce rules, the more resistant people become. Laws create outlaws. With people gaining the consciousness of the Highest Good and acting accordingly, we will have need of far fewer rules.

In this country, people's lives have been virtually enslaved by being at the mercy of over-regulation and over-regimentation and the complications of laws and rules that people are at the mercy of. We have more and more reporting, i.e. income tax is a major annual ordeal, and the government wants more and more information on all of us and where our assets are, etc. People live in fear of and obsession about laws, taxes, bills, and balancing their own personal finances while trying to save for an uncertain future (especially given what the government is doing and how many services will still be around). Then if we want to do something or if we need to protect ourselves from someone wanting to do something to us, we often, because the rules are so complicated, have to hire a lawyer for $200 plus per hour to represent us. In fact, our judicial system is now really a throwback to the old trial by combat. You hire your mercenary (lawyer) and they hire theirs. Usually the outcome has more to do with who has paid for the best combatant rather than anything having to do with truth or fairness.

In a consensus decision-making system, we don't need to live with the outside control that has preoccupied so much of people's time and life-force. Solutions arrived at where everyone is heard and all needs are considered have the effect of simplifying our lives and causing us to relax, knowing that we don't have to protect ourselves from others. Our life-force needs to be spent with personal growth, making a contribution, service, pleasure, and having fun.

MISTER BOFFO By Joe Martin

HOW DO WE BEAUTIFY OUR ENVIRONMENT?

Boy, how did we come up with this question for the subject of architecture and Community design? Again, it's important that we ask questions and what questions we ask, and we struggled with what the question was for this area. Traditionally, nature has not been considered in the design of towns, cities, and even an individual's use of land. It seems that the question our culture has asked is "How we can remove a few more trees, cover more land with concrete, and add a few shopping centers and malls so that we can get people out shopping so we can make money without the objections from these damned environmentalists?" Because we need to restore the environment rather than keep imposing on it, when we considered what we would design, we always came back to the question of how we would beautify our environment. The architectural design then comes out of that. But we have to start with considering the whole, the impact that anything would have on the whole area and its use, and not just consider the buildings and the architecture in isolation. Living in a beautiful place that is in harmony with nature also has the effect of greatly enriching our lives, and that resource is a major part of how we can all live abundantly.

Our Community Planet Foundation's overview for this area reads:

HOW DO WE BEAUTIFY OUR ENVIRONMENT?

Imagine looking at a Community and being struck by the natural beauty of the environment. Imagine also walking in a natural setting along natural paths surrounded by trees and hearing birds singing even in the Community center. We can design a Community that is so integrated with nature that, not only is it visually pleasing, but also the disruption of nature is kept to a minimum.

With people sharing resources and having the Community as their own, both the number of structures and the amount of personal space needed diminishes. (The co-housing movement has verified this.) Without fences and boundaries, we are left with beautiful vistas and the uninterrupted flow of nature.   (Imagine living without fences, where the land is open, the field of vision beautiful, and you can walk anywhere.)

ESSENCES: *How do we beautify our Environment?*

- *By being in harmony and balance with nature.*
- *By creating esthetically pleasing structures and landscaping while harmonizing with the natural beauty of the area.*

(We kept the essences pretty simple.)

GUIDELINES:

- *Have houses and structures make the least visible impact.* (The idea we had was to more fully enjoy the natural beauty of an area and even to restore the natural beauty if it had been previously damaged. Of course, some architectural designs could also add beauty while still bringing nature back into our lives.)

- *Make them an extension of the environment (i.e. depending on the area, they could be partially under ground, integrated with the trees, ivy, etc.).*

- *Use building materials natural to the area.*   (As much as possible we need to be locally responsible by practicing sustainability, and we have to be globally responsible by cutting down on the mass transport of so many materials, which has the effect of exploiting the land in distant areas while also using up energy and producing pollution.)

- *Build on the basis of need.*

  * *Community structures are multi-use in nature.*

  * *Individual houses/living units are built on the basis of need in terms of rooms, square footage, and design.*   (This is really not a limitation, because if a person/family has a need for more space, it can be easily provided. We're not doing a poverty imposition trip here. I've always wondered what people do in these houses that are so big that they can't possibly live in all the rooms. Do they play hide and seek? They have to hire people to even maintain

them. At the same time there are many who live in situations where there are ten or twenty people living in one or
two bedroom houses. When we share a Community and
no longer have to encapsulate and feel that we have to
protect our possessions within our walls and fences, we
can all live more abundantly. Thoreau, who led a very
abundant existence in the quality and joy of his life, wrote
that the key to happiness was to "Simplify, simplify,
simplify."[24])

- *Honor the environment and climate.*

  * *Utilize visually non-obtrusive agriculture.*

  * *Avoid using big blocks of land that would disrupt the
  environment.*   (Which is what our current agricultural
  practices have done.)

  * *Use high-tech production methods, such as permaculture, etc.*

  * *Use edible landscaping.*   (Fruit and nut trees don't
  have to be in faraway orchards.)

- *Encourage the wildlife natural to the area.*

- *Encourage the vegetation natural to the area.*

- *Keep the landscaping (i.e. trees, water areas, etc.) in
  harmony and balance with nature.*

- *Plan recreation areas within the landscaping.*

- *Allow no vehicles within the Community unless needed
  for construction, people with mobility limitations,
  emergencies, etc.*

  * *Limited or no concrete or asphalt roads or walks within
  the Community—use all natural surfaces while at the same
  time main areas and structures are accessible to all.*

  * *Parking is on an outskirts area.*

- *Utilize no above-ground wires.*   (How often we've
  thought, "What a beautiful view, except for the wires.")

- *Keep outside night lighting to a minimum.*   (So we can see
  the beauty of the night sky. The average number of stars

visable on a clear night in the wilderness is 2500; in a suburb, it's 250.[25])

One of the problems of the American housing industry is that living situations are generally not being designed and built for the needs of the people. The building industry still builds homes as if most of us are married people with children. Also, even if most of us were in that status, our housing needs change during our lives. We would go from being single to being married to having children to the children growing up and leaving home. These stages all require different housing, and this is hindered by the current economics of buying and selling and moving.

The Community will offer a whole new concept in housing where flexibility is the key. With the Community as a whole, and not individuals, owning the housing, and with resource sharing, we will be able to create innovative designs to provide different options to people in different stages of life and with differing needs. We will demonstrate cheaper housing with the option for shared spaces and the opportunities for more social interaction. However, there will also be the opportunity for and respect for private space both within one's living space and in outdoor sanctuaries.

Designing a Community as a whole before anything is built, such that the Community would be in harmony not only with our lives but also in harmony with nature, would be an eco-architect's dream. The structures would be designed for energy efficiency, be built with natural, non-toxic materials, be earthquake proof, and would even capture and store rainwater. The innovations in this area are already here and being built on an individual basis, but the creation of an entire cooperative Community built for The Highest Good of All residents and nature would truly be a thing of wonder—like the Epcot Center idea I described in "How Do We Interact With our Environment?"

In thinking about having less personal space within your walls than you would have in a conventional house, some of you may think that that's a lot to give up in going for the Highest Good. However, remember that the entire Community with all its amenities and opportunities for recreation and creative expression is

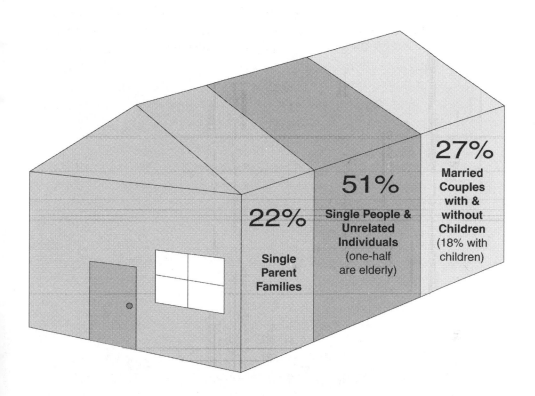

WE HAVE DIVERSE HOUSING NEEDS

now yours. Also, some interesting information comes from the co-housing movement. Co-housing residents are people who have decided to live together usually with less personal space (which is individually owned) and with some shared areas such as a dining/meeting room big enough for all residents, possibly some multi-use rooms, and outdoor areas. The individual co-housing homes normally have a kitchenette, small living room, bedroom(s), and bathroom(s). Interestingly, after some years of living in this experience, what the residents almost universally say they would do differently, if they were to redesign their co-housing, is to build their individual areas smaller and create more and larger group areas.

HOW DO WE ENJOY OURSELVES?

Most towns and cities have a parks and recreation department, theaters, museums, events to partake in the arts, and various other opportunities for leisure time activities. For us, though, we thought that we needed to ask a broader question. Our lives don't have to be so compartmentalized that we don't build enjoyment into every fabric of our lives. We need to do that, we need to start designing our lives so that they are a living affirmation of self-actualization, learning, and enjoyment. Too often the question our society has asked us is how we can get people more regulated, squeeze more time and money from them, and get them to bear down harder and produce more and have less free time (and spend money with the free time that is available). While our society is suspicious of free time, our Community will focus on bringing joy and creativity into every aspect of our lives.

In our largely urban society, we spend hours in our cars commuting to work, shopping, running errands, and driving to where we can play, be in nature, and exercise. As a result we are increasingly losing time in our lives for family, friends, and recreation. According to a Harris poll, we have one-third less leisure time than in 1973.[26] This is having an adverse effect on both our physical and emotional well-being. Depression is now our fastest growing medical problem. Remember when we were younger and recreation and play were very much a part of our lives? Not

"... the wider human habitat, far from being humanized and ennobled by man's activities, becomes standardized to dreariness or even degraded to ugliness. All this is being done because man-as-producer cannot afford 'the luxury of not acting economically' and therefore cannot produce the very necessary 'luxuries'—like health, beauty, and permanence—which man-as-consumer desires more than anything else. It would cost too much; and the richer we become, the less we can 'afford.'" [27]

—E. F., *Schumacher*, Small is Beautiful

"We are so trapped in this frenetic world of clocks and computers, schedules and programs, that most of us are counting the days until our next vacation." [28]

—*Jeremy Rifkin*, Time Wars

"Everything in life is somewhere else, and you get therre in a car."

—E. B. Wilhite

being burdened with responsibilities and having other young people around us ready to play, recreation with family and friends was readily available.

Now, for many of us, play and recreation have become something we yearn for and struggle to build into our lives. But often people come home from work with so little available time and energy in our isolated and alienated lives that reaching out to others is not even an option. It's so much easier to just ease into a recliner or lie on the sofa and watch the box. Also, quite often exercise has become going to a gym and exercising by ourselves as opposed to the group sports and activities we used to enjoy. A large part of the problem is that we have such divergent lifestyles. If we try scheduling fun on a regular basis among friends, we bring out our planning books only to find that our schedules don't match up. Maybe there's a Tuesday next month on the 17th when we can meet in the evening, but not too late because we have to drive home and get up early to get back on the treadmill. How did we ever get so caught up in our lives? Remember high school days? It was always possible to get people together on a regular basis to play.

Most adults have forgotten how to have fun. It's been so absent from their lives that they actually become frightened of it. Instead, they just make adjustments to the reality of having less and less fun and don't want to be pressured with the thought of anything more. Just as people adapt to oppression, diminished opportunity, stress, and poverty, people also have adapted to a world of little fun.

Do you know what our national pastime is now? It's no longer baseball, football, or any other sport—it's now gambling.[29] Far more people spend their time in casinos than in any other recreational venues.[30] Also, the net $50.9 billion lost on gambling in 1997 exceeded the amount we spent on movies, sporting events, theme parks, and recorded music combined![31] This is just another sign of the isolation, alienation and economic stresses that characterize our lives at the start of the 21st century. As a result, the increasing number of people addicted to gambling is one of the

DEEPEST ASPIRATIONS ARE NON-MATERIAL

"When people were asked to rate what would make them more satisfied with their lives, the responses were striking: non-material aspirations consistently outranked material ones by huge margins. Only small fractions said they would be significantly more satisfied with life if they had a nicer car, bigger house, or nicer things in their home.

"But a majority of Americans would be much more satisfied if they were able to spend more time with family and friends (66 percent rating 8 or higher on a scale of 1 to 10) and if there was less stress in their lives (56 percent rating 8 or higher). Also, nearly half (47 percent) would be much more satisfied if they felt they were doing more to make a difference in their community.

"Despite the cost in time and stress, many people say they feel stuck on a treadmill—striving for material goals that seem ever-harder to attain. ... "In our survey, 82 percent agreed that most of us buy and consume far more than we need."[32]

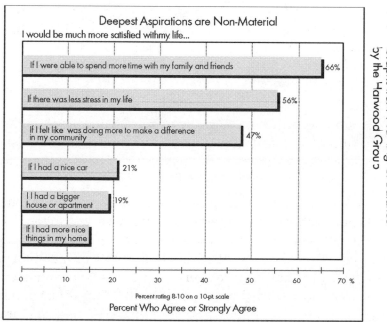

—*The Harwood Group, "Yearning for Balance" a 1995 study of citizen perspectives on the issue of consumption, commissioned by the Merck Family Fund. Reprinted with permission of the Merch Family Fund.*

"We're unhappy because something is missing in our lives, something that all the fancy gadgets and fun toys in the world can't replace.

"Lifestyle choices surround us, beckoning from glossy magazines and flashy commercials. Despite all these choices, few of us really feel much freedom to choose. There's little sense of creative expression. We're always going somewhere, *never* being anywhere. *As soon as we do opt for something, it begins to chafe ... because it never really fit us in the first place. We get trapped into thinking we'll be happy if we behave a certain way, live a certain lifestyle, and purchase all the products that go along with it.*

"...We think, 'Oh, I just need something else, one more thing and then *I'll be happy.' It's the catalogue-shopping approach to the good life. The problem is that every few weeks (or around the holidays, every other day), there's a fresh crop of new catalogues. So we're kept in a constant state of unfulfilled desire. The things we buy don't satisfy us, but we keep grabbing for more. We're addicted to accumulation, but our tolerance level is so high that enough is never enough. No wonder so many people see their own lives described in* The Overworked American, *the best-seller by Harvard University economist Juliet Schor. As she points out, since mid-century, when given the choice, Americans have consistently opted for higher salaries and more money over more time for leisure and family. Yet has this made us happier? Polls indicate the answer is no. Thus, she notes, we are trapped on a treadmill of more work, more consumer goods, and more destruction of the earth.*

"And on that treadmill, what happens to one's smile? Well, look around. See the expression so many people wear: half grimace, half fear. Lots of us look like we just ate a bad burrito—with great determination. We're not sure what's going to happen, but we're damn sure not going to let it affect us.

"Many of us who have worked hard our entire careers reach a point, usually around middle age, when we examine our lives and say, 'Hey! Is this all there is? When does the fun start?'"[33]

—*Richard J. Leider and David A. Shapiro,* Repacking Your Bags,
Lighten our Load for the Rest of Your Life.

fastest growing addictions. We've got to wake up, folks. When our lives are being eroded with concrete, over-regulation, stress, isolation, and alienation, it's no wonder that people are turning to a desperate attempt to try to buy some freedom or, at the very least, to try to beat the system. Also, I thank God that I was not raised with video games because I have seen so many people get hooked on the ease and isolation of playing alone vs. the joy of participating with others. Instead, I had my support network of friends to go out and play ball. This may be unpopular to say, but all the people I know who have visited Cuba were struck by how happy the children were. Without all the trappings of consumerism, the children get together to play with whatever resources they have.

Most of us yearn for more fun and more time for fun in our lives. To me that's what will be one of the most transformational things about the Community. This Community will be a really great place to have fun.

Living with nurturing and loving friends, a "family," we will design recreation and creative opportunities back into our daily lives. Just think about it—if you're into music, there are people who get together to jam and to dance; if you've ever wanted to act, there's a community acting group. When was the last time you played basketball or volleyball or softball? Well, the Community would have days and evenings with all sorts of organized recreational and creative opportunities. Bridge, anyone? Whatever you want, we can build into our lives on a regular basis. Also, we will not only have a host of high quality friends to participate with, but it will all happen within easy walking distance. Plus, in a world where recreation and creative pursuits can be expensive, the residents of the Community have access to far more opportunities through resource sharing. And, because our usual mode of transportation within our pedestrian Community is walking, exercise becomes a normal part of our daily lives, and, in addition, we have access to walking in nature.

With the increased social/recreational interaction, we will be able to see and study the effects that breaking down barriers between people will have and the effects that creating more connecting and bonding will have on our mental and physical health. The Community will also have a really good recreational therapist, a sort of Minister of Fun position, who can enter into the Community work situations and show how people can work and have fun at the same time. Having a good time working increases the quality of our lives and also results in increased production.

Here's what we wrote in the Community Planet description:

HOW DO WE ENJOY OURSELVES?

We feel that it is important to set aside time in our daily lives purely for enjoyment. We also believe that we can facilitate experiencing joy in every phase of our lives. To accomplish this, the "How do we enjoy ourselves" Hub coordinates a variety of opportunities for creative expression, interactive play and viewing pleasure with participation being an individual choice. This Hub looks for ways to create fun in all facets of Community life. An enjoyable aspect already built into our Community is the beauty and tranquillity of our natural surroundings. It is our experience that we can have joy in every phase of our lives and that enjoyment all starts with how we relate with ourselves and having loving communication and supportive relationships with each other.

ESSENCES: How do we enjoy ourselves?

- *By recognizing that joy is a way of life, rather than an activity.*
- *By encouraging creativity.*
- *By encouraging uplifting humor.* (Notice we singled out humor—we need to laugh more.)
- *By having all recreation within our Community freely available to all members.* (Money is no longer a limitation to the potential for enjoyment in a Use and Access world.)

GUIDELINES:

- *The Enjoyment Hub will generate, plan, and coordinate activities including:*
  - * *Organized sports and play time.*

*WE'RE GOING TO
HAVE TO LEARN
TO START LIVING
WITH MORE FUN
IN OUR LIVES.*

* *Plays, music events, etc.*
* *Time and resources for group and individual creativity.*

- *The Hub will also:*

  * *Receive and act on ideas from Community members.*

  * *Requisition items for enjoyment.*

  * *Encourage and suggest ways to bring fun into all Community activities.*   (Even in the work we do, we need to be experiencing enjoyment. If we're not, then we need to creatively redesign what we're doing.)

- *Our Community has natural opportunities for enjoyment built into our daily lives through:*

  * *Walking and cycling everywhere within our Community on natural pathways.*

  * *Enjoying the beauty and serenity of nature.*   (Simple things in our lives can be so enjoyable. I've worked with inner city youth in Los Angeles who have never been in the mountains or around trees or at the beach.)

  * *Loving communication and sharings.*   (This has been so absent from so many lives that it will be an adjustment to live with more loving on a daily basis—and all of us can use more.)

- *Our Community will have recreation facilities, including:*

  * *A multipurpose theater with a seating capacity for the entire Community population. This structure is designed to have many uses including meetings and conferences, movies, plays, etc.*

  * *A multi-use building with hardwood floors for sports, exercise, dance, etc.*

  * *A natural outside water area (i.e. lake), if possible, and/or an Olympic size pool.*

  * *Kids' play area and equipment.*

  * *Resource centers where one can pursue creative pursuits, i.e. artistic, inventive, etc.*

One last note about playing. In our current everyone-for-themselves competitive society, most sports and games are based on the principle of there being a winner and a loser. In both team and individual sports, a lot of emotionality and self-esteem can ride on whether we win or lose. Man, I hated to lose! But what if there was no one to play with? There wouldn't even be a game. So the truth is that we need the playing "partner" to even have an outcome, and I say that the "partner" therefore really assists in the win. In a Highest Good society, those earning the winning point totals need to acknowledge that the person(s) heretofore thought of as the "opponent(s)," by assisting in the win, therefore share an equal part in the win. There are no losers, and graciousness requires that we give all close calls to those we are playing because bringing in loving and kindness really does make for more loving and interesting competition where we are all left with a good feeling.

HOW DO WE ENRICH OURSELVES?

In our everyone-for-themselves world, the question here has usually been "How can we get enough money to be able to survive or to do what we want in the world?" When we consider ourselves as one family, it gives us a certain basis of support and freedom to look at the bigger picture of what freedom and wealth is. We don't have to live with the pressure we all individually experience when it comes to finances. As we relax into that realization, we start to get the bigger picture of what wealth in the quality of our lives really is, and how much more wealthy we can be by living in a Community based on the Highest Good For All. We start to look in a holistic way at how we can truly enrich ourselves.

Still, to be successful, this prototype Community must have the capacity to financially support itself. Although there will be a tremendous savings in the cost of living (through both the sharing of resources and correctly designing a Community, in the first place, for efficiency), a Community still needs to be able to provide goods and services to markets outside of the Community in order for it to be financially viable. These products and/or services could be almost anything, so there is no need here to get into specifics. However, in keeping with the sustainability of the planet, whatever is produced must be of positive value to the planet and must be totally recyclable.

"*And yet, deep down, we know that life has to be better than what most of us are experiencing. We feel so fragmented, our personal life, friendships, and spiritual values are often so separate from our work life that we feel schizophrenic. We drive hours per day across town to get from home to work to shopping center to entertainment to friends' homes, to church. Our life is compartmentalized, not whole. We feel alienated in our huge impersonal cities, suffering from pollution, the noise, the crime. We feel the grayness of our urban/suburban lives.*

"*Community can offer a way out, a solution to our dilemma. In community we can live on less income by sharing resources and 'living lightly on the earth.' At the same time, we can be doing something to heal the environment by reducing our consumption of energy and caretaking the earth. With reduced living expenses, there is less need for work and more time for relaxation, hobbies, and self-development. Stress is reduced and personal growth is enhanced.*"[34]

—*Corrine McLaughlin and Gordon Davidson,*
Builders of The Dawn

*Reprinted with permission of The Center
For Visionary Leadership.*

Ideally, much like the Mondragon model, these businesses would be owned by the Community as a whole, although several variations are possible and would be limited only by our creativity and keeping in mind The Highest Good of All. Also, existing businesses, realizing that we must start making life work for everyone, may wish to relocate into an intentional Community setting.

From our Community Planet description:

HOW DO WE ENRICH OURSELVES?

When we consider enrichment, we are looking at two main areas of wealth: material wealth and the enrichment of the quality of our lives. As we look around the Community we are creating, we find that the most striking form of wealth comes from the integration of technology, the sharing of our resources, living in harmony with nature, and the caring support that we share with each other.

At the same time, we view our Community as an enterprise where the value of our exports must equal or exceed that which we purchase. (At least until the world becomes a collection of Communities.) *To do that, the Community will have a variety of businesses and we will produce as much as is practical for our own use. This often has side benefits such as being able to consume the freshest and most natural food. Also, the Community will realize the savings that come with planning as a group and sharing our resources.*

ESSENCES: How do we enrich ourselves?

- *By being dynamically open to all possibilities of enrichment.*
- *By building time for communion with Spirit into our daily lives.*
- *By focusing on the quality of life within ourselves, with each other, and within the environment.*
- *By sharing our wealth as one family.*

GUIDELINES:

SOURCES OF INCOME

- *Encourage a variety of income-producing businesses owned by the Community.*

- *Receive contributions from residents working and/or earning income from outside the Community.*
- *Secure grants and fund-raising (i.e. through fostering research, etc.).* (The Community Planet Foundation is set up as a non-profit entity for this purpose.)
- *Receive contributions and fees from seminars, workshops, publications, and educational programs both inside and outside the Community.*

GREATER EFFICIENCY AND QUALITY THROUGH COMMUNITY SELF-PRODUCTION

- *Produce consumables (i.e. food, energy, etc.) and other needed products when feasible in terms of expense, energy, and time.*

    * *The quantity of our production must not detract from the quality of our lives.*   (There's a unique idea for our society.)

    * *Our production is through the consciousness of excellence* (Any job worth doing is worth doing well.)

    * *We will constantly strive for innovation and efficiency.*

SAVINGS THROUGH SHARING RESOURCES

- *Pool our abilities to do various tasks and projects.* (Currently there is so much waste in the way we do things.)
- *Eliminate non-productive jobs (i.e. middlemen, bureaucrats, etc.).*
- *Create group purchasing power.*
- *Share structures designed to be multi-use and multipurpose.*

ENRICHMENT OF THE QUALITY OF OUR LIVES

- *Focus on the quality of life rather than overproduction and overbuilding.*
- *Plan time into our daily lives for communion with Spirit.* (We often get so distracted by the obligations and stress in our lives that we don't even check in with ourselves to find out how we're feeling and what we can do to really nurture ourselves.)
- *Enjoy the beauty of and harmony with nature in our daily lives.*
- *Enjoy quality and simplicity rather than over-consumption.*

HOW DO WE COORDINATE WHAT WE LOVE TO DO?

Who does what job? Those who have been in control for thousands of years have asked how they can get people to do the jobs they don't want to do. The rest of the people have dealt with what they have to do in order to survive. As I wrote earlier in the "Seeds of Change" chapter, even in our society, a multitude of people work in jobs where their health is severely at risk. Others just work in uninspiring jobs that basically suck the life out of them. We need to do better than that; we need, in fact, to enjoy what we do. If that takes overhauling how we do things, then that's what we must do. The question of work, therefore, needs to become, "How do we coordinate what we love to do?"

This area concerns the work that people do. All work would fall within the 12 focus areas, and this focus Hub would coordinate that work. Two key elements of doing the work are focusing on the spirit in which the work is being done and using a creative approach to that work which people may not want to do. We tend to think of undesirable work as inevitable—"It's a dirty job, but someone's got to do it." But we'd like to approach that differently and ask how can we change things so that we can either make the task more enjoyable or perhaps eliminate it altogether by redesigning what we're doing. Whereas it's very difficult to do that with the economic forces at work in the everyone-for-themselves model, the creativity inherent in the Highest Good approach will enable us to redesign and/or eliminate tasks, and, with the elimination of stress-related illnesses and boredom, it's also more cost-effective.

Remember, most of our current jobs based on the everyone-for-themselves economic model are also unnecessary—especially the most tedious ones like accounting for what's mine and what's yours and the sitting or standing around trying to sell you something. The 8-to-5 workday would be a thing of the past unless one so chooses. With the elimination of unnecessary jobs and unnecessary work, there would be opportunities during the day for personal time for rejuvenation through play, retreat, creative pursuits or whatever one chooses.

"Less than one-sixth of the total population is engaged in actual production."

"(Our industrial working model) has had the inevitable effect of taking all normal human pleasure and satisfaction out of time spent at work. Virtually all real production has been turned into an inhumane chore which does not enrich a man but empties him."[35] *

—*E.F. Schumacher, Economist*

* (However, in Communities designed for The Highest Good of All, we can eliminate the tedious and nonsense jobs and make working fun.)

"Workplace stress worldwide has increased to the point where the U.N. issued a warning calling it 'one of the most serious health issues of the 21st century.' … In the U.S. stress-related diseases cost about $200 billion/year in lost workdays and medical claims."[36] **

—*Paul Hawkin, Economist*

** (The inevitable result of our everyone-for-themselves paradigm.)

When one can easily walk to work or anywhere else, the days do not have to be carved up into different sections as we now do by compartmentalizing our lives in our non-cooperative economic model. In leading more integrated and more creative lives, the standard question when first getting to know someone, "What do you do (for work)?" will change. How we think of ourselves and others will be different as we expand our identity and our worth beyond what we "do" and, instead, give our lives much more credit for *who we are* as whole human beings.

Through sharing work and resources related to childcare, parenting can also be a much different experience in the Community both for the parents and for the children. Because the Community as a whole becomes the support system for families (if they so choose), the parents are freed up to have time to be involved with many nurturing and re-energizing pursuits. As a result, the parents and other residents get to interact with children more when they want to than when they have to. Think of how that can increase the quality of adult/child relationships. Existing intentional communities have been experiencing these benefits for years, resulting in the maturing of confident, responsible, well-adjusted young people into adulthood.

In physically designing the Community, the architects will include designs that are not only safe for children, but also child-friendly. This means that most of the areas will be safe for the child to explore without an adult having to say, "NO! Get out of there, NOW!" We all have been a little scarred (and scared) from that "No" word and the power struggle which that set up inside ourselves. Designing things to support all of us in the first place is just such a logical thing to do to support us all, to go for The Highest Good of All.

In our society we have also often not considered the needs of older people. We put them aside when they retire, and because so many retire dependent on the meager amounts from the government, they often end up in facilities where they are grouped with other people waiting to die. Yet we have many examples of older people who continue to be vibrant because they continue to make a contribution. In a Community with common ownership, an opportunity to participate with diverse people of all ages, and a wealth of opportunities to be involved, we would expect people to be more active, live longer and healthier lives, and make a valuable contribution to all. We can do better than abandoning people to a fate of isolation and alienation.

From our Community Planet description:

HOW DO WE COORDINATE WHAT WE LOVE TO DO?

Consider the possibility that the work that you do in life could be a source of constant upliftment, learning, and joy. Imagine being a part of a team (your Focus Hub group) where all the members not only strive towards excellence but also share a family feeling where group support and fun are built into the workday. By constantly incorporating flexibility, innovation, and technology, we can also create greater freedom through efficiency.

We can do all this when we all work together as a Community and when we focus on the quality of life of the people involved. Knowing that people want to be contributing members of society, the Community will provide meaningful and useful work for all its members. As an example, older residents will not be forced to retire but encouraged to continue to contribute and share their wisdom.

ESSENCES: How do we coordinate what we love to do?
- *By focusing on Spirit in all that we do.*
- *By being flexible and innovative.*
- *By incorporating simplicity and efficiency in what we do.*
- *By encouraging volunteer service as a source of growth, balance, love and joy.*
- *By bringing fun into our work.*

GUIDELINES:
- *Every facet of the work within the Community is divided into the twelve focus areas, and the Focus Hubs within each area are responsible for the work.*

  * Some focus areas may have several hubs (i.e. "How do we enrich ourselves?" may consist of several Hub

groups in that focus area).

* *Hub groups do the work as a team.*

* *Focus Hubs are responsible for focusing on joy, love, and Spirit* (Does that happen in your work situation?) *as well as the accountability for their work.*

* *Focus Hubs begin the day with a short sharing and are responsible for supporting each member.* (When people are in alignment and attunement, they are also much more productive.)

* *People of all ages and abilities continue to be involved in the Hubs.*

* *Older residents are encouraged to continue to contribute, and they have the option of "retiring."*

* *Each member will have vacation and health leaves which are coordinated by the Focus Hubs.* (No more having to ask the boss—it's up to you and your work family.)

* *Focus Hubs' leadership is rotated.*

* *Focus Hubs consider all twelve focus questions in the work they do.* (The "systems" principle—everything is interrelated.)

* *The Community encourages "job" rotation while respecting each person's inner knowing and their abilities.*

* *Openings in Focus Hubs are filled through the process of the applicants listening to the description and deciding amongst themselves by consensus who gets the position.* (Part of the essence of consensus is creativity, and it's amazing what people can come up with to accomplish something.)

* *People working outside the Community are also in Focus Hubs.* (There could be "Enrich" Focus Hubs consisting of people who work outside the Community.)

* *Focus Hubs record pertinent information of their activities in the Community computer bank.* (Open information for all residents.)

- *The Community and teams focus on the Spirit in which the "work" is done.*

  * *We encourage love, joy, and learning in all that we do. The work is done in a positive environment (i.e. with singing, music, and laughter).*   (Again, we need to have fun in our lives.)

  * *Focus Hubs decide the degree of support for individual time allowances to pursue ongoing education and research including time at the Community creative centers.*

  * *We take a look at the least desirable work and find a creative, useful approach to do it, do it as a group, or eliminate it.*

  * *We make sure that we understand the purpose and value of everything we do in order to come into cooperation with the work.*   (So often in our society we keep doing work that really has little value or purpose, and these are usually not fun jobs.)

  * *We encourage flexibility in how we do the work and constantly look at bringing in new innovations.*

  * *We create freedom through developing low maintenance work wherever possible.*

  * *We include long-range planning in what we do.*

  * *We coordinate what we do with the seasons.*   (One of our more intuitive members kept pointing out that we need to get back in touch with the natural cycle of life.)

  * *We recognize the underlying principle of taking care of ourselves so that we can take care of others.*

  * *We encourage volunteer service as a form of balance.* (Performing service has been found to be a major factor in longevity.)

  * *We give recognition and acknowledgment to individuals and teams for their work, contributions, and service.*   (We need to acknowledge and stroke each other as a natural part of our lives.)

  * *We bring the consciousness of fun into all that we do.*   (I

haven't read this for awhile, it's nice to know that we ended our description with the bottom line.)

HOW DO WE NOURISH OURSELVES?

How we feed ourselves has been a constant part of the history and prehistory of man. In fact, the quest for food is obviously essential for all physical life. As population has proliferated and densified into areas that can no longer support it, the food industries' question has become, "How can we subjugate and manipulate our environment to make a profit growing food on huge tracts of land?" and "How can we produce all kinds of essentially junk food with no real food value, but which will generate a big profit?" When we consider the question of nourishing ourselves, rather than just feeding ourselves, we again have to look at the bigger picture. To really nurture ourselves, we need to look at how we relate to the land and to all the life on the land. We also need to look at how we can put the best possible nourishment, on all levels, into our bodies.

Current agricultural practices are depleting and polluting our groundwater, our topsoil, and our forests, and providing us with food having toxic levels of pesticides and preservatives. As towns and cities have been built in the good bottom lands and as population growth has squeezed us together, this trend has also squeezed agriculture further and further away from population centers. This, combined with economic pressures, has resulted in fewer and fewer small farmers and concentrated farming in huge tracts with the resultant harm to the environment. The average produce, often picked unripe and treated with preservatives to keep it from rotting before being sold, now travels over 1500 miles to market in the U.S. The clearing of huge tracts of land for farming has brought chemicals to the forefront in the past half century as the natural predators of the pests have been eliminated and superbugs resistant to the chemicals have emerged. The process of hybridization for large-scale agriculture, resulting in our now having a lack of variety within plant groups, has also left our produce vulnerable to insects and disease as well as decreasing the food value.[38] In fact, we have lost most of the

"Instead of searching for means to accelerate the drift out of agriculture, we should be searching for policies to reconstruct rural culture, to open the land for gainful occupation to larger and larger numbers of people, ... and to orient all our actions on the land towards the threefold ideal: of health, beauty, and permanence."[37]

—*E.F. Schumacher, Economist*

strains of our plants and seeds, and we must reverse this through local, smaller scale growing.

Noting the problems associated with the recent growth of large-scale intensified agriculture, Dr. David Tillman of the University of Minnesota concluded, "A hallmark of modern agriculture is its use of monocultures grown on fertilized soils. Ecological principles suggest that such monocultures will be relatively unstable, will have high leaching loss of nutrients, will be susceptible to invasion by weedy species, and will have high incidences of diseases and pests—all of which do occur. ... The tradition in agriculture has been to maximize production and minimize the cost of food with little regard to impact on the environment and the services it provides to society."[39] Dr. Tillman also observed that, "... greater diversity leads to greater productivity in plant communities, greater nutrient retention in ecosystems, and greater ecosystem stability. ... (Studies have shown that) each halving of the number of plant species within a plot leads to a 10 - 20% loss of productivity. An average plot containing one plant species is less than half as productive as an average plot containing 24 - 32 species."[40] Therefore, as opposed to the traditional monoculture agriculture, growing a diverse crop of plants within the Community will not only replenish and sustain the soil, but will also result in increased productivity and fewer pests.

As I wrote earlier, perhaps the most distressing aspect of current agricultural practices is that the toxic chemicals have now spread to our waters where they are genetically altering animals, birds, fish, and reptiles, rendering them unable to reproduce. Likewise, as I showed earlier, our own immune systems are being damaged as our consumption of the chemicals takes a steady gradual toll on us. We are inadvertently involved in a gigantic genetic experiment because of our agricultural and other pollutive practices. For our own health and the health of the planet, we need to demonstrate non-toxic agricultural systems that are in harmony with the environment.

"The genetic uniformity of a crop amounts to an invitation for an epidemic to destroy that crop. The uniformity itself may result from the market place (machine harvesting, processing, etc.), as well as the absence of genetic variety in the crop breeding programme."[41]

— Pat Mooney, Seeds of the Earth

"In biology, rigidity and uniformity work against species survival. The diverse will (and do) inherit the earth."[42]

—Jeremy Rifkin, The Green Lifestyle Handbook

"Seventy-five percent of the genetic diversity of major agricultural crops important to human survival was destroyed because of the Green Revolution in Asia and Africa and Latin America. The genetic base of crops like wheat, rice, sorghum, maize— even cowpeas and potatoes—has been destroyed in the field, has become extinct in the field, as new Green Revolution varieties were introduced in their place. The Green Revolution was an agricultural strategy to introduce high response seeds; seeds that were sometimes described as 'semi-dwarfs,' that had shorter stems. They were more able to utilize irrigation and fertilizers. And so there was a real pressure to ... and under ideal conditions they would vastly out-yield farmers' varieties of seeds that farmers have developed over the centuries. The problem was that they required the irrigation and fertilizers to do well. In the absence of irrigation and fertilizers they would still do well, but they would mine the soil. They would just draw so much out—they would demand so much from the soil—that agriculture would no longer be sustainable. And so we had a short term boom in crop yield because of the Green Revolution, which is in a sense quite beneficial, but over the long term the Earth has suffered. And because a single, high-yielding wheat, for example, might be grown from Mexico to India—or just right across a belt of the Third World—all of the traditional diversity of wheat was absorbed into that and lost."[43]

—Pat Mooney, researcher for the Rural Advancement Foundation International.

[Because of Globalization we have forced these countries to adopt our Green Revolution (so they could export crops) to make them players in the world marketplace— at the long term cost of the world's food supply.]

When we plan our food as a whole Community, we have the resources to produce most of our own food—vine ripened and without pesticides and preservatives. Using edible landscaping, permaculture, natural pest control, composting, hydroponics, aquaculture, crop rotation, and other proven natural methods, the Community will show how people can locally take care of most of their food needs without disrupting the environment. This will not only cut down on transportation costs and pollution but will also provide an important model for urban planning and for addressing poverty and hunger both here and abroad. This model of food production will also preserve the environment, replenish our topsoil, and return many devastated areas back to nature.

Having once worked with people with physical disabilities, I am also quite concerned with the plight of the farm workers. Bending over to pick food all day soon creates life-long back injuries. Breathing the chemicals in the fields and orchards creates a variety of lung problems, and the toxicity is also absorbed through the skin. Our farm laborers often sacrifice their health in poverty-level jobs with terrible living conditions, and most of us don't even think about anything more than the cost of what we're buying. But what of the human cost? Clete Daniel, a professor of farm history at Cornell University, wrote about California farm workers, "Every gain, every farm worker achievement is being eroded. If we consider ourselves a modern, humane society, I don't know how we can allow people to live under such degrading conditions."[44]

The point is that mass production of food is costing us too much in terms of our environment and people's health—both farm workers' and consumers.' In the cooperative Community, many people can participate in the growing and harvesting of organic food. This even offers a therapeutic opportunity for those of us who love to participate in gardening, but whose current lifestyles preclude that.

The Community will have one or more restaurants where people will have the opportunity to eat (at no additional cost) every meal if they so desire. Of course, most of the living units

HOW EFFECTIVE IS CHEMICAL WARFARE ON INSECTS?

• *Each year about one billion pounds of pesticides is applied to United States crops at the cost of more than $4 billion.*[45]

• *Increase in overall pesticide use since 1945 (when petro-chemical based agriculture became popular): 3,300%*[46]

• *Increase in overall crop losses due to insects since 1945: 20%*[47]

• *Increase in the amount of pesticides applied per acre of corn since 1945: 100,000%*[48]

• *Increase in corn crop losses since 1945: 400%*[49]

"What exactly is 'new improved lettuce'?"

would also have a kitchenette for those who choose to make any or all of their own meals. In any case, the Community will provide a variety of great fresh and natural food, which will have a very positive effect on both our health and longevity. It will also have a positive effect on the environment as we buy in bulk that which we can't produce ourselves, and thus we cut the waste from our consumption of food packaging materials by 99 percent.

Many people live on fast foods both because they feel that they have little time to spend on eating and/or they don't want to go shopping and prepare food for themselves. If you've reached this point in reading the book, you're a person I don't need to point out anything to about the healthiness of our country's fascination with the fast food businesses. In the Community you will be able to get a variety of some really healthy food, prepared for you quickly and lovingly, and be able to eat it in a peaceful place while being around some great people.

From our Community Planet description:

HOW DO WE NOURISH OURSELVES?

In nourishing ourselves, we will coordinate in the same Focus Hub the jobs involving the growing, purchase, and preparation of the food. (This is necessary to deal with the issue of food holistically.) *When we plan our nourishment as a whole Community, we have the resources to utilize the technology now available to produce our own food. In doing so, we benefit by being able to eat the freshest natural food and by eliminating preservatives and chemical insecticides. In keeping with our respect for the environment, we will also replenish the earth in natural ways to keep it bountiful.*

ESSENCES: *How do we nourish ourselves?*

- *By blessing the food we grow, harvest, prepare, and consume.* (How can we say this other than to say that people have had phenomenal results by acknowledging their partnership with all life. The scientific research on the sensitivity of plants verifies this.)
- *By respecting the earth and the environmental balance through the foods we grow and the animals we raise.*

- *By providing nutritional education and encouraging inner wisdom in nutritional choices.*

<u>*GUIDELINES:*</u>

- *We will grow as much of our own food as possible with the following guidelines.*

  1) We will plant and grow what will naturally grow in our environment.

  2) We will create artificial environments to produce foods not natural to the Community's environment.

  3) We will import food not available naturally or which cannot be grown in an artificial environment in an efficient and economical way.

- *We will use the best and most healthful means available in organically producing our food. These options may include:*

  * *High quality water purification including a watering system that will not build up salt in the earth.*

  * *Permaculture.*   (With local farming we can return the trees and natural pest control and replenish the topsoil.)

  * *Natural pest control.*

  * *Crop rotation.*

  * *Natural fertilizers (i.e. composting).*

  * *Aquaculture.*

  * *Hydroponics.*

  * *Waste recycling.*

  * *Edible landscaping both outside and inside (individuals have the option of growing food in their own homes).*

  * *Animals for consumption.*   (I've been a vegetarian for over 20 years, but everyone's body chemistry is different. Still, most people consume an unhealthy amount of animal products.)

    ** *Naturally fed, no artificial substances to stimulate growth.*

    ** *Space to move without overpopulation.*

    ** *High health standards.* (i.e., it's almost impossible to buy chicken in this country that does not have an unsafe level of bacteria.)

- *The Community will coordinate the purchasing of the food with the food production and will offer communal eating.*

  * *The Community purchases food in bulk that we do not produce.*

    ** *We observe healthful standards.*

    ** *Individuals purchase personal preference items on their own.* (We had to add this because, while we don't carry Snickers bars, we also allow for personal choice.)

  * *Every resident has the option of having their own kitchen in their home and/or eating communally.*

  * *The Community may have restaurant(s) both for residents and visitors.*

  * *The Community has a large well-equipped kitchen(s).* (With great cooks who put their loving energy into the food.)

  * *The Community has a large food storage area(s) with emergency food and water storage.*

  * *The kitchens are designed to be energy efficient.* (Remember that exchange of heating and cooling.)

- *We will encourage good nutrition through classes and individual consultation which are available through the Community Health Center.* (Eating in harmony with our bodies has been such guesswork, and yet it's such an important part of our lives and well-being. Help is on its way.)

HOW DO WE VITALIZE OURSELVES?

What to do about health care, now there's an ongoing quandary. With the financial limitations of the everyone-for-themselves paradigm, the questions that are now asked by our society are, "How can we pay for health coverage?" and "How can we cut back what health services are covered so that the government, businesses, families, and individuals can afford to have coverage?" These are very limiting questions and have caused much suffering on the part of people who need cared for physically, mentally, and emotionally. Again, using money as an excuse for not providing needed services just means that we continue to have an illusion control us. Besides, I think we all deserve far more than just basic services. I think that every one of us deserves the opportunity for maximum health on all levels, and that means the mental and emotional levels as well as the physical. Thus, we ask the question, "How can we vitalize ourselves?" which is to say, how can we have the most vibrant lives and vitality that we can possibly have? We have the manpower and the resources to provide excellent holistic health coverage for everyone, and, in cooperative Communities, we can demonstrate this reality.

The preventative approach to health is now at the leading edge of medicine. The old model was to approach health in a piecemeal fashion and go to doctors to fix the pieces instead of looking at the big picture of what may truly be causing our dis-ease. The Community will provide a full array of optional workshops, classes, and individual consultation on this preventative approach—i.e., proper breathing, nutrition, developing inner knowing on how to take care of oneself, keeping clear and balanced with ourselves and each other, the importance of and opportunities for exercise and fun, etc.

The Community will therefore be an observational haven for researchers looking at the impact of proper foods, emotional health, belonging rather than isolation and alienation, a joyful approach to life, a nurturing family/support system, etc. Seldom before has there been the opportunity to study the effects that a vastly different lifestyle has on health. The Community will truly be a living laboratory for preventative medicine. Its lifestyle will be contrasted against our current model of waking up to go someplace to be unhappy while being on the treadmill earning money based on ticks of the clock. We can't wait to leave so we can commute home, try to recover, and get ready to do it again tomorrow. Imagine instead being able to get great exercise everyday in fresh air, eat the most nutritional food, and even get regular massages—all at no cost. We all deserve them in a Highest Good For All Community.

Writing about their Sirius Community, McLaughlin and Davidson said, "Because we eat home-grown organic foods and use self-help, holistic health practices, we have very minimal medical bills compared to the average American."[50] If most of us had to choose between health and money, we'd choose health because the wealth of feeling healthy and being able to have fun with a healthy body is more than money can buy. Living and playing in natural surroundings with great people will be very vitalizing to the health of the Community residents. Being intimately involved with the Community, people will be able to live much longer and healthier lives. The process of living will be very stimulating as opposed to the isolation and alienation that most older people (as well as people of all ages) now experience.

From our Community Planet description:

HOW DO WE VITALIZE OURSELVES?

If we look at our well-being in a holistic way, we see that health services in our Community involve much more than medical services. We have chosen the word "vitalize" in order to consider the area of health in the broadest sense. For instance, in preventing and treating "dis-ease," it is just as important to treat the causes on the emotional, mental, and spiritual levels as it is to treat the physical symptoms. In our Community we will continually focus on peace and harmony both within ourselves and with each other. In addition, on the physical level, we will treat our bodies to the finest available air, water, and food and will create time in our daily lives for exercise, fun and inner attunement. We also will have a fully equipped healthcare center that not only treats people for specific complaints but also focuses on preventative medicine and healthcare education.   (Imagine the incredible support system for health and vitality that will be available in this Community.)

ESSENCES: How do we vitalize ourselves?

- *By respecting the body.*
- *By stimulating the body, emotions, mind, and spirit to create the energy and enthusiasm for greater growth and health.*
- *By vitalizing ourselves in a holistic way.*
- *By clearing imbalances and disharmony on all levels.*   (Our

The other rats do not like it when you
take a break from the race.

mental and emotional states have more to do with health than almost anything we do on the physical.)

- *By providing loving support for ourselves and each other.*
- *By emphasizing positiveness in our thoughts and feelings.*
- *By working with the Light in all we do.*

<u>*GUIDELINES*</u>:

- *The Community has a Health Center which coordinates the health services of the Community members.*

  * Health services are also available for paying non-residents. (In fact, people may visit the Community to gain their health and vitality.)

  * Community members have group insurance for medical costs at outside facilities.

  * The Health Center treats the whole person by combining modern Western medical technology with non-traditional practices in a spiritual perspective. (Treating the whole person.)

  * The Health Center focuses on a preventative approach to health including:

  > *** Educational workshops on personal growth and development.*
  >
  > *** Regular holistic check-ups for residents.*
  >
  > *** Training on body awareness.*
  >
  > *** Proper breathing techniques.*
  >
  > *** Sharing practical health tools.*
  >
  > *** Nutritional consultations.*
  >
  > *** The development of individual inner knowing and individual responsibility on how to take care of oneself.*

- *We will consume the purest, freshest, and highest quality food and water that is possible.*

- *We recognize the importance of exercise and fun in vitalizing ourselves.* (I can't stress enough the importance of the Fun Factor to our well-being.) *We will build recreatiion and pleasure into our daily lives through:*

Walking on the earth and natural pathways.

Organized and individual recreational activities available daily.

Looking at "work" as a form of both fun and exercise.

- *We utilize the environment for self-nurturing through the healing qualities of:*

Beauty in our field of vision and in our surroundings. (When I recently moved from Los Angeles to Santa Barbara, I noticed how much more peace was available just through the beauty of trees.)

Pollution-free surroundings.

Working and eating in attunement with the seasonal cycles. (This idea of eating whatever we want whenever we want—like melons in January—is not in harmony with both our bodies and our the planet's environment. Let's get back to enjoying the seasons and what they each uniquely have to offer.)

- *We recognize the importance of balancing ourselves mentally, emotionally, and spiritually by:*

Loving ourselves and each other.

Speaking kind works to each other.

Keeping clear and balanced with ourselves and with one another.

Encouraging individual responsibility to health.

Using the hubs as support systems.

Having time built into our daily lives for individual spiritual attunement.

Keeping spiritual attunement as a priority in our daily lives. (For example, researchers have thoroughly proven the tremendous value of meditation to health.)

Having a retreat area available.

Allowing no smoking or recreational drugs within our Community.

From the above description, I hope you get the picture that we can have vitality in our lives. We need to realize that we don't have to live with all the stress and the environmental and chemical threats that currently have such a tremendous effect on our well-being. In fact, if we're not experiencing joy and pleasure and growth in our lives, we really need to address that. When we do, we find that the key is how we choose to live together on this planet.

HOW DO WE COMMUNICATE?

How do we relate with each other in this society? The first thing that may come to mind is that this is the information age and we are technologically improving our communications systems all the time. We also have the media, which now, unfortunately, feeds us short bursts of sensationalized stories. But how are we relating with one another on a personal level? That question goes largely unaddressed except as it is played out in our everyone-for-themselves paradigm. We know, for instance, that there are laws that govern how we relate with others, and stepping out of line can have consequences (unless you can afford to hire a really good lawyer). We also know that there are rules of etiquette with certain social consequences if those rules are broken. Some of us were raised to be nice and not say anything if we can't say something nice (so we became passive-aggressive instead), and some of us were raised to express ourselves regardless of the effect (and damage) that may have on others. Our different backgrounds and styles in communicating make for some often volatile relation-ships, be it with friends or strangers. Yet no one really takes on the question of communication for society as a whole, and we are left to sort out this most important component of the quality of our lives by ourselves or, much more rarely, by seeking counseling.

We need to learn to live without acting against others and taking from others. We must reeducate ourselves and teach our children not to return harsh words for harsh words or a fist for a fist, but instead to act in kindness and loving, and to hold the consciousness of going for The Highest Good of All Concerned. In my experience, many people do not really know how to make friends or even how to get in touch with how they are really feeling inside. I grew up in a family where if someone had asked me how I felt (which never happened), I could have said in all honesty, "I'm sorry, I don't speak that language." It took me almost 30 years and a lot of heartache before I was able to start genuinely sharing with myself and with others. My story is not that different from many people in our culture. However, in a supportive, nurturing Community, there will be abundant opportunities for close friendships, and clear, loving communication. It will be almost impossible to experience the isolation and alienation that typify our society. I believe that the ability to get in touch with and connect with one's self and with other people has more to do with success and happiness than any academic skill.

The second part of communication involves the information/technology highway of which most of us are now a part. This technology will play a major role in the Community both in terms of accessing information within the Community and interfacing with information outside the Community. As you will read in our description which follows, communication technology enables consensus decision-making to be practical on a Community-wide basis. With everyone having the capacity to communicate with each other at any given time, this will also increase the closeness and Community-wide connections that are the cornerstone for cooperative living.

When we asked the question, "How do we communicate?," we intentionally chose to marry the technology of communicating with the quality and essence of our interpersonal and Community communications. We believe that these are two parts of the bigger picture, and, when we are creating a Community of several hundred people, we are going to have to be both responsible and creative in our communication so that we can successfully and joyfully live together. So far, though, it's a very unequal marriage in our society where technology has far outstripped the level of our interpersonal and media communications, which often display our individual and collective immaturity. Essentially our question gets back to how we can communicate For The Highest Good of All Concerned. Again, at this point in our planet's history, we can't settle for anything less. Peace and Loving need to be at the core of all our communicating,

"The greatest obstacle to communication is the illusion that it has occurred."

—*Harri Kallio*

and, in doing this, we will find that our lives become incredibly richer.

From our Community Planet description:

HOW DO WE COMMUNICATE?

The cornerstone that makes our innovative ideas on "consensus" and "sharing our abundance" work is communication. Effective, open, and loving communication creates the bonding, the respect for one another, and the willingness to act in consensus. To facilitate this process, we will offer ongoing training and practice in communication skills. Workshops on personal growth and development will emphasize how we as individuals and as a Community can act for The Highest Good of All Concerned, while at the same time realizing personal needs and goals. We will also utilize technology to make information and communication easily accessible to all residents.

ESSENCES: How do we communicate?

- *By listening to the truth within each other and responding with kindness, consideration, and loving honesty.*
- *By creating a safe space to communicate.* (This is the bottom line for communication and consensus to really work.)
- *By having workshops to continually improve our communication skills through emphasizing personal growth.* (Effective and Loving communication is too important to be left to chance. This is among the most glaring of errors in most of the world's cultures.)
- *By calling in the Light.* (It never hurts, and often helps, to ask for assistance from a Higher Power and to realize our oneness in Spirit.)
- *By respecting confidentiality.*
- *By recognizing our oneness with everyone and everything.*
- *By having Community information accessible to all residents.*
- *By acting in consensus.*
- *By keeping communication fun.* (We often take ourselves too seriously.)

GUIDELINES:

- *We will use the best available communications technology to make information easily accessible to all residents.*

  * *There will be a Community-linked computer within each home or hub that will serve several functions:*

    ** *A bulletin board for announcements about activities, news, innovations, etc.*

    ** *A log of all Community and Hub records and meeting notes so that all residents have access to all Community information.*

  * *There will be a Community communication system so that residents can talk to one another within the Community at any time and anywhere.*

  * *To facilitate the process of Community consensus, we will have an audio-visual system with the capability to:*

    ** *Telecast live and taped Community consensus meetings.*

    ** *Telecast presentations from any of the Essence Hubs to both the Main Hub and all other Essence Hubs.*

  * *There will be a shared information center/library that also contains tapes of all Main Hub meetings, Community records, etc.* (Community information must be freely and readily accessible to all residents—mostly so that people have the opportunity to contribute their creativity to all aspects of the Community.)

- *We will provide training on specific techniques and methods for effective and loving communications.* (Where was this when I was trying to learn by trial and error how to relate more effectively with others and with myself?)

- *We will offer ongoing training on personal growth and development.* (As a resident, you won't have to pay for those very good, but very high-priced, workshops.)

- *We will encourage an atmosphere for consensus by:*

  * *Giving each person the chance to be heard.*

  * *Recognizing all ideas as having value.*

    * *Using the concept of "Po" (putting ideas not in consensus*
    on hold). (We've had great success with this. When we
held different and entrenched points of view on a decision
to be made, we'd essentially call a time-out and bring the
issue up in the next week's meeting. Given a chance to
mellow and get in touch with how important an issue was
or a chance to come up with creative, win/win solutions,
we always got past our hurdles and came up with even
better decisions.)

- *We will communicate on many different levels including
creative endeavors, cultural activities, growth exercises,
etc.* (We can and do communicate on many other levels
other than just verbal.)

HOW DO WE BRING FORTH INNER WISDOM?

    Education has been a hot political issue. But what questions
has our society asked about education? Society has generally
asked us to learn what they want us to learn, complete with profi-
ciency tests. Our society has even asked us to learn history from
an incredibly one-sided point of view, the point of view of the
Western civilization that has subjugated the planet. What we have
essentially been asked to learn is how to be good and obedient
citizens to support the status quo of the everyone-for-themselves
paradigm. Creativity is allowed, but only within that framework,
and we are taught that stepping outside that box is to be ungodly.

    Whereas the process of education traditionally has been
pouring information into us, we believe that true education
involves bringing forth the best of what is already inside all of us,
and this applies to every one of us no matter what our age is. We
all have a vast storehouse of inner wisdom that transcends
anything that can be stuffed into us from the outside. Sure,
learning information is often important, but it must be the servant
to our inner wisdom and not the master. Communication is a
major aspect of that, and in our present society the ability to effectively communicate probably has, as I previously wrote, more to
do with success than any other single factor.

    I've heard it said that one of the values of school is that it taught us to be bored so that we had practice for eventually working. How many of us have dreamed of revamping the educational process to make it more relevant, more interactive, and more interesting? We can do that in a Community where people have access to participating in every aspect of the Community and all its businesses, services, and enterprises. The totality of life needs to be our stage for learning rather than just depending on what we can learn within the walls of crowded classrooms with often uninspiring curriculum. That curriculum has become even more uninspiring recently as more and more of our creative classes that would enrich us have been eliminated due to financial constraints, even though we can spend billions on weaponry.

Recognizing that the roots of learning and communication start early, the children of the Community will find many nurturing people of all ages to learn from and participate with in all aspects of Community life. But education is not just for our youth—we believe that it is a life-long process in which we all need to be participating. Stagnation is often the first sign that it's time for changes.

From the Community Planet description:

HOW DO WE BRING FORTH INNER WISDOM?

An essence of the educational process is bringing forward the inner wisdom that each of us has within us. We see learning as a life-long process in which there is value to be gained from all our experiences. To facilitate our inner wisdom, we encourage creating the time in our daily lives for inner attunement. (Most of us are too caught up in our outer lives that we don't take the time to access our inner wisdom.)

A major aspect of education is the Community itself. With all its innovations, the Community is intended to be a school of life to explore how the people of this planet can live in greater peace and harmony with each other and with all life. Utilizing the latest educational techniques, we offer classes, workshops, and shared learnings in an atmosphere of joy and loving support. In addition, both children and adults will be given the opportunity to learn by doing through participation in various aspects of the Community.

ESSENCES: *How do we bring forth inner wisdom?*

- *By recognizing life as the classroom where we are learning all the time.* (We believe that life is the classroom.)
- *By utilizing the Community as an educational laboratory.*
- *By supporting and respecting the inner guidance in each of us as a source of direction, learning, and truth.*
- *By encouraging all positive expression and experiences leading to inner growth, self-knowledge and expansion.*
- *By encouraging learning by doing and by being of service.*
- *By using everything for our advancement.*
- *By encouraging natural curiosity and creativity.*
- *By making learning joyful, entertaining, and available.* (Again, the fun factor.)
- *By acting and sharing with loving, honesty, and integrity in whatever we do.*

GUIDELINES:

- *We will consider several educational options:*

  * Students may attend public or private schools outside the Community. (This encourages broader experiences and perspectives.)

  * Depending on our resources and on Community choice, we may have Community schools.

  * Parents have the choice to send their children to whatever schools are available.

  * There may be a student support group.

  * Child care is available and emphasizes inner wisdom, responsibility, learning skills, group interaction, communication, creativity and fun.

- *Community members can explore vocational choices by participation in various aspects of Community life.*
- *We recognize that inner wisdom is brought forward through inner attunement which we will focus on by:*

  * Making it a priority in our Community.

  * Building time for it into our daily lives.

Creating a retreat/meditation area(s).

- *We recognize that every situation or circumstance throughout our lives is an opportunity to learn and grow.*
- *To facilitate bringing forward inner wisdom, both individually and collectively as a Community, we will encourage:*

* Innovation:

        ** By maintaining an openness for change and improvements.

        ** By making our Community a haven for new positive technology.

        ** By using the newest and best educational techniques.

* The acquisition of learning skills.

* The recognition that people learn at different rates.

* The availability of learning resources including a resource center.

* People sharing their wisdom:

        ** By inviting in resources from outside our Community.

        ** By offering learning experiences to people outside our Community.

* Spiritual awareness and inner attunement in the educational process.

* Loving.

* Opportunities for being of service.

* The acquisition of effective communication skills.

* Learning about cooperation, sharing, and fulfillment.

* Learning about being in harmony with our environment.

* Learning by doing:

        ** By participating in various Community activities.

        ** By becoming aware of how our Community works.

        ** By focusing on teaching through "hands on"

Teachers Often Left to Deal With Pupils' Medical Needs

■ Schools: The ranks of disabled students rise as on-site nurses are cut. It's an equation for disaster, some fear.

By MARLENE CIMONS
TIMES STAFF WRITER

WASHINGTON—One of the boys in Michele Daly's kindergarten class had diabetes, and several times a day she would prick his finger, squeeze out a few drops of blood and test his blood sugar to make sure it was at a safe level.

She was terrified of making a mistake.

"If I was wrong, he could go into a seizure or eventually suffer heart failure," said Daly, who teaches in West Jordan, Utah. "I have no medical background. I shouldn't have to do that."

Her predicament is becoming increasingly common. Across the nation, teachers and other school personnel without medical training are being asked with growing frequency to perform medical duties for which they feel ill-equipped and ill at ease.

These range from dispensing medication to more complicated procedures: administering finger-stick blood tests and insulin injections, performing breathing treatments, even feeding children through stomach tubes and changing catheters.

And some, like Daly, are called upon to make medical judgments for which they feel they lack expertise.

This situation has developed in recent years as more children with disabilities have, by federal law, **Please see SCHOOLS, A24**

Just as I was editing this section, this article appeared in the Los Angeles Times.[51] *This is a statement about our priorities and the quality of our educational institutions in our everyone-for-themselves world.*

experience in addition to classroom learning.
** By rotating to different Focus areas so people
have the option of having different experiences.

I notice in reviewing our "Guidelines" for "How do we bring forth inner wisdom?" that I have nothing of note to add to it. To me the description paints an exciting picture of what education and learning can be. As opposed to the very limited way that our society approaches education, I feel that we have a format for making it a joyful, life-long experience when we approach it as life itself being our canvas and our entire Community being the educational support system.

HOW DO WE EXPAND OUR COMMUNITY?

When I first started thinking about an intentional Community that could provide the model to transform the planet, I read many books on actual and fictional utopian societies. It seemed obvious to me that in order to have a so-called utopian society, what was needed first were utopian people. At this stage in our planet's history, with the survival of the planet and the prospect of an adequate life for everyone and anyone now at risk, we must replace the old everyone-for-themselves model that has led us to the precipice of being engulfed by our ignorance concerning the balance of nature. Now, perhaps more than ever, people seem to be willing to embrace the concept of going for The Highest Good of All Life. Teaching people this concept is the essence of what the people in this Hub group would be doing, for we must expand the Highest Good approach to include all life on the planet.

In order for the Community to be able to make decisions by consensus, it will take residents who both have a real commitment to what the Community is and have the consciousness to work consensus. There are, of course, skills that one can learn to better be able to work consensus, but still there has to be the absolute choice to commit to working consensus and going for the Highest Good, rather than running one's personal stuff at the expense of others.

For us to successfully live together, we must know ourselves; we must seek self-awareness and realize our collective oneness.

Without that, we cannot move forward to making the planet work for everyone. But, with a Community of people demonstrating the Highest Good consciousness along with abundance on all levels (including fun), then people will be inspired to realizing our collective oneness as taught by all the great spiritual teachers. More than anything else, the Community will show the world the value of people willing to go for The Highest Good of All.

Therefore, for this model to succeed, we will have a very comprehensive (but also fun and interesting) screening process. The residents who pass this process and come into the Community will have the commitment, ability, and support necessary to work consensus. If not, persons not yet ready to come into the Community will come out with solid feedback on what to work on if they wish to reapply. This is not an againstness process, it's just that for this model to succeed we must be able to be successful and to show people the value of choosing to go for The Highest Good of All. Historically, cooperative communities were not good at screening members, and this later usually led to their demise. I can't stress enough the importance of people willing to go for The Highest Good of All, for it is time to change the basic paradigm of human interaction. There is just too much at stake for the future of the planet to do otherwise. Those who are "cooperation challenged" will have to wait and learn the value of a different approach before trying to inflict their out-of-date ways onto others in this New Age of cooperation we are entering.

Some people, upon first hearing some very basic information about this Community concept, have said that this would be a great thing for homeless people. But that's not what this project is. Instead, the initial model Community will have rather exceptional and successful people as residents because it is extraordinarily important that the Community be able to demonstrate both an abundance of lifestyle (that would appeal to almost everyone) and the Highest Good consciousness that will teach others what is necessary to create other Communities around the planet.

This demonstration Community will be a revolutionary model, and, as such, will be a mecca for both research and for media coverage. Besides screening for new residents, this Hub also has the job of communicating to the world what we are doing. Because the everyone-for-themselves model has been so entrenched in our consciousness, for many people the only way they can perceive of a way that we can all live for The Highest Good of All Life and live more abundantly and happily at the same time is to actually see a model that demonstrates the concept. This Hub group will make sure that people all over the world get an opportunity to see, through the various forms of media, the Community and how it operates.

From our Community Planet description:

HOW DO WE EXPAND OUR COMMUNITY?

Our purpose is for the Community to serve as a living laboratory for demonstrating a successful model for living—one in which there is harmony with ourselves, each other, and our environment. This Hub has the responsibility of sharing with the world the concept, experiences, and acquired knowledge of our Community, screening applicants for membership, and expanding the concept of our Community to other locations. To support the integrity of our Community, the entrance requirements for a new member include having a willingness to cooperate with the focus areas' essences and guidelines and having an enthusiasm for participating in the vision we are creating. To give applicants the information and experience they need for choosing to apply, the Expand Focus Hub will offer a variety of opportunities for participation.

ESSENCES: How do we expand our Community?

- *By sharing a successful model of Community living with the world so that the vision can expand.*

- *By accepting new residents who share the concept of our Community and have a willingness to participate.*

- *By making the Community experience available to all people regardless of race, color, nationality, or age.* (We intentionally left out "creed" because some creeds may currently not be in alignment with having respect for all people and being committed to The Highest Good of All.)

GUIDELINES:

- *We will share with the world our Community's structure,
  workings, goals, experiences and acquired knowledge through:*

  * A visitor's center.   (Which will showcase our eco-
  technology as well as our Highest Good model of living.)

  ** An internship program—i.e., quarterly programs where
  people can come and study Community living and other
  areas of innovation.*

  * Housing available for visitors.

  ** Seminars, workshops, and presentations both within and
  outside our Community.*   (Given that we are successful,
  we'll take our show on the road.)

  ** Publications of our research and our experiences—both
  successful and unsuccessful.*

  * Public relations outreach.

  * Area service projects.   (Sharing our abundance with our
  neighbors)

  * Sharing innovative technologies that can assist the world.

  * Assisting others to start their own Communities.

- *The "How do we expand our Community" Focus Hub sets
  the criteria for screening new members and creates an
  application which may include letters of recommendation,
  employment histories, credit checks, etc.*

  ** The focus hub may create and/or coordinate classes and
  workshops for prospective members to come for a week
  or weekend in order to experience the Community and
  give the Community a chance to experience them.*   (Since
  we wrote this description, we came up with what may
  turn out to be a very effective screening process utilizing
  consensus. It also allows applicants to gauge their own
  readiness to participate successfully in consensus
  decision-making.)

  ** The focus hub may also set up opportunities and experi-
  ences for non-residents to be participant-observers.*   (In

"THE WORLD IS NOW TOO DANGEROUS
FOR ANYTHING LESS THAN UTOPIA."

—*Buckminster Fuller*

other words, we will use a variety of ways—not limited to those above—that will offer diversified participation opportunities to people interested in checking out the Community.)

The focus hub is available, if needed, to set up procedures for new residents to ease their integration into the Community.

- *Entrance requirements to be a Community member include:*

Sharing the vision of the Community and a willingness to participate enthusiastically.

Being willing to cooperate with the essences and guidelines of the 12 focus areas.

Agreeing to the financial guidelines of "How do we share our abundance."

Agreeing that the Community is their primary residence.

Agreeing that if they work within the Community, they will be available to participate for a certain minimum amount of time.

Agreeing that they will treat Community property with respect and be responsible for any damage they may do.

Agreeing that parents are primarily responsible for their children. (Although the Community is an incredible resource for support.)

A non-resident marrying a resident must meet and agree with the same guidelines as any other resident. (This is necessary to ensure that all people are committed to The Highest Good of All.)

Meeting the entrance fees (see "How do we share our abundance" for details). (Remember, these are not prohibitive.)

Meeting their financial obligations to others. (An applicant whose financial and legal obligations could not be met by living in the Community would not be accepted.)

No applicants will be accepted over the preset maximum

of residents per space in keeping with living in harmony with our environment. (To heal the planet, we can't afford to continue our society's same area overpopulation route.)

* *Members may be asked to leave the Community for falsifying their application, conviction of a serious crime, or failure to cooperate with Community guidelines. When dismissal is being considered, the Expand Hub investigates and presents (only when making a recommendation for dismissal) findings to the Main Hub for consensus on whether or not a person remains a Community member.*

LIVING IN COMMUNITY/FREE AT LAST

Many years after I first realized that, in order to heal the planet, we had to redefine how we lived together on the planet, it dawned on me that I had an idealized, yet fuzzy picture of what living in this prototype Community would be like. It therefore seemed that one of the first necessary steps to creating the Community was to create a written description of what the Community was like and how it would operate. To accomplish this, I formed a class that I thought would meet weekly for 10 weeks, at the end of which time we would have a finished descriptive product. Well, as soon as we really started questioning the assumptions that our society has made regarding how we have to live together and started to really think creatively, our timeline started stretching. To create the description, we met weekly for about two years. Each week was an adventure in massaging each of the questions in order to ascertain exactly what we wanted to say. The process, with its laughter along with occasional harsh words and stuckness, was incredible. As my fuzzy picture merged with the collective wisdom and intuition of the group, we came into a descriptive reality that far exceeded anything that I had imagined. I think that my friend, Mike Feeney, best described our journey with the "preface" that he wrote for our Community Planet description:

"The class met with the purpose of planning a New Age Community where people live and learn in peace and harmony with themselves, each other, and their environment. After the class members realized how strong our collective vision was, we dedicated ourselves to seeing it becoming a reality.

"Our first challenge as a class was how to merge all our individual visions into one. Although we shared pretty much the same larger vision, we often differed greatly when it came to details. Our solution was CONSENSUS. We saw the process of consensus being one where everyone is encouraged and given an opportunity to express themselves, and then an elucidation is found that all can agree upon and come into harmony with.

"Everything that was produced by the class, including this write-up, was done through the process of consensus. We started every class by each member taking time to share what was going on in their lives. We discovered that this helped us come into harmony with each other and to reach consensus. It also helped us to remain loving friends when reaching agreement was difficult. Out of these sharings sprang the idea of Hubs, which are the modular units that make up the Community. Each Community member would belong to one or more of these Hubs, small groups of people meeting together for support and decision-making.

"As a beginning exercise, the class started by imagining that we were all from a planet named 'Kungawungajungo,' a word we coined to represent all the positive qualities we wanted in our Community. On our 'home planet' we consider everyone in our world as family and the needs of the one are the responsibility of everyone. In our native language there are no such words as lack or poverty, which are comparative words that describe some people as having less than others, a condition unknown on our planet. The dual purpose of our adventure was to create a home where we could live in peace and prosperity and also to create a Community that would serve as a model of successful cooperative living for those on earth.

"Our first task was to observe the way the people of earth did things, to take note of where they excelled, and to observe where their actions did not serve them. From these observations, plus the vision we held coming into the class, we formed the ideas that became the Community Planet."

B.C.

By permission of Johnny Hart and Creators Syndicate, Inc.

While we realized that our description was probably not complete (and it wasn't intended to be), we aimed for it to be readable in a few pages rather than a several hundred page document. You may be able to see some difficulties or holes, but I can testify that people getting together and looking at an issue via the process of consensus can come up with some amazingly creative solutions. The current crises our planet faces demand nothing less. Truly, if wise beings from another planet were to visit us, they would wonder how we created such a mess out of a place where everyone could be living abundantly and in harmony with all life.

Every focus area we looked at includes how we can attain more peace and harmony in our lives. People, all people, need to be free and supported—with time, opportunity, Loving, and nurturing—to fulfill their individual destinies, missions, and creative expressions here on the planet. We need to realize that each and every person is important and has something to contribute. But, the support is not there in our everyone-for-themselves paradigm. Right now we're living as victims of the structure of our society rather than being able to create fully positive choices. The structure of our lives is way too controlled by society and the hoops that an uncooperative system makes us jump through. Instead of giving us freedom, that system has sucked up our time, resources, and creativity as well as damaging all life on the planet. If we want to have more vital and more fun lives, we must unburden ourselves from the over-regulation that has fragmented our lives. Our living paradigms need to be set up to have a lot more peace and harmony so that people's energy can go to creativity, growth, and fun rather than survival and oppression.

ANOTHER PIECE TO THE PUZZLE

In the twenty years I've been involved in teambuilding training, rarely have I ever seen groups—whether they be corporate, educational, or civic—model effective teamwork. Recently I was working with a group that was comprised of the very best thinkers and innovators from a major international automobile/jet engine manufacturing company. Our lead facilitator cautioned our facilitators that we might have to really challenge these people because of how sharp they were. Well, they were just a little worse than the average group I work with in accomplishing the challenges. It's not that they didn't have the information available in the group to do the task, it's just that they had difficulty in effectively communicating as a group.

During the next few days I wondered about that—how a very hi-functioning group of individuals could be so bad working as a group. In observing hundreds of challenge-based teambuilding trainings, I've seldom ever seen a team truly model excellent communication and leadership. I've seen groups get "in sync" somehow and do really well on the group challenges, but usually they just did it without really knowing how it happened. Therefore, it would be uncertain as to whether they could move into a cooperative place were they to be given a new and different set of challenges.

Then it dawned on me, as I was out walking at night and was observing cars drive down concrete streets lined with dark, empty stores, that my community and society itself had been created haphazardly—because people had a very limited concept of how to work together in groups. People coming together to live in the same place did not know how to effectively work together. Thus, not possessing either the skills or the consciousness of how to work together for The Highest Good of All, we accommodate by taking the path of least resistance and making decisions individually and/or haphazardly. As well-intentioned as they might be, politicians, business and civic leaders—you name it—they all didn't have any more ability to effectively work together than all the groups I've seen for the past twenty years. So, everything in society evolved pretty much individually and not with a consensus and a spirit of oneness from a highly-functioning team approach. Therefore, with most people feeling powerless to work effectively in a group, what typically happens is that power is usurped by those who want power over others or power to get what they want—often at the expense of others. This is the everyone-for-themselves legacy that we have been doing for so many thousands of years that our very cultural pattern became the mindset that we think alone rather than being able to think as a group.

But wait, weren't there examples of hi-functioning teams that have accomplished great things. Militaries have sometimes gotten miraculous things done. For that matter, so have some regimes throughout the ages. But these are top-down, autocratic forms of leadership which both do not usually gather the collective wisdom of all involved, and their goals are almost always accomplished at the expense of others, rather than being for the benefit of all. For instance, if we were truly thinking of The Highest Good of All militarily, we would have put our resources and our trillions to work sending people and technology out to improve the lives of people throughout the world who are on the edge of survival. That act of goodwill would have protected our security far more than any military act. People often fight both because of limited resources and because they, like the rest of us, also do not have the experience of how to work together as a group.

But what of sports teams that have accomplished great things? Though these teams may have worked well together, they have done so within a win/lose, us vs. them, competitive system. Look at the bigger picture—everybody didn't win, there were far more losers than winners. Yet, this competitive model is virtually all that is presented in the media in sports and any other achievement. Who is the best? We must show or prove that we are better, and it starts subtle or sometimes outright wars between people.

We live with this consciousness of scarcity and lack—that there isn't enough for everyone to win—and this comes into play with people participating in groups. Thus, people either cooperate out of greed or get very competitive for perceived limited resources or opt out of the decision-making process altogether. We have been so ingrained by our limited cooperative abilities that we don't hold the consciousness of how we can make something work in the most expansive way possible for everyone. Instead, we go to our survival response.

Because we haven't been able to function well working in groups, we've put together our world by a combination of haphazard or autocratic, win/lose decisions. People have remarked to me, "Wouldn't consensus decision-making take too much time?" Well, yes, it might take more time as people educate themselves to tap into the consciousness of the Highest Good instead of the simple legacy of againstness. But, once that is done, it becomes easier, and the decisions that are made are more creative, long-sighted, save time in the long run, and work for all life.

We are not wrong for not knowing how to work coopera-tively—few have been trained both in how to access that consciousness and how to implement it. Most of us still have to deal with the underlying everyone-for-themselves issues we still hold. We have trouble even in groups of two where 50 percent of our marriages result in divorce and where many of the remaining 50 percent have learned how to accommodate their partner rather than absolutely going for creating the best, most dynamic relation-ship that they can possibly have. The same is true in families. It just seems easier to take the path of least resistance, rather than to learn and apply the skills.

We will change only when we see a better model of relating. With the consciousness of the Highest Good being the key along with the skill of how to work together as a group, Communities—based on this principle of the Highest Good For All—will be what transforms the world. People must see that there is an alternative way to succeed or else they will continue to survive at the expense of others or by making others wrong.

Indeed, if we were truly to grapple with virtually any decision from the consciousness of the Highest Good, it would necessitate being creative, thinking out-of-the-box, and ultimately changing the way we live together. Let's take recycling and trash as an example. It is possible to recycle 100 percent of what we create, but the recycling itself is just part of the issue. How trash is created— by packaging, overconsumption, making products purely from the self-interest of the maker, designed obsolescence, etc.—must be addressed hand-in-hand with how to recycle. Thus, as I wrote earlier, we have to look at not creating or supporting anything that can't be reused or recycled. But, even beyond that, we have to look at anything that even wastes people's time and life-force due to lack of cooperation. We have to look at all the paper and office products that are created for an everyone-for-themselves society and all the hours that are spent supporting that system. If one Community of four to five hundred people could demonstrate this, then a cluster of Communities demonstrating the value of living together for The Highest Good of All could really show what is possible through consensus-based cooperation as opposed to our current haphazard approach to living together.

"It is possible that the next Buddha
will not take the form of an individual.
The next Buddha may take the form
of a community;
a community practicing understanding
and loving kindness,
a community practicing mindful living.
This may be the most important thing
we can do for the survival of the Earth."

-- Thich Nhat Hanh

Chapter 5

COMMUNITY CLUSTERS

So, once we get the model demonstration Community going, what's the next step? Given its success, one of the things that will happen rather quickly is that this "Highest Good For All" model for living will be replicated at various places around the planet by people who see that this holistic systems-approach to the planet's challenges is not only what is needed but needed immediately. Therefore, the next major step would be to create a cluster of cooperative Communities all physically connected to each other. A cluster of Communities would be able to provide the social, intellectual, cultural, recreational, and economic diversity to not only help stabilize the Communities, but also provide ample opportunities for enrichment on all levels of living.

Let's take an area of, say, ten thousand acres where we're planning on creating a cluster of Communities. We would create the first Community on only a small portion of the land, and then later create Community #2, then #3, etc., until we had five or six Communities of four to five hundred people each. Naturally, the area of land needed for each Community would depend on the particular area and what the land could naturally support in keeping in harmony with *all life*. These Communities would be planned in harmony and cooperation with each other so that they could share many of the same resources, thereby also limiting the number of unnecessary buildings. In addition, through sharing resources, the Communities would be able to reduce the total amount of equipment per person that they need and also eliminate several job duties. However, the Communities are close enough together so that it is easily possible to walk, ride a bike or

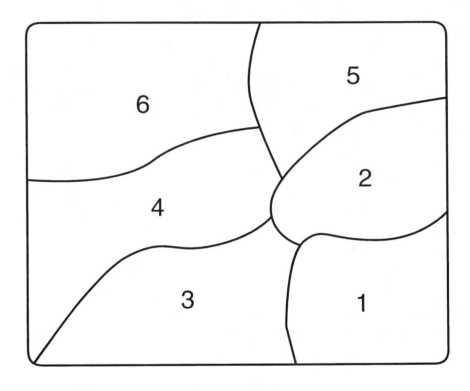

WE START WITH ACREAGE LARGE ENOUGH TO CREATE ONE COMMUNITY AND THEN GROW INTO A CLUSTER OF COMMUNITIES.

electric cart from one Community to another on natural paths and a minimal road system. But again, the key is that all the residents are committed to acting for The Highest Good Of All and to enjoying the abundance of that approach rather than the limitations of the everyone-for-themselves, win/lose, let-me-fence-off-my-area system.

A most important benefit of the clusters will be that they will generate many times the attention of the initial single model Community. When people hear that a couple of thousand people in one area are living what can only be considered a very successful and happy yet radically different lifestyle, then that will really grab their attention. This will become of progressively greater importance as people search for solutions against the backdrop of the planet's progressively greater problems. The mindsets of people, which have been based on thousands of years of programming, will be challenged and changed as they see a different and better way of living for all life. There will be media coverage dwarfing the amount of coverage that, for example, the Biosphere project near Tucson, Arizona received. There will be scientific studies in all the various disciplines as the very fabric of the world's system of interrelating economically, socially, politically, and interpersonally is challenged.

COMMUNITIES COOPERATING

Now let's take a town of about 10 thousand people made up of 20 to 25 Communities of four to five hundred people each, all operating on the principle of the Highest Good For All. First of all, through the commitment to make this larger Community work for all of the residents, we no longer need to consider the question of unemployment, even though we can eliminate many traditional jobs which, as we discussed earlier, are based on the lack of cooperation between people. We also have no need for welfare or disability benefits because, in a cooperative Community, there is always something that every resident can do to contribute to the Community, the larger Community, and/or to the planet. Given the number of traditional jobs that are no longer needed, other jobs will be created as we restore the environment locally, produce more of our own food locally, and begin to build fun and nurturing back into our lives. Although we obviously can't replace all the jobs, there's nothing wrong with reducing the number of hours that people spend working. It's interesting that this seemingly liberal approach to changing the way we live together is actually more in line with the conservative agenda of eliminating public assistance, returning decision-making to the local level, and downsizing the need for government.

This larger Community would also have the ability to share many additional resources not practical in the four to five hundred person Communities. For instance, they might have a hospital, a large recycling facility, etc. But, again the principle is that the number of buildings are kept to a minimum, they are multi-use, and they are available for the use of all the people in all the connected Communities at no cost, because this entire cluster of Communities is based on the philosophy of cooperating for The Highest Good For All. Thus, we have little or no use for lawyers, accountants, and paper shufflers of all types except for those who are necessary in the Highest Good model for tasks such as inventorying and ordering.

The elimination of those jobs which are based on lack of cooperation frees up a tremendous amount of space as well as jobs. Just look at any business street and see how much space is used for stores with huge inventories of products, products which may sit there for long periods of time before being sold to individual homes where many of them may sit around in disuse for years before entering landfills. Then check out the number of stores that are selling the same things but are in competition with each other. These jobs, born out of the everyone-for-themselves' need to create jobs and amass money, along with the space they occupy and the resources they use, are not necessary in a cooperative model. In fact, they diminish the quality of life we could have. This Community of ten thousand would truly demonstrate that people can live cooperatively on a large scale with all residents able to afford the richness of what the Community has to offer. If one Community has a need, the representatives of all the Communities get together to figure out how to deal with the

MISTER BOFFO By Joe Martin

MISTER BOFFO © Joe Martin. Dist. By UNIVERSAL PRESS SYNDICATE.
Reprinted with permission. All rights reserved.

issue. Without the influence and restrictions of government, very creative systems-approach solutions can also now be found—solutions which heretofore were not possible in traditional living models. Using money as an excuse for not being able to do something becomes a virtual non-issue as compared to the way our lives are currently set up.

The larger Community could also grow just about all of its own pesticide-free and chemical-free food as well as start to renew the topsoil. Some of the Communities would choose to grow certain more specialized foods (sometimes in specially created environments), and it would now make more sense to grow the larger grain and legume field crops. The key, though, is that the food is still being grown locally as opposed to our present day practice of shipping it over 1500 miles to market.

However, as contrasted to a current typical town of ten thousand, we have many times more open area and nature with natural habitat. While our lifestyles are far more abundant, we have far fewer structures, far less space under roofs, and more than 95 percent less land under concrete. This larger Community is also mainly a pedestrian Community with no traditional street system leading up to individual houses, no driveways and garages (remember that the few number of cars necessary for the smaller Communities are kept on the outskirts of those Communities). Instead, there are walking and biking paths and a minimal road system interconnecting the Communities, and these roads are used mostly by solar electric powered carts, transports and shuttles. In fact, the larger Community would plan all the Communities in such a way as to create a beautiful, balanced interrelationship with nature.

Of course, my personal favorite aspect of the larger Community is that the capacity to have fun in our lives increases exponentially. Through the benefits of sharing, the larger Community will enable us to have the option of spending even less time working. Also, the kinds of resources that the larger Community can provide create the opportunity for almost any kind of recreational, artistic, and creative interests that one may have—from hang gliding to playing in an orchestra. All these pursuits then suddenly become affordable and available to all residents as opposed to what we now do, which is dream about doing these things if we had the equipment and/or the money, the time, the proximity, and the friends with whom to do these things—which translates to "we just don't get around to doing many things on a regular basis that would add more enjoyment and excitement to our lives."

SO THE WORLD CAN SEE

Imagine the impact that a Community of this size would have on the world. We would be addressing the environmental concerns by being basically non-polluting, by being energy self-sufficient, by eliminating the need for almost all packaging and other landfill materials, by making it easy to recycle almost everything, etc. We would also reintegrate our lives with nature while at the same time bringing fun, creativity, nurturing, and really connecting with others back into our lives. With a Community on this scale which boldly redefines how we as people can live together, the media coverage will bring this model to the attention of the world.

Just as the current model of the way we live together continues to disintegrate, people all over the planet will be quick to respond to a better way of living both for themselves and for the planet. It is then just a question of how long it will take before most of the world starts forming Communities based on the concept of *The Highest Good For All Life.*

As Communities spring up around the planet, they will have different looks depending on the area and climate. One of the exciting things design-wise is that, in planning Communities for The Highest Good Of All, it opens up some interesting opportunities for improving the quality of life in relationship to the whims of our weather. For example, as I described earlier, it's possible to put domes over Communities to lessen the inconveniences of winter snowstorms. These domes can be of any size from the 350 person Community I saw the blueprints for to a whole town. Imagine still being able to enjoy the snow while also having the

CONCEPTUAL DOMED COMMUNITY DRAWING BY THOMAS SLAGLE

option of being able to live and go to work in the Community without having to negotiate the trials of the season.

Is it possible that we can successfully live together in Community?   Well, it's actually happening and has been happening for hundreds of years. There are many books in print about the multitudes of today's intentional communities.   The authors of one of the most informative intentional community books, *Builders Of The Dawn*, state that "Information of today's communities is lacking" and "The majority of communities shun publicity."[1]   It's like what has been happening in the very successful Basque cooperatives—the news hasn't been getting out that cooperative living and working has been very successful.

The early American colonists shared resources and were like the intentional communities of today, so what we are proposing is not un-American. However, unlike anything else that has been done, what we are proposing is a much larger model which integrates technology and the kinds of amenities, opportunities, and nurturing that would make Community life appealing to almost everyone in terms of lifestyle. The other big difference is that this model would not shun publicity but instead would make sure that the world takes notice that we can make life work abundantly for everyone.

But again, let's keep in mind that this Revolution in the way we live together involves both the change in the form to the Highest Good model and *the commitment in consciousness* to go for The Highest Good Of All. As this Revolution then spreads around the world, improving life all across the planet and bringing prosperity—while also restoring the environment in even Third World countries—the quality of life evens out to a very high level worldwide. As people gain years of experience in being committed to The Highest Good and as the Community model for living that principle spreads across the planet, we not only will be sharing resources in the larger cluster Communities and seeing ourselves as part of the local areas, but we will also be seeing ourselves as part of the worldwide network of Communities. With that global consciousness, we will be committed to life working abundantly for all Community members (and for everyone) everywhere.

Chapter 6
COMMUNITIES AROUND
THE WORLD

So, let's take a look at what would happen with this future global Highest Good model. Right now we are hooked into a world economy that has been a blessing in terms of the opportunities it creates to share some resources and products and for some degree of ingenuity. But it is also a monster, not only for the environmental damage, but also because we have no idea, in our everyone-for-themselves economic model, of how to improve the quality of life for all people. This damage has happened even though, as we have pointed out many times, we have all the resources and manpower to have life be abundant, nurturing, and fun for *everyone*. In fact, with what is happening to the environment, a case can be made that the idea of having more or less than someone else doesn't really matter anymore. Rather, the important thing is having the absolute most available for everyone while still keeping in harmony with the planet and restoring the environment. (Of course, as we have described, living in Communities and sharing resources represents abundance rather than sacrifice.)

A USE AND ACCESS WORLD

With the Community model redefining wealth as use and access rather than as possessions and as cooperation rather than power, let's look at what would happen if we replaced the out of control, "sorcerer's apprentice" money exchange system with something that would work for the Highest Good For Everyone. First of all, with the Communities more integrated with nature and locally growing the food that is needed, we no longer have to ship food the huge distances to market (while simultaneously enjoying fresh and natural rather than processed foods). With hothouses and hydroponics, Communities could also choose to grow most foods anywhere on the planet.

While the sharing of resources locally means that we will have to produce far fewer of the products that can easily be shared, we have also, with the Highest Good model, eliminated the need for the nonsense products—since we no longer have to invent ways to individually make a living. However, we still would have many products which are necessary and helpful to people that need to be distributed across the planet. So, how could we both produce and distribute those products in a worldwide Community system? One big change would be that, in the Highest Good model, there would be the cooperative commitment to create the very best possible products that can be made. No longer bound by the profit motive, there would be no secrets, and the people with the best ideas could get together to not only produce products that would last a long time, but, with our absolute commitment to the environment and to health, would also be 100 percent safe and recyclable. Nothing but material that can easily and safely decompose need ever go into the ground—goodbye landfills.

In the U.S. the advertising expenditure per capita is about $500.[1] Think of the resources that are tied up in that. In cooperative Communities, with the very best products being made, there would no longer be any need for the marketing industry. There would be no reason for hype or for trying to convince people that they need something, and all the information on a product would be available on computer. Then when a product is no longer necessary, the Community(ies) producing that product would simply stop making it and start doing something else to contribute to the Highest Good of the planet.

Even in our current system it would make more sense to just provide people with the best possible products as opposed to continuing our market economy. For instance, if Ontario Hydro in Ontario, Canada gave away energy-efficient appliances to every home in the Province at a cost of $7 billion, this would save enough energy to save them from building a nuclear reactor at a cost of $17 billion.[2] Likewise, if we produced 250 million refrigerators for

DOONESBURY By GARRY TRUDEAU

DOONESBURY © G. B. Trudeau. Reprinted with permission of
UNIVERSAL PRESS SYNDICATE. All rights reserved.

MISTER BOFFO By Joe Martin

MISTER BOFFO © Joe Martin. Dist. By UNIVERSAL PRESS SYNDICATE.
Reprinted with permission. All rights reserved.

prospective new buyers, and these refrigerators were seven times more energy efficient (we can already do this, even though we don't), it would save enough electricity to save building $90 billion of coal powered generating plants or $200 billion of nuclear plants. Just giving the refrigerators away costs only $6 billion.   In addition, every dollar spent on building nuclear-power plants would be seven times more effective in diminishing the greenhouse effect if that dollar were invested in energy efficiency.[3]

The same is true of both electric cars and solar energy collectors—it would be far cheaper to just provide these items than to continue our current economic approach. That doesn't even take into account the ultimate environmental costs of fossil fuel use—everyday the world's economy burns an amount of energy it took the planet 10,000 days to create.[4] Stephen Lewis, former Canadian ambassador to the U.N., warned that we're not going to get away with anything less than "an all-out assault on the whole process of fossil-fuel combustion, everywhere, in order to save the planet."[5] We have the technology available to stop using both nuclear and fossil-fuels for energy, but there are powerful economic forces at work that prevent this from happening. As I've said, our current system into which we've boxed ourselves seems to be really crazy.

A WORLD OPEN FOR ALL—COOPERATING FOR THE HIGHEST GOOD

In the Highest Good system, information on what is needed for people and for all life on the planet would be compiled and representatives of areas would decide which Communities would be best suited for making and providing those needs. Government in the Highest Good system is no longer a patriarchal power/money-based system, but instead would consist of rotating representatives whose job is to look for the needs of the planet and coordinate production, distribution, and assistance. In the Highest Good system, the needs of the one are the concern of everyone—where there is a need, it just gets provided. When we take out the money/power factor and its complications and replace that with unfettered cooperation, we can just do it—it really can be that simple.   Remember, of course, that the people living in the

*"The inhabitants of planet Earth are quietly conducting
a gigantic environmental experiment. So vast and so
sweeping will be the impacts of this experiment that,
were it brought before any responsible council for
approval, it would be firmly rejected as having potentially dangerous consequences. Yet the experiment goes
on without significant interference from any jurisdic-
tion or nation. The experiment in question is the
release of carbon dioxide and other so-called greenhouse
gases to the atmosphere."*[6]

—Wallace S. Broecher, a Geochemist at Columbia University

*"We cannot have all the conveniences of our lives—the
VCR's, the all-terrain vehicles, the 2-car garages,
homes filled with all kinds of gadgets—and an easier
life, if they're powered by the combustion of fossil
fuels."*[7]

—Doug Scott, Sierra Club

Communities have also transitioned into the *consciousness* of going for the Highest Good and into seeing themselves as citizens of the world and as part of the oneness of humankind.

The "government," like the smaller Communities, would also use consensus for decision-making. There may well be a Community cluster (a global Community), which would consist of rotating representatives from all the regions of the world. Their job would be coordinating the equity distribution system and monitoring the planetary conditions. There would no longer be Third World countries (if the idea of countries still even makes sense in our new role as citizens of the world), and the quality of life would be elevated throughout the world. This would not only produce a very high quality of life anywhere on the planet but would also enable us to restore the planet's forests and ecosystems, which are currently being destroyed in good measure by the need for profit and survival in the everyone-for-themselves paradigm.

With the system of Communities, how can we transport products that may need to be shipped long distances? Well, remember that, when sharing resources and eliminating many nonsense products and products that now go to support jobs (that do not need to exist in a cooperative system), the shipping of many things will be cut down immensely or completely. However, there will still be a need to transport many items, so how can we do that if the shippers themselves are also members of Communities, yet have to travel? In the equity distribution system, there will be centralized warehouses with inventories. Then when a Community needs products, they can transport in the product(s) they produce and pick up what they need. Also, people involved in transportation in a Highest Good system can be at home anywhere by just stopping in at any Community because every Community has a certain amount of "guest" accommodations— just call ahead for space available. Airports and seaports are also still easily handled because they are the primary function and contribution of a Community or cluster of Communities. Since we are no longer in competition with others, the time factor involved with pickup and delivery is not the urgent priority necessitated by our current system. This allows us to be much more efficient in the shipping that we still have to do.

One of the things I get excited about when thinking about Communities around the globe is how much easier travel will be for all the citizens of the world. One could simply look at a computer for openings in Communities around the planet and become a part of that Community for the duration of the stay, which could be a day or a year. In fact, relocation also becomes very easy when one can come to a Community and be a full partner in that Community. Moving is no longer an ordeal as we don't have to worry about furniture and the myriad of other possessions that often create more confinement than freedom. Whatever we need is available at the next location if we so choose. If one chooses to, one could travel the world living in one area and then another and having interesting experiences with a variety of loving, supportive people.

Certain Communities will have the primary function of catering to vacationers because of their locations. Right now most of the people on the planet do not have the means to vacation at all, let alone travel far away from home, but, in the cooperative model, everyone on the planet can travel without having to worry about what it costs—because it would cost nothing. I think that most people, even in a culture such as ours, which has more access to the resources to travel, would enjoy the ability to take vacations that were heretofore unthinkable, unaffordable, and/or undoable because of the constraints of time and money. However, to people in cultures that have never been able to travel, this would create opportunities these people have never known. It's all possible when we decide to make the world work for everyone.

As the need for most traditional transportation diminishes, we can remove the vast amounts of extra concrete and asphalt and either fill up the quarry holes or we can use existing concrete-eating machines to turn most of those three million acres per year of concrete back into productive farmland. In a Community system, we can utilize group transports more because there is really no need to have a hurry-hurry, rush-rush life to be anywhere at a given time. That idea is linked to our

Western world everyone-for-themselves, "If you snooze, you lose" approach to life.

But what about the jobs in today's society that you may think that no one wants to do? Two things come into play with this. The first is that the very foundation of the Highest Good system is that, not only has the form of how we live together changed but also there has been a profound change of consciousness to go for the Highest Good Of All. This change is reinforced by the tremendous change in lifestyle with increased abundance on all levels. So people who have come to embrace the Highest Good will want to make a contribution. We are now trained to work for money and conditioned to the struggle for money, and, with that struggle laid to rest, people are more motivated to do whatever it takes to be of service. However, the second factor that comes into play is that in a cooperative model and in a cooperative world we can creatively design products and systems up front to eliminate many of the jobs that are either unpopular or unnecessary. In our competitive model it's very difficult to eliminate these jobs because people cut corners to create profit, and then others must do the undesirable, make-work for them later to clean up the waste. For example, garbage disposal is one of those kinds of jobs. It's far easier for most companies and households to just throw "trash" away and have someone then haul it away. But, in the Highest Good system, there would be very little packaging and everything would be produced both to last and with recycling in mind. As opposed to how difficult it is now for those of us who recycle, the Community would be designed for ease of recycling and composting. Therefore, it becomes a very easy task for all of us to do, and we do it with the satisfaction that we are taking care of the planet.

Now, what of those jobs which require many years of educa-tion? Will anyone be ambitious enough to spend eight plus years to be a medical doctor? Actually, I think that we'd find that probably more people would pursue higher education in the Community clusters supporting universities. First of all, the finan-cial limitation factor would be eliminated so that young doctors, for example, would not emerge a hundred thousand dollars in debt, and the high-pressure competitive system could be replaced by a more supportive system. Rather than the information stuffing torture that medical students are currently put through, the new system would focus on truly learning from a variety of disciplines and treating patients with loving and caring. Imagine being able to go to school in a nurturing, supportive setting where everyone is focused on the goal of learning in order to both expand one's inner wisdom and creativity and to serve one's fellow man. I think that a lot more people would choose to expand their inner wisdom in the Community University clusters.

Because we haven't laid out a complete, detailed, thousand-page blueprint on exactly how the worldwide system of Communities would work, people could easily say at this point that the system would break down here or there because we haven't addressed this or that. The intent of this book is to create a workable framework, not to present all the detail. Within the Highest Good framework, the evolving detail will be created in the consensus process for each Community. However, let's remember that the point is that what we are doing now is not working, and there is only a small window of time to do something drastically different about that. We cannot have the current everyone-for-themselves paradigm in place 50 years from now without also seeing the devastation of the planet's environment, the degradation of lifestyle for almost all of us, and probably more conflict and war as a result of people fighting over what little is left.

With the Highest Good approach, for any problem that we can identify, we can also *create a solution*. The reason that we can do that is that the Community/Highest Good model is a systems-approach to living on the planet and there would not be the blocks to doing what has to be done on *all* levels to resolve an issue. Thus, we can creatively change or alter whatever has to be changed in order to create balance and abundance. In our everyone-for-themselves paradigm, it is hard to affect workable solutions because there are so many factions and special interests with power/control and profit motives that we end up not being able to change what then usually creates more problems a few years or generations down the line. Looking at how we currently do things, it's easy to get stuck thinking that things can't change. But

the model we are proposing makes things possible that are virtually impossible in the everyone-for-themselves system. Again, the
key is the major change of consciousness to that of going for the
Highest Good Of All. With that consciousness, with the systems-
approach of the Community model, and with the magic of
consensus and its innate creativity, then almost all things become
possible—*for all people.* With the world living in cooperative
Communities, not only are people enjoying their lives more, but
also it works for all life as we return the world to more of its
natural state by regrowing the forests and healing the land, the
water, and the air.

*I think that Thoreau best expressed the danger of the
well-intentioned, Band-Aid approach (vs. the systems-
approach) in trying to solve our problems:*

*"There are a thousand hacking at the branches of evil to
one who is striking at the root, and it may be that he
who bestows the largest amount of time and money on
the needy is doing the most by his mode of life to
produce that misery which he strives in vain to
resolve."*

— *Henry David Thoreau,* Walden

Chapter 7
SEEDS OF CHANGE REVISITED-
ADDRESSING OUR PLANET'S NEEDS

As I wrote before in the Highest Good chapter, individuals, cities and countries alike now use the lack of money as the excuse for not getting things done. But, if the world had a format for all of us cooperating together for the Highest Good, then money would not be an issue and we would just do whatever was necessary for ourselves, for each other, and for the Earth. We have the manpower, the resources, and the technology available to do all that we have described, so what's the worldwide problem? It's just that our systems are not set up for cooperation. We're still in the age-old system where the many really serve the few. The few think that they can have much more (except, of course, in terms of the real quality of life, which transcends materialism), and the many, blinded by thousands of years of history, are still unaware that another choice is possible.

Again, in attempting to resolve the severe challenges that now face mankind and threaten our continued life on Earth, unless we address the quality of all life all over the planet, we are simply taking a Band-Aid approach that will at best just delay the inevitable by a few years. We must take care of all life in a loving and caring way. We must address both wealth (the quality of life on all levels) and sustainability simultaneously to make life work bountifully for all. To eliminate the isolation, alienation and powerlessness that is the root of many of these problems, we must reinvolve people in the decisions that affect their daily lives.

With the technology now available, we have a tremendous source of support to have life work for everyone. You probably know that we have the capability to put cameras in satellites that

*"I have the audacity to believe that peoples everywhere
can have three meals a day for their bodies, education
and culture for their minds, and dignity, equality and
freedom for their spirits. I believe that what self-
centered men have torn down, other-centered men can
build up"*[1]

—*Dr. Martin Luther King, Jr., from his Nobel*

Prize acceptance speech Dec. 10, 1964

can literally photograph and identify us individually. We're even working on being able to view a pin on the floor from 500 miles up. We can make "smart bombs" that can be programmed with the picture of a target, for instance a particular building within a city, and we can drop these bombs and they will go and seek out that particular target, identify it, and then destroy just that target. If we have the technology to do these kinds of things, we can produce energy and other products without pollution. We can recycle all that we make. We can create a high quality of life for all. So far, however, in the everyone-for-themselves system, science is expensive and technology follows the money that is available to be spent. The pentagon pays for most of it—70 percent of all science funded in the U.S. is paid for by the military. Worldwide, the military budgets are $800 billion per year, and $80 billion goes for military research and development.[2] We can change all that in a cooperative system and create some really positive miraculous things to improve our lifestyles while also restoring the planet.

In revisiting the problem areas identified in Chapter Two, let's look again at the challenges facing us to see what the Community approach would do to resolve some of these issues.

ECONOMICS

The idea of some people having great wealth while others live in poverty doesn't make sense anymore because of the conditions now on our planet, specifically the environmental crisis and the diminishing resources and food production problems. Yet, what has been described here in this revolutionary approach to cooperation is that we can all live very abundantly. Remember being or seeing children at play and the issue of sharing toys and then getting into "that's mine and you can't use it"—even if you weren't playing with it at that moment? Now we are adults, and the system is not set up to share our world. It was children's toys then, but now it's our adult toys like property and possessions, even if we rarely use them. There is enough wealth in terms of resources and manpower for *everyone* to have a really incredible, abundant life.

Military Nears Revolution in Weapons, War Strategy

■ Defense: New technology points to end of traditional structure, combat tactics. One result will be leaner force.

By ART PINE
TIMES STAFF WRITER

FT. BENNING, Ga.—High above the 200-mile-long battle zone in the Middle East, a pilotless Air Force radar plane controlled from a U.S. air base in Missouri charts the precise location of all American and enemy troops, weapons and equipment. It transmits the information to U.S. air, land and sea forces all over the globe and, almost simultaneously, jams enemy air defenses and attacks military and civilian targets with super laser beams.

A hundred miles offshore, a newly developed Navy "arsenal ship"—partially submerged and almost invisible both to radar and to the naked eye—fires hundreds of long-range, precision-guided missiles capable of hitting within 10 feet of their targets every time. A few moments later, Army attack helicopters and ground-launchers

■ LAST OF THREE PARTS

use laser-guided missiles to knock out enemy tanks and ammunition depots from miles away.

Small teams of soldiers and Marines—most of them flown in from bases in the United States—race into enemy urban areas, able to stay in touch via belt-carried mini-computers that pinpoint enemy soldiers and keep American troops
Please see MILITARY, A13

IF THE TECHNOLOGY IS AVAILABLE TO DO THIS, THEN WE COULD CHOOSE TO REDIRECT OUR TECHNOLOGY TO MAKE OUR WORLD WORK FOR EVERYONE.

REAL LIFE ADVENTURES By Wise and Aldrich

Learning the *real* facts of life.

HERMAN By Jim Unger

"The bank will lend you the money, but you have to prove to us that you don't really need it."

"We have to give importance to the next generation and the next. See, it was only when we failed to include them in our scientific theories and in our pursuit of growth that we placed all living systems in jeopardy. Just contemplate that horrifying fact that we are all leaving to our children the most poisonous of wastes— plutonium. It's going to remain poisonous for the next generation and the next and the next. In fact, it's going to remain poisonous for half a million years. We should never have accepted that theory: knowledge is power. We should never have accepted that theory that what's good for General Motors is good for America. We need a sustainable society, one in which our needs are being satisfied without diminishing the possibilities of the next generation."[4]

—*excerpt from the movie,* Mindwalk

Future economics must involve sustainability, otherwise the well from which we take our resources eventually runs dry. Obviously we need to not only stop destroying the environment but to begin to restore the planet. We know that consumption— largely through the consumerism of the Western societies—uses up the vast majority of the world's resources. We also know that the trickle-down effect of the present polarization of the world's wealth has resulted in poorer countries destroying their environments to service those Western societies and the tremendous financial debt owed to them. Through living cooperatively as we have described, we can eliminate unessential jobs and the resources they consume, we can eliminate nonsense products and still have more play and pleasure in our lives, and we can cut back on many essential products through sharing. We can even provide all of the people in the world with products that are beneficial, and we can eliminate all the absurd indebtedness that has enslaved people and countries to the point where the environment and the quality of people's lives have been compromised. Thus, everyone and the environment can win in a cooperative system of Communities.

We live with the unnecessary restriction of how we see society and wealth. Isn't wealth and abundance much more than money? It's what money can do that makes it valuable, and, in an individual Community and as Communities spread across the planet, you will be able to do incredibly well. As I said earlier, we need to redefine wealth as "use and access" rather than as possession. Yet, in this transition phase, perhaps until all the people realize that we can all basically have it all, we don't want to keep people away who have more, or who like having more, so we created a model (in the "How Do We Share Our Abundance" section) that would work for them, too, during this time of transition.

In the Highest Good Community system there really is no such thing as employment because there is no unemployment— everyone in a Community contributes, even those with perceived limitations. I learned through working many years with people with disabilities that we all have abilities and limitations and that everyone can make a contribution on some level no matter what those abilities or limitations are. Welfare and social security also

Everyone-For-Themselves Economics VS.

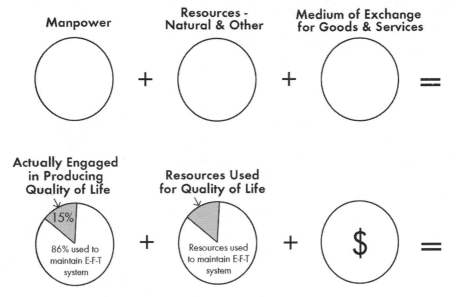

Everyone-For-Themselves Economics

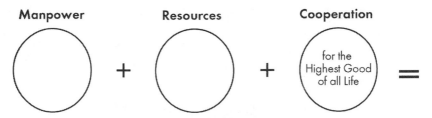

Highest-Good-For-All Economics

Only goods and services/resources and manpower have real value, and yet money, the artificial contrivance we invented as the medium of exchange, rules. Most of our manpower and the accompanying resouces go to fuel our Everyone-For-Themselves economy and produce no

Highest-Good-For-All Economics

Quality of Life/Abundance

The Economic Model

Abundance + Inequality/Poverty + Conflict, Isolation, Alienation, Depletion of World's Resources

Everyone-For-Themselves Economics

Abundance for All on All Levels + **Sustainability** and Replenishing of World's Resources + PEACE

Highest-Good-For All Economics

real value. Using "not enough money" as an excuse for not supplying needed human services and not restoring the environment is nothing short of in-the-box mass hysteria.

become archaic concepts in a cooperative system, as that which is needed can just be provided. People are naturally cared for in a Community, and, if services are needed, i.e., medical care, they can be provided for in a high quality way because they are now, with the old system out of the way, made a priority. We would have the resources and the technology to do that which was impossible in the everyone-for-themselves paradigm.

Yet, with "full employment" realized in the Community system, we have also eliminated some 80 plus percent of the existing jobs, thereby giving us both the ability to have the time to restore the planet and to have more time to enjoy our lives. Entire industries—including insurance, middlemen, sales and marketing, retailing, legal, governmental bureaucracies, and everything having to do with money—will be eliminated. The whole money system will eventually be replaced in the Highest Good system by representatives, working without the excuse of "there is not enough money," to coordinate production and distribution so that *all* the world's people can prosper. Again, until we do something about the wealth and poverty gap in the world and the corresponding rip-off of the environment, the environment that is our lifeblood will continue to decline.

Skeptics may speculate, probably based on their own feelings and lack of experience with working with people for the Highest Good, that people in Communities will become lazy and not want to work in a more idyllic life setting. However, the statistics I wrote about earlier from large cooperative systems like the Mondragon cooperatives in the Basque country prove that people willing to cooperate for the Highest Good can be far more productive. In Israel, the kibbutzim, with less than 4 percent of that country's population, were producing 40 percent of Israel's agriculture and 7 percent of the industrial exports in addition to supplying their own food, housing, medical, and entertainment needs.[5] The ones I visited were also very pretty places to live.

"Various places are witnessing a resurgence of a certain capitalistic neoliberalism, which subordinates the human person to blind market forces and conditions the development of peoples on those forces. We thus see a small number of countries growing exceedingly rich at the cost of the increasing impoverishment of a great number of other countries. As a result, the wealthy grow even wealthier, while the poor grow ever poorer." [6]

—Pope John Paul II from an open air mass in Havana

on Jan. 25, 1998

"How is it that we have created an economic system that tells us it is cheaper to destroy the earth than it is to maintain it?" [7]

—Paul Hawken, Economist

"Together, population growth, high rates of resource consumption, and poverty are driving the global economy toward ecological bankruptcy—a process that can only be reversed if their root causes are eliminated. We have filled up the planet's ecological space, and it will take reducing excessive consumption, redistributing wealth and resources, accelerating the development of more environmentally sustainable technologies, and slowing population growth to achieve a world in which all people may have a decent and secure life." [8]

—Lester Brown, State of the World 1994

"The hard truth is that our economic system is partially blind. It sees some things and not others ... GNP treats the rapid and reckless destruction of the environment as a good thing." [9]

—Al Gore

THE ENVIRONMENT

Many experts feel that the major problem we're dealing with is the rampant increase in the planet's population and thus the over-taxation on the planet's finite resources. But we must look at this in a holistic way and address the causal factors of population growth. It's in the poorer countries where we see the population explosion. People have felt that they needed large families in order to survive. Ironically, the Kerala State in India is the one glaring exception in the world. Although one of the world's poorest areas, they have a fertility rate lower than America's, a 100 percent literacy rate, and even a life expectancy about the same as ours.[10] The reason for this startling contradiction is that the people have chosen to cooperate to a higher degree than any populous State in the world is currently doing. Overpopulation per se is not a problem, but a symptom of our lack of cooperation in the world. The most effective birth control continues to be social and economic gain resulting in a high quality of life. There is an old saying: the rich get richer, and the poor get children. As we make the world work for everyone through Communities, the need for large families dissolves into the realization that we are all family. The Communities will provide the family support that people have heretofore looked for in biological families. Then, as we realize through the worldwide Communities that we are all one family on this planet, we can choose to spread the population around in ways that make sense beyond the issues of national borders.

In a talk before the United Nations, Robert Mugabe of Zimbabwe said, "They [the Third World peoples] know that cutting down trees and the deforestation of tropical forests will lead to soil erosion and future disasters, but their problem is survival today. ... To ask us to plan for our survival tomorrow when our survival today is in doubt, is to ask too much of us. For it is only when we can survive today that we can talk of tomorrow."[11] In 1987, the World Commission on Environment and Development published the results of a four-year study on environment and development. Their report, *Our Common Future*, found that "Poverty is a major cause and effect of global environmental problems. It is therefore futile to attempt to deal with environmental problems without a broader perspective that encom-

"Increasing human demands are damaging the natural resource base—land, water and air—on which all life depends."[12]

—The State of World Population 1988

"There are many signs that the next general international crisis is going to be about the environment. There have been warnings about environmental abuse for decades, but concerns were separated from high politics and security. Now convergence has begun."[13]

—*Flora Lewis,* "The Next Big Crisis"

"Deep inequalities drive environmental degradation, cause explosive social conditions, and fuel ethnic conflicts."[14]   *(I included this quote just in case you were still wondering what's been fueling these ethnic conflicts and how we must address them by making life work for everyone.)*

—*United Nations,* Report of the World Summit for Social Development (Copenhagen, March 6-17, 1995)

"The depth of the rift between rich and poor was illustrated as Pakistani Environmental Minister Anwar Saifullah Khan spoke for the developing nations' caucus (at the 1992 Earth Summit). 'It is difficult,' he said, 'for a man scavenging on the garbage dump created by affluence and profligate consumption to understand that protecting a bird is more important than protecting himself.'" [15]

"The (World Commission on Environment and Development's (WCED)) report cites preventable poverty as one of the major causes of environmental degradation. It argues that poverty pollutes our environment. Those who are poor and hungry will often destroy their immediate environment in order to survive. They will cut down their forests. Their livestock will overgraze the grasslands and in growing numbers will crowd into congested cities. They will overuse marginal land. This explains why the greatest damage is occurring in developing countries. These countries are poor. They are faced with falling commodity prices, a rise in protectionism, a crushing debt burden and dwindling or even reverse financial flows. If their commodities bring little money, they must produce more of them to bring in the same amount or at times even less. To do this, they cut down trees, bring under cultivation marginal land, overgraze their pastures and in the process make deserts out of previously productive land. But in these actions the poor have no choice. They cannot exercise the option to die today so as to live well tomorrow. Developing countries are caught in a vicious circle, which the Commissioners have acknowledged in their report." [16]

—Robert Mugabe, Prime Minister of Zimbabwe

"We [WCED] early came to recognize that poverty is the main cause and effect of environmental degradation in many developing countries. Clearly it is totally unacceptable and incompatible with human decency and solidarity even to suggest that the poor must remain in poverty in order to protect the environment." [17]

—Gro Harlem Brundtland, WCED chairperson

passes the factors underlying world poverty and international inequality." Therefore, the report concluded that improving human welfare through sustainable development is the key to protecting the environment."[18] Ms. Brundtland, the Prime Minister of Norway, who headed the Commission, added that there was no way to improve the environment without improving people's life conditions generally, and that, "The Commission became collectively convinced that present development patterns cannot be allowed to continue. While economic and social development suffer from severe national and global imbalances, threats to the environment are becoming global in scope and devastating in scale and effect. The survival of this planet requires that we act now."[19]

Yet, in improving people's lives in order to try to rescue the environment, we cannot emulate the Western free market economics because the Western world's impact on the environment has been a disaster. We have been operating under the myth that nature was infinite and could absorb all our waste with no—or at least limited—adverse effects. Economic development and environmental protection must proceed together, which means sustainability and restoring the Earth's resources. We think that what we've described in this book—a system based on the Highest Good For All Life— may be the only way to do it. We're going to have to make the world work for everyone or it will work for no one.

Because we have the technology to eliminate the production of just about all the pollution (if we choose to do so), the production of pollution is mostly economically driven. So, when we combine the predicament of the Third World countries and the developed countries, we see that the environmental problems are economically based. With worldwide Communities, there no longer would be people living on the edge and having to destroy their own habitats to survive, nor would countries have to sacrifice their environments to service their massive debts. There would also be Community based agriculture rather than the economically driven system of eradicating nature from vast tracks of land for large-scale agriculture. Here and in the Third World we will be putting back trees and ecosystems to replenish the topsoil and provide natural insect control so that there is no longer a need for harmful

"We must learn to live together as brothers or perish together as fools."
—Dr. Martin Luther King, Jr., from a March 22, 1964 speech
in St. Louis

"If we're going to continue to have a world, we're going to have to start making the world work for everyone— or it will work for no one."
—members of the Community Planet Foundation

From "The Urbanity of Toxics," Jay Levin, *Los Angeles Weekly*, Dec. 1-7, 1989.

Conceptual Community industrial area drawing by Thomas Slagle

chemicals and pesticides which pollute both our planet and our bodies. Also, with education and the nutritional way our Communities will prepare our food, we'll be using less meat and dairy, which will help restore the land and improve our health.

In a Highest Good Community system, there is no reason why we cannot restore the Earth to the state of being the green planet, a virtual ecological paradise that is a pleasure to see—with clean air, water and land. There no longer have to be landfills, vehicles that pollute, or even traffic. Yet, at the same time, all people have more time and access to see more of this magnificent planet.

Remember the boiled Frog syndrome that I described earlier? How do we get the people of this planet to respond to the environmental changes before it's too late? I believe that the answer is to show the frog that there is a much better pond available. That better pond is a Highest Good For All way of living on our planet.

"The dramatic threat of ecological breakdown is teaching us the extent to which greed and selfishness—both individual and collective—are contrary to the order of creation, an order which is characterized by mutual interdependence. ... Modern society will find no solution to the ecological problem unless it takes a serious look at its lifestyle."[20]

—Pope John Paul II

"To commit a crime against the natural world is a sin. ... We're all connected—there is no separation. Polluting the environment is blasphemous—we are ruining God's work. There's only one planet and one people."[21]

—His Holiness Bartholomew I

HEALTH

As I understand it, the key factors in health are our mental/emotional state, good water, good air, and nutritional food. According to experts in longevity, with these factors in place, we should now be able to live healthily in excess of 120 years of age or so. The Communities will enable us to greatly improve our health on all levels. Perhaps most important is the freedom from stress that we will experience as we are involved with a loving, supportive family of people, as our work actually becomes meaningful for everyone, and as our lives are greatly simplified in the Highest Good paradigm. Currently in the U.S., all seven top selling drugs are for stress-related diseases, and Zontac, the top selling drug in the world, treats ulcers.[22] Further reducing stress and adding to our well-being on all levels, regular exercise and play in nice surroundings with nurturing people become daily Community activities rather than events to try to squeeze into our too-busy lives. Even regular massage becomes commonplace for all rather than a luxury for the few that can afford it.

Given the reallocation of manpower and resources in the Community system, there will be more resources available to all for medical treatment. Of course, with better water, air, and food and with less stress and more of a holistic approach to preventative medicine, we will also have a tremendous reduction in the medical drug industry as well as much less of an incidence of many of the preventable diseases that are caused by stress, pollutants, and improper nutrition. Still, medical services will no longer be limited by insurance or to those who can afford them. In our current system, we have made some tremendous medical advances, but, with spiraling medical costs, it has more and more become medicine for the rich. Health services are all too often determined not by need but by money. Meanwhile, a major injury or health crisis can devastate many families. We also can't afford to get regular preventative treatment, which would cost less in the long run. Worldwide, millions of people die from preventable diseases. To me, that's a tragedy that is attributable to our everyone-for-themselves system and preventable in a Highest

DOONESBURY © G. B. Trudeau. Reprinted with permission of
UNIVERSAL PRESS SYNDICATE. All rights reserved.

THE WIZARD OF ID By Brant Parker and Johnny Hart

By permission of Johnny Hart and Creators Syndicate, Inc.

This is medicine in our everyone-for-themselves paradigm. We can do better tha
that, we can create an abundance of health and wealth for everyone if we choos
to live for the Highest Good For All.

As I was editing, this perfect example of the "Us vs. Them" consciousness–that is an integral part of our everyone-for-themselves paradigm–played out in the media. As the EPA came out with a proposal for tougher smog and airborne particles standards, the opposition by the money interests standing to be financially impacted was immediate and fierce.[23,24]

EPA Proposes Tougher Limits On Soot, Smog

By Marla Cone
Times Enviromental Writer

Fueling a fervent debate on capitol Hill and in corporate boardrooms, the U.S. Environmental Protection Agency on Wednesday unveiled a far-reaching proposal to strengthen standards aimed at protecting over 130 million Americans from health dangers posed by urban smog and tiny airborne particles.

Pressured by powerful industries and Republican leaders in Congress on one side and environmental and health advocates on the other, EPS Administrator Carol Browner recommended pollution limits in the middle of the range endorsed by her staff and scientific advisors. ...

Hundreds of major corporations and business groups, led by the nation's oil and auto industries, contend that the new health limits are unjustified, impractical and would add tens of billions of dollars a year to an already intense bill for smog control.

Some Republican Congress members and governors have warned that they will not only try to block the EPA from implementing the new proposal but will mount campaigns to overhaul the Clean Air Act, which gives the EPA sole authority to set air pollution standards.

U.S. Poised to Toughen Air Quality Standards

•**Pollution**: Opponents say new ozone and particulate limits are unrealistic

By Marla Cone
Times Enviromental Writer

The long-awaited new limits on ozone and particulates—two of the nation's most pervasive air pollutants—will establish more rigorous requirements for what is considered healthful air.

U.S. Environmental Protection Agency Administrator Carol Browner plans to sign a proposed rule as early as Tuesday, unleashing a fierce, nationwide debate that will cumulate when a final version is adopted in June.

Even before the proposal has been unveiled, it has been under attack from a broad base of foes, including more than 500 powerful corporations and business groups—led by General Motors, Ford, Chrysler, Chevron, Mobile and other oil companies—as well as many governors and members of congress.

Industry leaders say tightening the health standards will launch the nation on a multibillion-dollar impossible mission of trying to clean up pollution to unrealistic levels. ...

"The question has to be, how clean can we afford the air to be?" said Gerald Esper, director of the American Automobile Manufacturers Assn's environmental department.

The last paragraph of "U.S. Poised..." contains this astounding quote, "The question has to be, how clean can we afford the air to be?" said Gerald Esper, director of the American Automobile Assn.'s environmental department." Who are the "we" in the "How clean can we afford...? I don't think it's the estimated 60,000 Americans who die annually from breathing the pollution particles in the air, and I don't think it's the millions of others whose lungs and breathing are affected, not to mention that smog is really ugly. Yet, as long as we continue with the everyone-for-themselves approach, people will make decisions based on "us vs. them" and there will be the tradeoffs of financial consideration vs. the well-being of all life on the planet. The stakes are too high to continue this approach, especially when there is such a wonderful alternative.

Good system. All the planet's people deserve and can have access to needed, preventative, and vitalizing health care.

Do you know that in some countries whole villages of poor people are selling their "spare" body organs just to survive financially? The organ brokers take these organs and sell them to those who can afford this service. Excuse me, this not only gives me the creeps, but is just plain wrong. This is not "survival of the fittest," but "survival of the richest."

On a personal note, pain is one of my least favorite things. Since we can plan our planet in a way that alleviates the most possible pain on all levels, including emotionally and mentally for all people, there is no really good reason not to do it. We have just had thousands of years of everyone-for-themselves which has blinded us to the possibilities.

SOCIAL

I previously proposed that isolation and alienation are two of the key causal factors for the dysfunction in the world today. As a consequence of this, people have tried to escape their feelings of powerlessness through crime, drugs, cynicism, resignation, and lapsing into uninspiring lives. With the support, nurturing, and creativity available within the Communities and with abundance being a given in our lives, the key factors to the escapist behavior of addictions and crime are eliminated. We also can end the separation we impose on people with disabilities and people who are elderly as they become valued, integrated members of our Communities. Obviously there would also no longer be homelessness or refugees as we make the planet work for everyone.

What would you really like to do with your life if you really had the freedom to choose and the time to express that choice(s). Would it be to express yourself more creatively, perhaps even for the benefit of humanity, or would you like to have a peaceful life in beautiful surroundings that would support you to go inside and discover more of who you truly are? Whatever your dream for self-actualization, in your life as it is now you may feel that you just don't have the time to pursue your dreams. With the unessential jobs and products eliminated via a cooperative world of

"I come from a country (the U.S.) where they use 40 percent of the world's resources to support 6 percent of the world's population, which makes the population so happy and peaceful that we're the world's biggest drug market. Half our teenagers contemplate suicide, one in five girls has tried it."[25]

—*excerpt from the movie,* Mindwalk

(By the way, if you haven't seen this movie, rent the video—it's a must as an introduction to the System's Theory—the interconnectedness of all things.)

Communities, people not only will have more time to enjoy themselves but also more time and cooperative resources for actualization—and we're talking about *all the world's people,* including those that have heretofore been disenfranchised by their struggle to survive.

In going for what works for all of us in the Highest Good system, we find things getting simpler. There are fewer responsibilities to fill up our lives, especially in the stressful area of finances and security, and there is more natural space to facilitate our attuning within. Who knows, we may even spend a lot less time as media spectators, as we choose to participate more than watch. Given the choice through accessibility to a variety of fun pursuits and fun people to participate with, I think that most of us would rather play than to watch others play. Of course, there would still be the opportunity to enjoy the performances of others, but you no longer would have to pay big bucks to watch multi-millionaires play and perform. Instead, you would see good and talented people perform for the joy of it.

Awhile ago I talked with a person from Armenia who told me that, while poverty was rampant in her country, the people in the area she was from were much happier than the people here. When I asked her why, she said that the people would sit down and talk with their neighbors and do things together. She said they had a sense of community there and that that was the big difference. Here, a lot of the older houses have porches, but who even knows their neighbors anymore, let alone participates with them. In the abundant Highest Good Communities, the support would be phenomenal and opportunities for nurturing, play, creativity, and having needs met would be almost unlimited for all the people. Imagine living in a happy/Loving world.

POLITICAL

It's interesting that I saved this area for last. In one of Buckminster Fuller's talks, he said, "I hear a lot of people say 'I don't like machinery and technology, it's making a lot of trouble, upsets all the old things.' So we're going to take all the machinery away from all the countries of the world, all the tracks and wires and the works and dump it all in the ocean. And you'll discover that within six months two billion people will die of starvation having gone through great pain. So we say, 'That's not a very good idea; let's put the machinery back the way it was.' Then we're going to take all the politicians from all the countries around the world, and we're going to send them for a trip around the sun, and you find that we keep right on eating. And, with the political barriers down ... the scientists say very clearly that you could make the world work and take care of 100 percent of the humanity ... but you can't do it with the barriers; ... it is an organic whole."[26] Bucky Fuller, perhaps our foremost futurist, knew that we are going to have to change business-as-usual to free up the resources for everyone. He said that "The only way we can possibly take care of everyone is through a design revolution—doing more with less."[27] Also, he noted that "Our bedrooms are empty two-thirds of the time, our living rooms are empty seven-eights of the time, our office buildings are empty half the time, it's time we gave this some thought."[28]

Of course, the basis of the design revolution has to be on the level of how we choose to live together, it has to be choosing to live in a way that works for everyone, and, as Fuller correctly noted, sending politicians around the sun would be helpful. The political process in our everyone-for-themselves world has virtually always broken down into power struggles between two or more groups, political parties, or power brokers positioning themselves for financial gain. The bulk of humanity has been left on the outside of this struggle—while also being at the effect of the struggle— with no one really getting their needs met in terms of the real quality of life.

The only way we can change is to show something completely different—as different as a Highest Good system is to our everyone-for-themselves institution. We must reinvolve people in the decisions that affect their daily lives and help them learn effective, harmonious communication. In Communities operating for the Highest Good Of All Concerned, the fundamental difference between the Communities' method of making decisions by consensus and other traditional forms of decision making is that

*"THE WORLD IS IN A RACE BETWEEN
EDUCATION AND CATASTROPHE."*
                              —BUCKMINSTER FULLER

*"WE CAN HAVE A DEMOCRATIC SOCIETY OR
WE CAN HAVE THE CONCENTRATION OF
GREAT WEALTH IN THE HANDS OF A FEW. WE
CANNOT HAVE BOTH."*

*"WE DO NOT HAVE A REPRESENTATIVE
DEMOCRACY IN THE UNITED STATES. WE
HAVE AN UNEQUAL DEMOCRACY WHERE THE
MAJOR DECISIONS THAT AFFECT OUR LIVES
ARE DRIVEN BY POWER/MONEY INTERESTS.
WE NEED TO RETURN TO THE PEOPLE THE
DECISIONS THAT AFFECT THEIR EVERYDAY
LIVES."*
                  —SUPREME COURT JUSTICE LOUIS BRANDEIS

*"FASCISM SHOULD MORE PROPERLY BE
CALLED CORPORATISM, SINCE IT IS THE
MERGER OF STATE AND CORPORATE POWER."*
                              —BENITO MUSSOLINI

we have fundamentally similar ideas rather than that we are fundamentally different. Of course, this depends on the consciousness of the people, but, in seeing that the Highest Good can benefit all and having the commitment to go for that, we can have a revolution in making the world work for all. It becomes much easier to give up something, like a holdout dissension position, when people can see that through cooperation they can have so much more in return, both in terms of the quality of their lives and actually having more say in the decisions that affect their daily lives.

As this educational process spreads across the planet through worldwide Communities, the power will go to the people, and the political process will be taken away from the power brokers and the accompanying philosophy currently committed to protecting the status quo. In a peaceful, evolutionary/revolutionary process, the power will be taken away from the few controlling the many through their philosophy of conflict and the hoarding of the resources. We will then have essentially sent the power brokers around the sun. If they still want to play, they will find an ever-shrinking audience. Besides, the quality of their lives would also improve by choosing to become part of a Community and finally experience the caring and Loving that they were trying to seek through having control over others.

There are good things about countries and certainly about cultures, *and we need to move into peace and cooperation*. In the Community model, we can let go of nationalism, racism, sexism, etc., where everyone has a point of view that is "right"—a position that probably can be justified on any side by hundreds or thousands of years of history. However, because of the destruction of the environment, we must now be willing to move into a greater oneness, into the brother/sisterhood of all humankind. That means that we must make life work very well for everyone every-where to eliminate inequity, one of the key sources of againstness. We are now all interconnected because of the world's environ-mental problems and economics, and practicing nationalism and other "isms" has led us away from the solutions.

"Nationalism is an infantile sickness. It is the measles of the human race."

—Albert Einstein

"It's foolish for a society to cling to its old ideas in new times just as it's foolish for an old man to squeeze into a coat that fit him in his youth."

— Thomas Jefferson

"In Spirit, we are one family, and we're unified across the planet. Do you remember when Jesus said, 'When you've done it to the least of them, you've done it unto me?' That's quite a statement of compassion, a statement of responsibility if we're going to follow the Christ."

— John Morton, Educator

"Every once in awhile a man oughta do something just because it's right."

— Sam Rayburn

While we're at it, let's also discuss religious differences because they have too often been the source of conflicts between individuals and groups for thousands of years. We must move into acceptance and understanding, which are qualities beyond merely tolerance, where everyone can pursue whatever Spiritual path they choose—as long as they don't inflict on others and as long as their choice includes an absolute respect for all life. Within the Communities and their Highest Good consciousness, that will be the requirement. I think it's great to have diversity in religion as long as there is acceptance and understanding for the choices of others. We are all on our path to realizing who we truly are, and there are likely different approaches that work best for different people. Even if one disagrees with that, demonstrating a happy life, acceptance, and loving service to others without expectation is always more persuasive than any other approach.

Now is a good time to address the possibility that some people may, in seeing that the Highest Good system is not the "acceptable" capitalistic system, mistakenly put an erroneous label like socialism or communism on our model. In many cases, the people who sit on the boards of the print and broadcasting media are the same ones who sit on the boards of the multinational corporations. Through the propaganda of corporate America, free enterprise has come to be equated with freedom, which equals nationalism, which equals Christianity, which equals God. However, as we've noted, "free" enterprise has enslaved the world economically, and more and more people fall into poverty as more and more gets concentrated into the hands of fewer and fewer. Meanwhile egalitarianism has come to equal equality, which equals socialism, which equals unionism, which equals communism, which equals Satan. Remember, though, that American communities began with the Plymouth pilgrims who set up our first towns by pooling their resources. Also, the early Christians practiced communal living and held all things in common. Funny how times have changed—these early Americans and Christians would now be seen as anti-Christian and branded as evil.

With capitalism, communism, and socialism alike, the power is in the hands of the state and the ruling elite, and thus these models

are basically more alike than they are different. The Highest Good
For All Community model that we have described is fundamentally different from any existing models because we are a group of
individuals who make decisions for ourselves at the Community
level—not the State level—and everyone is involved in those
decisions. There is no elite group controlling everyone else. Also,
remember that what is unique here is that the Highest Good model
is the marriage of the *consciousness* of the Highest Good to the *form*
of the Highest Good. It has never worked to impose the form on
everyone—the consciousness of the Highest Good has to be there.
If it is not, then we are not talking about the same thing. This is,
therefore, neither socialism nor communism nor a State-controlled
social welfare system. Some of the social welfare countries, i.e.,
New Zealand and Sweden, are not doing well because they try to
do it on a State level within an everyone-for-themselves paradigm,
and this can never really deal with the intricacies of the problem,
because it is not a systems-approach.

   People need to be given opportunities, nurtured and cared for
as individuals, and included as an integral part of a Community
and not anonymously just given money. Using any current
system, when we try at a State level to provide for people, then
the economy supports a bureaucracy, middlemen, nonsense jobs,
unemployment, and welfare—none of which would exist on the
Community level. To me, capitalism, socialism, and communism, as they have been practiced, are also fundamentally more
alike than different in that they are all patriarchal varieties of the
everyone-for-themselves approach rather than a systems-
approach of making life work for all of us. Still though, a
systems-approach at any level won't work unless everyone is
committed to the Highest Good, and that's an educational
problem that people must first see demonstrated.

   Interestingly, if we were to use a consensus decision-making
approach to deciding how we as people would live together on
this planet, we would eventually come up with a system or form
of living that would work for everyone and for the planet. That
form would probably look a lot like the one that we have
described. It would be a decision that worked for all us on the

planet: it would encompass sustainability, it would put nurturing, fun, and joy into our lives, and it would eliminate unnecessary jobs and give us more time and fun and less stress. We would also stop polluting and unnecessarily using up our planet's resources and get back in touch with nature. Politically, it's time we start choosing to make our planet work for everyone.

If we do not start making our world work for everyone, the United States Commission on National Security 21st Century has some sobering predictions. This report was put together using our best security advisors. The report forecasts: "Thanks to the continuing integration of global financial networks, economic downturns that were once normally episodic and local may become more systemic and fully global in their harmful effects. Isolated epidemics could explode into global pandemics." Also, "... disparities in income will increase and widespread poverty will persist."[29] Because history tells us that desperate and disenfranchised people will do desperate things, the report also offers the dire prediction that "...mass-casualty terrorism directed against the U.S. homeland was of serious and growing concern." and "A direct attack against American citizens on American soil is likely over the next quarter century."[30] Even then will we have the wisdom to start making choices that support all life on the planet or will we go down the traditional road of separation, revenge, and retaliation. In order to change course, it's going to take a new paradigm of living together and relating together for the Highest Good For All, and this must be first demonstrated on a Community level.

A COMPETITIVE SYSTEM WILL ALWAYS HAVE PEOPLE AT THE BOTTOM WHO HAVE LITTLE TO BALANCE THOSE AT THE TOP WHO HAVE TOO MUCH.

Chapter 8
HOW DO WE START

"The time has come to break out of past patterns. Attempts to maintain social and ecological stability through old approaches to development and environmental protection will increase instability. Security must be sought through change. This Commission has noted a number of actions that must be taken to reduce risks to survival and to put future development on paths that are sustainable. Yet we are aware that such a reorientation on a continuing basis is simply beyond the reach of present decision-making structures and institutional arrangements, both national and international."[1]

—World Commission on Environment and Development (WCED)

This conclusion from the WCED's 1987 report to the U.N. warned the General Assembly that there were many imbalances that needed to be corrected to have a sustainable future, indeed, "to keep options open for future generations."[2] In response to the Commission's sobering report, the 1989 U.N.'s General Assembly mandated the 1992 Earth Summit in Rio do Janeiro, which brought together the world's leaders for the week-long U.N. Conference on Environment and Development. But, despite the dire warnings that we have only a limited time to make sweeping changes on how we go about life on the planet, what changed after that conference? Other than the creation of a good book, *AGENDA 21*, not much happened.

It's kind of puzzling that the WCED called upon the government leaders for a solution, since they had already concluded that political solutions would not work, that national and international decision-making structures were incapable of making the necessary changes to secure our future. The truth is that there are just too many fractional interests involved for governments to have much effectiveness. We can't save humanity on the political level because it's dictated by the age-old everyone-for-themselves paradigm that does not take into account The Highest Good Of All and the form that approach has to take in order to make the world work for everyone. That can only be done by a group of people who absolutely hold the consciousness of the Highest Good For All and have the vision to bring that into manifestation on the level of how we live together on the planet.

This Next Evolution that will change the world will start with just one model Community. It will not start nationally or even on the scale of a several thousand person Community. The reason is that most people will first need to see the concept and learn and commit to the consciousness of the Highest Good For All. There are many books written about Utopian societies, but most are big government models and/or provide us with no realistic road map for how to get to the endpoint—it's as if it just magically happens with people willing to move into cooperating. But four to five hundred people can create a model such as we've described and show that it's practical and doable while also showing the prerequisite consciousness of the Highest Good. I think that there has probably never been the consciousness to do cooperative Communities on a large scale. However, now, at the start of the 21st century, with the media coverage and technology that is available and with the environmental threat to the planet combined with the growing desire for more fulfilling and less isolated lives, we can transform the planet by showing a model of a better way to live.

The first step is to create a model on a piece of land large enough to later do a Community cluster. As the Community successfully demonstrates this rather radical but practical way of life, the media naturally covers the story and educational institutions come to visit and study this living laboratory. The Community would also become known through tourism as people come to see both the Epcot-like technology put to positive use in the way we live and to see what cooperative living looks like in an abundant setting. In addition, there would be a variety of workshops and internships available both for people to come to the Community to learn more and workshops and seminars given by request around the country and around the planet.

When there is enough interest generated by the first Community, then we can do a second Community, then a third, and so on, in a cluster. When, as previously described, we have about five, it will cause a huge media splash, and people all over the world will become aware that there is a happier and more abundant lifestyle available. At that point an international audience will want to come to learn and train so that the model can be taken globally. Also, some of the Community pioneers will probably want to go and help establish new Communities. The original Communities, with the greater abundance that is available to them, may also help fund the newer ones.

But, of course, it all starts with the first model, and following are the steps, as we see them, that are necessary to establish that first model. These steps are not necessarily in chronological order because many of the steps would be happening simultaneously.

1. Locate the site - It must be large enough to eventually do a cluster of at least five Communities and preferably more. Given that most of our zoning rules are now set up to serve the everyone-for-themselves paradigm, the choice of site must be one where we do not get stuck for years explaining that we're not going to have individual home parcels, but rather we're going to take a piece of land and design it to work for everyone.

2. Do an environmental impact study - Focus not only on how much can be done without adversely affecting the flora and fauna, but also on how the overall environment can be enhanced from any previous damage that was done before us.

3. Get the people - The key to doing a Community based on The Highest Good Of All is to screen for people who are committed and hold the consciousness. This is especially important for the first Community, because people must see that it can work and the kind of consciousness it takes. This requires a commitment both to do what it takes for The Highest Good Of All and a commitment to

personal growth. But we must start with a model that people can aim at so that they can get inspired to realize that there is a huge benefit in lifestyle available in going for the Highest Good. After all, most of the world's problems and conflicts fundamentally stem from the consciousness of separateness.

The Community Planet Foundation has developed a workshop on consensus decision-making that both teaches the skills and consciousness necessary to do consensus and also screens participants for Community residency. Once people are attracted to the lifestyle of the Highest Good, they will come for workshops to learn cooperative decision-making. You can also start in your own life by beginning to practice peace, cooperation, and Loving. In your relationships start committing to going for the Highest Good, creating a safe space for communicating, *and choosing Loving over all else*. Start developing a habit of putting yourself in another's place to see things as they see them. Also, start valuing and respecting them no matter what they do and start taking responsibility for everything you react to. There is a notion that respect has to be earned, but I disagree. I think that trust has to be earned by all parties in establishing safety in communication. But I think that everyone has a God-given right to respect no matter what. Until that happens, there will not be a Brother/Sisterhood of humankind.

4. Completely design the Community for the maximum number of people before anything is built - This is the reverse philosophy of most community planning where communities just happen by chance as people build individual houses and build-ings with lots of concrete roads and parkways. By getting experts from all the disciplines together for the planning process, our Community will be a well thought out, integrated whole for both maximum efficiency and minimal environmental disruption. Building design and multipurpose use, energy generation and efficiency, water collection and storage, edible landscaping, recycling, etc., will all be a part of the design process before anything is built.

5. Identify and secure income-producing businesses that would

be incorporated into the Community - This may cause some alterations in #4 and ideally would be done along with #4, but sometimes people like to look at a draft model first to get the vision.

6. Secure the financing - This first Community must be done correctly (and rather immediately to help the planet and minimize the ongoing environmental damage). Therefore, while the Community with its businesses will be a money-maker, the money for this first Community needs to be in place up front. The money can come in from a variety of sources and a variety of ways, but it also could take just take one person to fully fund this project—a person who has the resources and the vision to recognize that living for the Highest Good is what must happen. The lure is that this is not a Band-Aid approach to dealing with the world's problems, but rather a revolutionary approach that can transform the entire planet.

Because a lot of the design and technology of the Community will be either revolutionary or leading edge, the Community will be an Epcot Center concept complete with a visitor's center to showcase these technologies. Because manufacturers will therefore be able to derive a great deal of benefit from the Community using their design, product(s), and/or materials, a lot of these technologies and materials may be donated or provided at a reduced cost.

7. Move people into the Community in a logical sequence - Some people would be needed for the building and planning phases while others would come in with the businesses to get them established. A key is to start the consensus process on site and to have the people living together start using it and getting it in place. This would also include those people who may be living nearby while waiting for their housing to be ready.

8. Outreach/Education - Once the Community is functioning successfully, we will share with others what we are doing through workshops, seminars, media coverage, etc. (See the "How Do We Expand Our Community?" description).

9. Replication - We give our support both in expertise and funding to start other Communities. The first ones may be in our cluster while simultaneously happening in other states and other countries.

"Never doubt that a small group of thoughtful, committed citizens can change the world. Indeed, it is the only thing that ever has."

—*Margaret Mead*

Chapter 9
THE NEXT (R)EVOLUTION

Just like the Sorcerer's Apprentice in *Fantasia*, we, as a planet, now stand on the precipice, watching the seemingly out-of-control results of what we have created threaten the very survival of the planet or, at the very least, cause a greatly diminished lifestyle for almost everyone, as the ability of the planet to support life drastically erodes over the next 50 years. It's ironic that in this post-Cold War era, it's become increasingly clear that the real threat to our survival maybe never was nuclear war because no one really wanted to do something which would have been so fast and final. Rather, the threat we face is more insidious than war because the destruction of the earth's environment has been happening so much more slowly in its inextricable marriage to our everyone-for-themselves paradigm. Having taken place over hundreds of years, so many economic forces are involved in our world economy that it's now too complicated for anyone to bring into balance. All our efforts to date have at best been Band-Aid approaches, and the destruction continues. Therefore, we now find ourselves in World War III—the War Against The Earth. This war is not only against the environment but also against the quality of life which that environment supports.

OUR PLACE IN HISTORY

With all our crises, mankind now teeters at the precipice of its out-of-control creation. Which way are we going to go? If we do not in the next few years have a major (r)evolution in the way we go about life on this planet, it is absolutely predictable how historians will write about this period of time. What will they say fifty years from now when the quality of life on this planet is greatly

"And yet, while public awareness of all these (life-threatening environmental) problems is rising dramatically, they are strikingly absent from the American political dialog. We are about to see another presidential election without any substantive discussion of the real issues of our time.

"This constitutes a breakdown of democracy. While we applaud the emergence of new democratic governments around the world, our own democratic institutions are rapidly disappearing.

"The mass media do not offer independent reports and analyses, but merely echo the views of a small group of politicians who are controlled by corporate America. This means that at any time, important issues cannot be brought up on television or in the press, because the corporate owners of the media do not want these issues to be discussed. All this in spite of the First Amendment."[1]

—*Fritjof Capra*

diminished and as our depleted planet is no longer able to provide food and other basic needs for the ever-increasing population? The historians will say that we engaged in financially-driven chemical experimentation with the various products we made, which had devastating long-term effects on the air, land, and sea. They will also write about how we basically raped the planet's resources, treating them as if they were limitless, with no concern for future generations. Although those things are sometimes reported now, the historians will be unmerciful in describing how, even at the start of the 21st century, we still allowed many known poisonous products to be widely used because of the political/economic factors. They will write about how we the people bowed to big money and power broker interests, and then they will report that it didn't even work out for those people as the planet self-destructed.

The historians will compare this time to the decadence in the fall of the Roman Empire. They will decry us for choosing temporary greed over the well-being of the planet and of our grandchildren, and they will cite numerous examples of how we attempted to justify our economic decisions at the time while ignoring the long-term results of our choices. They will point out how television and the media became the opium of the masses by fixating people on the momentary sensational stories like the allegations against Michael Jackson, the Tonya Harding Olympics story, the emasculating of John Wayne Bobbit, the Menendez brothers' murder trial, the two-year daily coverage of the O. J. Simpson story, Monicagate, and Eilian Gonzales. They will also report how increasingly bizarre talk show topics and "Survivor"-type reality shows became all the rage.

The historians will question why, with what we knew about the depletion of the planet, we stuck or heads in the sand and focused on sensational momentary issues and profit instead of our using the media *24 hours a day* to report about the seriousness of the environmental issues. They will indict us for not using the media as a forum to explore possible solutions that would begin to restore our planet and keep the Earth healthy for generations to come. It's like there's a huge black cloud coming that can suffocate

FEIFFER

the world, and, although we have the evidence that it's coming, we choose instead to bicker about balancing the budget, affirmative action, taxation, crime, drugs, family values, etc. If that cloud finally settles upon us and it's too late, we'll say, "Oh, we should have been dealing with the issue that was looming over us with the capacity to destroy our way of life instead of arguing about what we now realize were, in comparison, petty differences."

The historians might say that we considered the planet's long-range problems to be too scary and too overwhelming to even think about, and thus most of us felt too impotent to really do what it would take to heal the planet. Sticking our heads in the sand, we hoped that the problems would just go away. It's sort of like what happens in a dysfunctional family. The family makes an unspoken covenant not to talk about the dysfunction because, if they did start to really talk about it, then they might have to start doing something about it. They might also have to face the reaction of the power brokers. Our planet is like that dysfunctional family. It was interesting to me to note that in President Clinton's 1995 State Of The Union Address, nothing was said about protecting and restoring the environment, even though Vice President Gore's, *Earth In The Balance*, detailed the environmental threat to the planet. Then, in his 1996 address, when the Republicans were more vulnerable on environmental issues, Clinton chose to say something.

Perhaps, though, the current alarming rate of environmental destruction and the rapid decay of social, political, and environmental systems can be seen as a good thing because they will force us to look for long-term solutions for survival. We will be forced to choose either cooperating and having more for all of us or continuing our everyone-for-themselves approach and watching our quality of life rapidly decline. So, even though it may not look that way now, our destructive changes can be seen as good. As Martin Luther King once said, "Only when it is dark enough do you see the stars." Think of the billions of people already in absolute have-not situations. Many of these people have been there for generations, even lifetimes as they daily live in abject poverty on the edge of starvation and survival. Long ago the planet stopped working for them. To restate one last time the simple truth that is the

THE FALL OF THE ROMAN EMPIRE HAD NOTHING ON US.

WORLD

BRITAIN

Woman loses 3 octuplets; others in peril

A British woman on Monday lost three of the octuplets doctors had advised her not to try to carry to term.

Mandy Allwood, 32, was in satisfactory condition at King's College Hospital. But the remaining five fetuses were still in danger.

"Sadly, she has lost three babies and the situation for the others is bleak," Donald Gibb, a consulting obstetrician, said in a statement.

Allwood sold exclusive British rights to her story to the tabloid News of the World and hired a publicist to seek further financial deals. While details of the arrangement were not released, the newspaper has indicated that the more babies she bears, the more money she gets.

She rejected doctors' advice to abort some of the fetuses, which were conceived while she was on fertility treatment.

Reprinted with permission of the *Santa Barbara News Press*.[2]

key to changing things while there is still time: *if we choose to make life work for everyone,* there are enough resources and manpower on the planet for all of us to live very abundantly.

THE (r)EVOLUTION

The problem has been that we're still choosing to go with the age-old, tired, and archaic everyone-for-themselves way of going about life. We've used the survival of the fittest philosophy as the justification for how the rich and powerful have continued to oppress the poor and disenfranchised. The philosophy is useful to the "haves" because, if God set the planet up as a "survival of the fittest" paradigm and that's just the way it is, then the "haves" get to exploit the people, the planet and its resources, and feel no guilt while doing it.

The solution is to change the way that we as people live together. Now, with the survival of the planet in question, it is truer than when Patrick Henry first spoke these words, "We must hang together or we will surely hang separately." We must now adopt a new "Declaration Of Independence" for the Next (r)Evolution. This must be a Declaration of Interdependence simply stated as "We choose to make life work for all of us, for The Highest Good Of All Life on the planet."

> *"The overall thrust of AGENDA 21 is that the global community must be set on a bold new course—a course which strives for a sustainable future for humanity—a course which fully implements an understanding of the impact of humanity on the natural world.*
>
> *"The world scientific community has seen into the abyss of environmental collapse and has sounded an urgent alarm. The leadership of the world has finally grasped the consequences of the failure to heed the warning to step back from the brink. AGENDA 21 is the call for an unprecedented global partnership among all nations and all citizens to confront and overcome the problems. It is now up to individual citizens to understand and grasp the crucial nature of the twin global*

problems of environmental destruction and poverty.

"The responsibility for our common future is in our own hands. The prospect of inevitable global environmental disaster or world-wide social upheaval must not be the legacy which we leave our children. Within the lifetime of a child born today, we have the opportunity to create a world in which concern for life is paramount—a world in which suffering is not taken for granted—a world in which nature is revered and not exploited—a world which is just, secure and prosperous—a world in which our children's children are assured of enjoying the bounty of nature and the splendor of life.

"This particular point in history offers a unique opportunity for humanity to make the transition to a global community which provides a sustainable living for all."[3]

—AGENDA 21

Indeed, as *AGENDA 21* points out, "The responsibility is in our hands," but we cannot depend on nations, politicians, and vested multinationals to make the changes. Instead, we must boldly show on the level of Community how we can not only save our planet's environment but also create the opportunity for all people to lead inspired and abundant (on all levels) lives.

We're not preaching sacrificing yourself to take care of others. We still want and need people to take care of themselves, but the old win/lose method is just not going to do it. Win/win is the only way to truly look out for Number One. Going for The Highest Good Of All is really the tremendous commitment to one's true self as we realize that immediate self-indulgence is the immaturity that has caused us to threaten the survival of our planet. The mature person knows that we are all interconnected and that one's own welfare is intrinsically linked to the well-being of all life on the planet.

If we can act for The Highest Good Of All and create a model to demonstrate how to do this, there will be a revolution like no other that there has ever been. This Next (r)Evolution will be how we choose to live together for The Highest Good Of All and how we came to have respect for all life on the planet. This (r)Evolution

"A human being is part of the whole, called by us 'Universe,' a part limited in time and space. He experiences himself, his thoughts and feelings as something separated from the rest—a kind of optical delusion of his consciousness. This delusion is a kind of prison for us, restricting us to our personal desires and to affection for a few persons nearest to us. Our task must be to free ourselves from this prison by widening our circle of compassion to embrace all living creatures and the whole of nature in its beauty."

—*Albert Einstein*

"Don't wait for the light at the end of the tunnel. Stride down there and Light it yourself. No problem can be solved with the same consciousness that created it." *

—*Albert Einstein*

*(... and we must shed light on the fact that our problems were created by the everyone-for-themselves consciousness and cannot be solved by that same consciousness.)

will change competition into cooperation. Technology will no longer serve greed but will be for the betterment of all. This (r)Evolution will redefine wealth and ownership and even what countries are until this truly is OUR WORLD. This (r)Evolution will change isolation and alienation into joy and loving and redis-covering play and creativity in our daily lives. This (r)Evolution will start because we choose to stop blindly going about our lives the way we have for thousands of years and start doing what will work for all of us. It will be a (r)Evolution perhaps a hundred years in the process as it spreads from the first model to all peoples throughout the planet.

People may respond to our solution by saying it's too simple to work or by saying that there would be economic chaos. It's easy to be a critic, and it's easy to be critical, but the truth is that the approach of making life work for everyone is very simple, and it's never been tried as we've described it. For thousands of years, out of the consciousness of againstness and everyone-for-themselves, we have complicated life to the point of not even considering that there could be a simple approach that would work for everyone. Remember also that the key to change is both having the *model* and the *consciousness* of The Highest Good. We will avoid chaos because the Next (r)Evolution will occur one Community and one cluster at a time at first until people really get the change of consciousness that is necessary. The key to creating a utopian society is to have fairly utopian people. Books have been written about utopian societies, but there's never been the consciousness and the tools to do it on a large scale. Now, with media coverage, technology, and our diminishing quality of life, people are seriously looking for a different approach, and that different approach is possible.

The truth is also that life as we've been doing it is no longer a viable choice for preserving life on the planet, so, despite how easy it is to be critical, we still have to do something radically different, and we have to do it while there is still time. So, as we learned from our experience with consensus decision-making, if you can see a problem with the approach we're suggesting, let's synergize creative solutions that keep us going along the path of having life

"Our country does not need cynics and skeptics. We need men and women who can dream about things that never were."

—*John F. Kennedy*

work for everyone.

When I think about the Next (r)Evolution, what gives me goose bumps is the realization that this greatest of all revolutions will be different than all the others. I have a good friend who defines peace as "the cessation of againstness." We must no longer be against poverty, hunger or pollution, but rather we must be *for all life*.

Created without any againstness towards anyone or any country, the Next (r)Evolution will be a totally nonviolent revolution as it sweeps the planet. Unlike other revolutions, there doesn't have to be any againstness because everyone's lifestyle will be improved as people experience not only more abundance in terms of access, but also more abundance in terms of having much more fun, creativity, and Loving in their lives. The isolation and alienation that most of the people experience will be replaced with truly connecting with each other. It is only logical that the greatest (r)Evolution ever on the planet will be that we chose to make it work for everyone. All the great spiritual teachers have talked about it, now it's time to do it.

A part of The Next (r)Evolution will be that we also take back our lives. It is all too commonplace now that people spend all their time and energy in pursuit of a better life, and, in that struggle, they lose all hope of a better life. Truthfully, the quality of our lives is not the amount of money or possessions that we have but rather the amount of Loving, nurturing, fun, creativity, friendship, and time spent in nature that we have access to. We can transform life into a less stressful and more enjoyable place for all.

Having brought the world to the place where it will no longer support us if we continue on our same path, we are not unlike the sorcerer's apprentice whose own creation was about to destroy himself. Can we find the Wizard within us so that we finally realize that we are all one.

From the postscript of the Community Planet description:

"We believe that the keys to world peace and prosperity are recognizing our oneness with all life, having a consciousness of sharing and cooperation, and acting in loving. If we lived in these ways, we could eliminate hunger, poverty, and the isolation and alienation of those who are perceived as being different from ourselves. The idea of Community has come forth to provide a working model for living together in greater harmony with ourselves, each other, and all life on the planet.

"It is our hope that historians will look at this time and write something like: 'The people of the early 21st century recognized that they had to wake up and stop doing life as it had been done for thousands of years. They realized that to survive, it could no longer be 'me vs you' or 'us vs them,' but that it had to be just US. They finally realized that they had all the resources and manpower to make life work for everyone, and they just did it.'"

"Nothing can withstand an idea whose time has come."

—Ralph Waldo Emerson

... and it is now time to make our planet work for everyone.

Let me leave you with a prayer that I wrote a few years ago:

MY PRAYER

Let us realize that we are all one.
Let us see that when there is even one amongst us
that needs assistance and loving,
that it is the concern of each one of us.
Let us know that there is enough for all of us,
that the world is for all of us to share and take care of.
Let us let go of the need to individually have more,
and move into the consciousness
that we can all have everything.
Let us look upon each one of us as sister and brother.
Let us see and experience the presence of God
within ourselves, in everyone, and in everything.

Never having written a book before, this process has been an odyessy. Please forgive any style or writing errors. I would rather have been at the beach, but this book had to be written by someone. I now issue you a challenge:

If you feel so moved, please join with us, and LET'S MAKE THE WORLD WORK FOR EVERYONE.

God Bless You,
I Love You,
Jack Reed
jack@communityplanet.org

NOTES

CHAPTER 2

[1]Royal Society of London and the U.S. Academy of Sciences, *Population Growth, Resource Consumption, and a Sustainable World*, London and Washington D.C.: 1992.

[2]Union of Concerned Scientists, *World Scientists' Warning to Humanity;* Washington D.C.: 1992.

[3]*AGENDA 21: The Earth Summit Strategy To Save Our Planet*, edited by Sitarz, Daniel, Earth Press, Boulder, CO: 1993, pg 20.

[4]Carrying capacity is the largest number of any given species or population (in this case, man) that a habitat (in this case, Earth) can support indefinitely.

[5]Meadows, Donella and Dennis and Randers, Jorgen, *Beyond the Limits*, Chelssea Green Publishing Co., Post Hills, Vt.: 1992.

[6]Caldicot, Helen, *If You Love This Planet: A Plan to Heal this Earth*, W. W. Norton and Co., New York: 1992, pg 194.

[7]"Final Conference Statement: Scientific/Technical Sessions," Second World Climate Conference, Geneva, Nov 7, 1990; U. S Environmental Agency, *Policy Options for Stabilizing Global Climate*, Washington, D.C.: 1990.

[8]Marshall, Tyler, "Rifts Cloud Conferences on Global Warming, Pollution," *Los Angeles Times*, Mar 29, 1995, citing address by Angela Merkel, Germany's Environmental Minister and conference chairwoman of the U.N.'s 1992 Earth Summit, to the 1995 U.N. Conference on Global Warming.

[9]Brown, Lester, et. al., *State of the World* 1997, W. W. Norton and Co., New York: 1997, pg 26.

[10]Russell, Dick, "The Critical Decade," *E Magazine*, Jan/Feb 1990, pg 31.

[11]United Nations Environmental Program draft report, "Environmental Effects Panel Report," Aug 1989.

[12]Gordon, Anita, *It's a Matter of Survival*, Harvard University Press, Cambridge, Mass.: 1991, pg 28.

[13]Global Tomorrow Coalition, Corson, Walter, Editor, *Citizen's Guide to Sustainable Development*, Washington, D.C.: 1989, pg 114; Mead, Mark N., Mann, John D., and Yarrow, David, 'The Fate of the Earth Depends on the Fate of the Trees," *Utne Reader*, May/June 1989, pg 50; Rainforest Action Network, San Francisco, CA.

[14]His Holiness Bartholomew I, addressing a conference on the environment, religion and science at St. Barbara Greek Episcopal Church in Santa Barbara on Nov 8, 1997 as quoted by Stammer, Larry, "Harming the Environment is Sinful," Prelate Says, *Los Angeles Times*, Nov 9, 1997.

[15]Hawkin, Paul, *The Ecology of Commerce*, HarperCollins, New York: 1993, pg 29.

[16]Meadows, as per note 5, pg 60; Rainforest Action Network, San Francisco, CA.

[17]Brown, Lester, et. al., *"State of the World 1994,"* W. W. Norton and Co., New York: 1994, pg 12.

[18]Goldsmith, Edward, et. al., *Imperiled Planet,* The M.I.T. Press, Cambridge, MA: 1990, pg 58.

[19]Rifkin, Jeremy, *The Green Lifestyle Handbook,* Henry Holt and Co., New York: 1990, pg xii.

[20]Hur, Robin, "Six Inches From Starvation; How and Why America's Topsoil is Disappearing," *Vegetarian Times*, March 1985, pgs 45-47.

[21]Pimental et al, "Land Degradation Effects on Food and Energy Resources," in *Science*, Vol. 194, Oct 1976; National Association of Conservation Districts, Washington, D.C., *Soil Degradation: Effects on Agricultural Productivity, Interim Report #4*, National Agricultural Lands Study, 1980, pg 20; King, Seth, "Farms Go Down the River," *New York Times*, Dec 10, 1978, citing Soil Conservation Service.

[22]Brione, William, State Conservationist, Soil Conservation Service, Des Moines, Iowa, testimony before Commission on Agriculture and Forestry, July 6, 1976.

[23]Carter, Vernon Gill and Dale, Tom, *Topsoil and Civilization*, Rev. ed., University of Oklahoma Press, Norman: 1974.

[24]Hur, as per note 20.

[25]*Organic Matters* magazine, Summer 1992, pg 20, citing United Nations' Resolution on Topsoil Production and Replenishment.

[26]Cited in Hur, as per note 20.

[27]Russell, as per note 10, pg 32.

[28]Brown, as per note 9, pgs 23-24.

[29]Gordon, as per note 12, pg 3.

[30]Brown, as per note 9, pg 23.

[31]Goldsmith, as per note 18, pg 144.

[32]Goldsmith, as per note 18, pg 148.

[33]Brown, as per note 17, pg 177.

[34]Robbins, John, *Diet for a New America,* Stillpoint Publishing, Walpole, NH: 1987, pg 352.

[35]Chu, Henry, "Yellow River Giving China New Sorrow," *Los Angeles Times*, Feb 18, 1999.

[36]Commoner, B., *Making Peace with the Planet*, The New Press, New York: 1992, pg 89.

[37]McEntee, Gerald, "Warning: Environmental Pollution!," *The Public Employee Magazine*, Aug/Sep 1989, pg 4.

[38]*Global Tomorrow Coalition*, as per note 13, pg 244.

[39]*Agenda 21*, as per note 3, pg 199.

[40]Russell, as per note 10, pg 31.

[41]*Los Angeles Times*, "Today on the Planet," Fisher, Dan and Engle, Jane, editors, May 26, 1992.

[42]Efron, Sonni, "Ecological Russian Roulette," *Los Angeles Times*, Nov 22, 1994.

[43]Gore, Al, *Earth In The Balance*, Houghton Mifflin Co., New York: 1992, pg 1.

[44]Paddock, Richard and Morain, Dan, "Pesticide Peril to Ozone May Lead to Ban," *Los Angeles Times*, May 26, 1992.

[45]Beder, Sharon, *Global Spin: The Corporate Assault on Environmentalism*, Green Books, Ltd., United Kingdom: 1997, pgs 91-92.

[46]Lesly, Phil, "Coping with Opposition Groups," *Public Relations Review* 18(4), 1992, pg 331.

[47]Gordon, as per note 12, pg 3.

[48]Russell, as per note 10, pg 34.

[49]Hawkin, as per note 15, pg 50.

[50]Rifkin, as per note 19, pg 11.

[51]"Eco L. A.," *Los Angeles Weekly*, Edited by Levin, Jay et al, Dec 1, 1989, pg 7.

[52]*Los Angeles Weekly*, see note 51, pg 7, citing an EPA report.

[53]*Pesticide Chemicals News Guide*, website: www.fcnpublishing.com, "Food Chemicals News," as of Jan 2000.

[54]The United States Food and Drug Administration website: www.fda.gov

[55]Lehmann, Phyllis, "More Than You Ever Thought You Would Know About Food Additives," *FDA Consumer*, Apr 1979.

[56]Tyson, Rae, "Toxin study finds risks in breast feeding," *USA TODAY*, Dec 18, 1987, pg 3A.

[57]Hawkin, as per note 15, pg 2.

[58]Robbins, as per note 34, pg 346.

[59]Robbins, as per note 34, pg 346.

[60]Carson, Rachel, *Silent Spring,* Houghton Mifflin, Boston: 1962.

[61]*Citizen's Guide to Sustainable Development,* as per note 13, pg 247.

[62]Richards, B., "Drop in sperm count is Attributed to Toxic Environment," *Washington Post,* Sep 12, 1979.; Brody, J., "Sperm Found Especially Vulnerable to Environment," *New York Times,* Mar 10, 1981; "Unplugging the Gene Pool," *Outside,* Sep 1980; Jannson, E., "The Impact of Hazardous Substances Upon Infertility Among Men in the U.S., and Birth Defects," *Friends of the Earth,* Washington, D.C., Nov 17, 1980.

[63]Cone, Marla, "Human Immune Systems May Be Pollution Victims," *Los Angeles Times,* May 13, 1996.

[64]Cone, as per note 63.

[65]Cone, as per note 63.

[66]"A Plague on Our Children," *NOVA,* WGBH Educational Foundation, Boston, 1979.

[67]Culhane, J., "PCB's: The Poisons That Won't Go Away," *Readers's Digest,* Dec 1980.

[68]Regenstern, L.ewis, *How to Survive in America the Poisoned,* Acropolis Books, Washington, D.C.: 1982, pg 295.

[69]Howlett, Debbie and Tyson, Rae, "Toxicity of dioxin even in trace amounts of breast milk," *USA TODAY,* Sep 13, 1994, pg 1A and 10A, citing 1994 EPA report.

[70]Noordland, R. and Friedman, J., "Poison at our Doorstep," *Philadelphia Inquirer,* reprint of Sep 23-28, 1979.

[71]Robbins, as per note 34, pg 321.

[72]Beder, as per note 45, ch. 9.

[73]Beder, as per note 45, ch. 9.

[74]Cone, Marla, "Destroying The Balance Of Nature," *Los Angeles Times,* May 12, 1996.

[75]*Los Angeles Times,* as per note 40.

[76]Russell, as per note 10, pg 32; *Global Tomorrow Coalition,* as per note 13, pg 161.

[77]Russell, as per note 10, pg 32.

[78]Gerstenzang, James, "Toxins Contaminate U.S. Water Supply, Study Says, *Los Angeles Times,* Oct. 27, 1995, citing report by Natural Resources Defense Council.

[79]Gerstenzang, as per note 78.

[80]Gerstenzang, as per note 78, citing National Resources Defense Council's 1995 report.

[81]*Los Angeles Times,* as per note 41.

[82]Cone, Marla, as per note 63.

[83]Brockley, Ross, "The Menace from Midland," *Multinational Monitor*, Jul/Aug 1991, pg 39.

[84]Matthiessen, C., "The Day the Poison Stopped Working," *Mother Jones*, Mar/Apr 1992.

[85]Global Tomorrow Coalition, as per note 13, pg 247.

[86]Phillips, R., "Coronary Heart Disease...Differing Dietary Habits: A Preliminary Report," *American Journal of Clinical Nutrition*, 1978, 31:181; Walles, C., "Hold the Eggs and Butter: Cholesterol is Proved Deadly and Our Diet May Never be the Same," *Time*, Mar 26, 1984, pg 62.

[87]Wright, Robin, "World View; Three Faces of Hunger," *Los Angeles Times*, Dec 15, 1992.

[88]Center on Hunger and Poverty, Tufts University School of Nutrition, Science, and Policy's website, in their discussion of hunger in the U.S. as of Nov 1999.

[89]Global Tomorrow Coalition, as per note 13, pg 68.

[90]Recer, Paul, "Scientists 'astonished' by finding on harmful effects of pesticides," *Santa Barbara News Press*, June 7, 1996.

[91]as quoted in *Citizen's Guide to Sustainable Development*, as per note 13, pg 133.

[92]as quoted in *Citizen's Guide to Sustainable Development*, as per note 13, pg 133.

[93]as quoted in *Citizen's Guide to Sustainable Development*, as per note 13, pg 133.

[94]as quoted in *Citizen's Guide to Sustainable Development*, as per note 13, pg 133.

[95]as quoted in *Citizen's Guide to Sustainable Development*, as per note 13, pg 161.

[96]Brown, Lester, as quoted by Resenberger, "Curb on U.S. Waste Urged to Help the World's Hungry," *New York Times*, Nov 14, 1974, adjusted using 1988 figures from USDA, *Agricultural Statistics 1989*, table 74, "High Protein Feeds," and table 75, "Feed Concentrates Fed to Livestock and Poultry."

[97]*Raw Materials in the United States Economy 1900-1977*, Technical paper 47, Vivian Spencer, U.S. Dept. of Commerce, U.S. Dept. of Interior, Bureau of Mines, pg 3; cited in Lappe, Frances, *Diet for a Small Planet*, Tenth Anniversary Edition, Ballantine Books, New York: 1982, pg 66.

[98]Barnard, Neal D. and Chaitowitz, Simon, "Eat Your Broccoli," *Santa Barbara News Press*, Apr 26, 1998, G1&2.

[99]Rainforest Action Network, San Francisco, CA.

[100]Barkin, D. and DeWalt, B., "Sorghum, the Internationalization of Capital, and the Mexican Food Crisis," Paper presented at the American Anthropological Association Meeting, Denver, CO, Nov 16, 1984, pg 16.

[101]Durning, A. and Brough, H., *Taking Stock: Animal Farming and the Environment,* Worldwatch Paper No. 103, Worldwatch Institute, Washington, DC, 1991, pg 29.

[102]Robbins, John, *May All Be Fed,* William Morrow and Company, Inc., New York: 1992, pg 44.

[103]Rifkin, as per note 19, pg 8.

[104]Borgstrom, Georg, presentation to the Annual Meeting of the American Association for the Advancement of Science, 1981.

[105]*Newsweek,* "The Browning of America," Feb 22, 1981, pg 26.

[106]Simon, Paul, "Are We Running Dry?" *Parade Magazine,* Aug. 23, 1998.

[107]Robbins, as per note 34, pg 367.

[108]*Los Angeles Times,* as per note 41.

[109]Kapstein, Ethan, "Collapse of a World Safety Net," *Los Angeles Times,* Jan 31, 1999; *Agenda 21,* as per note 2, pg 32.

[110]United Nations Development Programme (UNDP), *Human Development Report* 1996, Oxford University Press, New York: 1996.

[111]Fulwood III, Sam, and Healy, Melissa, "1.3 Million More Drop Into Poverty," *Los Angeles Times,* Oct 7, 1994.

[112]Sanders, Bernard, "What's Really Going on with the Economy?" *USA Today Magazine,* Vol. 125, Mar 1, 1997. Sanders is a U.S. Representative and member of the House Banking and Financial Services Committee.

[113]Sanders, as per note 112.

[114]Dyer, R.A., "Despite Good Economy, Many poor Texans Remain Penniless After Payday," *Ft. Worth Star-Telegram,* Sep 5, 1999.

[115]Gorman, Tom, "It's Home for the Holidays, *Los Angeles Times,* Dec 25, 1987.

[116]Renner, Michael, "Transforming Security," in *State of the World 1997,* as per note 8, pg 121.

[117]Sanders, as per note 112.

[118]Sanders, as per note 112.

[119]Sanders, as per note 112.

[120]Fullwood III and Healy, as per note 111.

[121]Sanders, as per note 112.

[122]Brown, as per note 17, pg 5.

[123]Wright, Robin, "Rich-Poor Gap Widens Around the Globe," *Los Angeles Times*, June 14, 1994, citing the United Nation's Development Report, "Human Development Report."

[124]Dentzer, Susan, "The Wealth of Nations," *U.S. News and World Report*, May 4, 1992.

[125]Mierzwinski, Ed, "House passes bill to overhaul bankruptcy laws," *Los Angeles Times*, Mar 2, 2001.

[126]Healy, Melissa, "To Some, Money Now Counts for Less," *Los Angeles Times*, Dec 24, 1996.

[127]Earnest, Leslie, "Household Debt Grows Precarious as Rates Increase," *Los Angeles Times*, May 13, 2000.

[128]Healy, as per note 126, citing Shilling, A. Gary, a financial consultant based in Springfield, N.J.

[129]Healy, as per note 126.

[130]Brown, as per note 17, pg 4.

[131]Balzar, John, "Doomsayers of Overpopulation Sound a New Jeremiad," *Los Angeles Times*, June 7, 1994.

[132]Daly, Herman, *Beyond Growth*, Beacon Press, Boston: 1996, pg 105.

[133]Daly, as per note 132, pg 38.

[134]Global Tomorrow Coalition, as per note 13, pg 47.

[135]Russell, Richard. *Richard Russell's Dow Theory Letters*, Sep 5, 1990, pg 5.

[136]Russell, as per note 135, pg.5.

[137]MacGregor, Hilary, "Japan's Jobless Generation," *Los Angeles Times*, May 4, 1996.

[138]*Trading Futures, Living in the Global Economy*, with David Suzuki, produced, directed, and researched by Poole, Mike, written by McConnell, Amanda, telecast on the Canadian Broadcasting Corp., Apr 4, 1993.

[139]Mander, G., "Reforming the Nonreformable," privately published paper, as cited in Hawkin, as per note 15, pg 108.

[140]Hawkin, as per note 15, pg 108.

[141]Mander, Jerry, *In the Absence of the Sacred*, Sierra Club Books, San Francisco: 1991, pg 78-79.

[142]Hawkin, as per note 15, pgs 8 and 111..

[143]Feingold, Sen. Russell D., as quoted by O'Conner, Anne-Marie, "Shadow Convention Focuses of Rebels With Cause," *Los Angeles Times*, Aug 14, 2000.

[144]Hawkin, as per note 15, pg 109, citing Art Levine's, "Join Congress, See the World—on Corporate America's Tab," *San Francisco Chronicle*, Apr 2, 1991."

[145]Peterson, Jonathon, "Washing Our Hands of Politics," *Los Angeles Times*, May 20, 1992.

[146]Broder, John M., "GOP Candidates Start Anti-Powell Research," *Los Angeles Times*, Nov 12, 1995.

[147]As quoted by Deardorff, Julie, "McCain, Bradley pledge to reform campaign finances," *Chicago Tribune*, Dec 17, 1999.

[148]Downs, Hugh, commentary on hemp for *ABC News*, New York, Nov. 1990.

[149]Downs, Hugh, as per note 149.

[150]Ryan, Nancy Ross, "Hemp for your health?," *(Chicage Tribune) Santa Barbara News Press*, Jul 25, 2000.

[151]Yiamouyiannis, Dr. John, *Fluoride the Aging Factor*, Health Actions Press, Delaware, OH: 1993, pgs 72-90.

[152]Community Health Studies volume 11, 1987, pgs 85-90; *Journal of the Canadian Dental Association* volume 53, 1987, pgs 763-765.; *Fluoride* Volume 23, 1990, pgs 55-67; Yiamouyiannis, as per note 151, pgs 114-132.

[153]Citizens For Safe Drinking Water, San Diego, CA.

[154]Goldman, Abigale, "Grandmother, 71, Arrested; Did Despair Lead to Crime?," *Los Angeles Times*, May 7, 1996.

[155]"Highlights," *Santa Barbara New Press*, Oct 1, 1996.

[156]Healy, Melissa and Marquis, Julie, "Rise in Mental Disorders Seen as Boomers Age," *Los Angeles Times*, Dec 14, 1999, citing Satcher's "Mental Health: A Report of the Surgeon General."

[157]U. S. Dept. of Health and Human Services, Centers for Disease Control and Prevention, "Youth Risk Behavior Surveilance Report, 1990."

[158]U. S. Dept. of Health and Human Services, Centers for Disease Control and Prevention, "Youth Risk Behavior Surveilance Report, 1995."

[159]California State Dept. of Rehabilitation's Stress Management Training, Sep 1988, citing the Public Employees Retirement Service (PERS) Actuarial Tables.

[160]Rifkin, as per note 19, pg 67.

[161]Lee, Don, "Employees Get a Real Workout," *Los Angeles Times*, Sep 4, 1995.

CHAPTER 3:

[1]*Los Angeles Times*, "A Day in the Life of Mother Earth: A Special Earth Summit Issue of World Report," May 26, 1992.

[2]Zinn, Howard, *A People's History of the United States*, Harper and Row, New York: 1980.

[3]*Trading Futures, Living in a Global Economy*, with David Suzuki, produced, directed, and researched by Mike Poole, written by Amanda McConnell, telecast on the Canadian Broadcasting Corp. Apr 4, 1993.

[4]*Citizen's Guide to Sustainable Development*, Global Tomorrow Coalition, Corson, Walter, editor, Washington, D.C.: 1989, pg 17.

[5]*It's a Matter of Survival*, Canadian Broadcasting Corporation, aired July/Aug 1989, unbroadcast portion of interview with Bill Rees.

[6]Hawkin, Paul, *The Ecology of Commerce*, HarperCollins, New York: 1993, pg 57.

[7]*Trading Futures, Living in a Global Economy*, as per note 3.

[8]*Trading Futures, Living in a Global Economy*, as per note 3.

[9]*Trading Futures, Living in a Global Economy*, as per note 3.

[10]Daly, Herman, *Beyond Growth*, Beacon Press, Boston: 1996, pg 40.

[11]Daly, as per note 12, pg 221.

[12]*The Unfolding Story* video, producers: Buck, James and Wileta, and Mardigian, Sandra, Baylands Production, 1993.

[13]*The Unfolding Story*, as per note 12.

[14]Holley, David, "Major Rebuilding Effort Could Aid Economic Growth, Analysts Say," *Los Angeles Times*, Jan 18, 1995.

[15]*Trading Futures, Living in a Global Economy*, as per note 3.

[16]Eisler, Riane, *The Chalice and the Blade*, Harper and Row, Cambridge, MA: 1987.

[17]Hawkin, as per note 6, pg 33.

[18]Kohn, Alfie, *No Contest*, Houghton Miflin Co., Boston: 1986.

[19]*Trading Futures, Living in a Global Economy*, as per note 3.

[20]*Trading Futures, Living in a Global Economy*, as per note 3.

[21]Motavelli, Jim, "Enough! (Dissatisfaction with the consumer culture)," *E Magazine*, Mar-Apr 1996 v7 n2, pg 28.

[22]Grunat, Diane, "Bye-bye Rat Race: Washingtonians who are getting off the fast track learning to live with less," *Washingtonian*, May 1996 v 31 n8, pg 43.

[23]Oldenburg, Don, "The Simple Life, Making Due with Less…and Loving It," *Washington Post*, Jan 9, 1996.

[24]Dominguez, Joseph and Robin, Vicki, *Your Money or Your Life*, Viking, New York: 1992.

[25]Hiltzik, Michael, "Taking Stock of CEO Pay," *Los Angeles Times*, May 10, 1996.

26"Who's Getting Rich And Why Aren't You?" *CBS Reports* aired Aug 8, 1996.

27Whyte, William and Kathleen, *Making Mondragon: The Growth and Dynamics of the Worker Cooperative Complex*, ILC Press, Cornell Univrsity, Ithica, New York: 1988, pg 5.

28Whyte, as per note 27, pg 5.

29Whyte, as per note 27, pg 5.

30Bradley, Keith and Gelb, Alan, "Cooperative Labour Relations: Mondragon's Response to Recession," *British Journal of Industrial Relations* 25 (1987): 85.

31*Trading Futures, Living in a Global Economy,* as per note 3.

32Schumacher, E.F., *Small Is Beautiful*, Blond and Braggs, London: 1973, pg 272.

33Petruno, Tom, "Bond Traders' Power Again Riles Markets," *Los Angeles Times,* Mar 10, 1996.

34Balzar, John, "Doomsayers of Overpopulation Sound a New Jeremiad," *Los Angeles Times*, June 7, 1994.

35Murphy, Kim, "Cairo Conferees Linking Growth, Environment," *Los Angeles Times,* Sep 12, 1994.

36Brown, Lester, *State of the World 1994*, W.W. Norton and Co., New York: 1994, pg 4.

37Dominguez, as per note 24.

38Shi, David, *The Simple Life, Plain Living and High Thinking in American Culture,* Oxford University Press, New York: 1985, pg 197.

39His Holiness Bartholomew I, addressing a conference on the environment, religion and science at St. Barbara Greek Episcopal Church in Santa Barbara on Nov 8, 1997, as quoted by Stammer, Larry, "Harming the Environment is Sinful, Prelate Says," *Los Angeles Times*, Nov 9, 1997.

40Hawkin, as per note 6, pg 80.

41Rumnalls, David, as quoted on the *Earth Chronicles —Environment and Development website*, http:/www.docker.com/~kattenburgd/envdev.htm

42Shiva, Vandana, as quoted in the *Earth Chronicles* website, as per note 40.

43Luhrs, Janet, as quoted in *Simple Living*, Winter 1996.

44Rees, William E., "Ecological Footprints" from *Yes/A Journal of Positive Futures*, Spring/Summer 1996, pgs 26-27.

45as quoted in "A Theology of Less," by Furtwangler, Tom, *Yes/A Journal of Positive Futures*, Spring/Summer 1996, pg 44.

46Rifkin, Jeremy, *The Green Lifestyle Handbook*, Henry Holt and Co., New York: 1990, pg xiv.

[47]Koenenin, Connie, "Let's Get Simple," *Los Angeles Times*, May 14, 1996.

[48]van Gelder, Sarah, "Sustainable America," from *Yes/A Journal of Positive Futures*, Spring/Summer 1996, pg 6.

[49]Clifford, Frank, "Which Comes First—Food or the Forest?" *Los Angeles Times*, July 24, 1997.

[50]Brown, Lester, *State of the World 1997*, W.W. Norton and Co., New York: 1997, pg 3.

[51]Grubb, Michael, *The Earth Summit Agreement: A Guide and Assessment*, Earthscan, London: 1993.

[52]Rifkin, as per note 46, pg 54.

[53]Rifkin, as per note 46, pg 26: Koenenin, as per note 47.

[54]Rifkin, as per note 46, pg xiii.

[55]Rifkin, as per note 46, pg xiii.

[56]as quoted in *Citizen's Guide to Sustainable Development*, as per note 4, pg 1.

CHAPTER 4:

[1]McLaughlin, Corrine and Davidson, Gorden, *Builders of the Dawn*, Sirius Publishing, Shutesbury, Massachusetts: 1986, pg 27.

[2]McLaughlin and Davidson, as per note 1, pg 122.

[3]Daly, Herman, *Beyond Growth*, Beacon Press, Boston: 1996, pg 15.

[4]Thoreau, Henry David, *Walden*, Franklin Library, Franklin Center, PA: 1976..

[5]McLaughlin and Davidson, as per note 1, pg 91.

[6]McLaughlin and Davidson, as per note 1, pg 91.

[7]Sarah van Gelder, "Real Wealth, Redefining Abundance in an Era of Limits" from *YES! A Journal of Positive Futures,*: Spring/Summer 1996, pgs 13-16.

[9]Motavelli, Jim, "Enough! (Dissatisfaction with the consumer culture)," *E Magazine*, Mar-Apr 1996 v7 n2, pg 28.

[10]Motavelli, as per note 9.

[11]Grunat, Diane, "Bye-bye Rat Race: Washingtonians who are getting off the fast track learning to live with less, *Washingtonian*, May 1996 v 31 n8, pg 43.

[12]McLaughlin and Davidson, as per note 1, pgs 27-28.

[13]Natural Resources Conservation Service, United States Dept. of Agriculture, "Natural Resources Inventory," Dec 7, 1999.

[14]Gordon, Anita, *It's a Matter of Survival*, Harvard University Press, Cambridge, Massachusetts: 1991, pg 224.

[15]Weisman, Alan, *Gaviotas: A Village To Reinvent The World*, Chelsea Green, White River Junction, Vermont: 1998.

[16]Schumacher, E.F., *Small is Beautiful*, Blond and Braggs, London: 1973, pg 125.

[17]Community Planet, "How Do We Reach Consensus?," a private paper.

[18]McLaughlin and Davidson, as per note 1, pg 165.

[19]Cooper, Richard, "White House Seeks to Still Criticism of Mrs. Clinton," *Los Angeles Times*, June 25, 1996.

[20]McLaughlin and Davidson, as per note 1, pgs 62 & 64.

[21]*1990-91 Directory of Intentional Communities*, Fellowship for Intentional Community, Evansville, IN: 1990, pg 97.

[22]Rogers, Carl, *A Way Of Being*, Houghton Mifflin Co., Boston: 1980, pg 195-196.

[23]McLaughlin and Davidson, as per note 1, pg 27.

[24]Thoreau, Henry David, as per note 4.

[25]Upgren, Arthur, Wesleyan University, Middleton, CT, quoted in Harper's Index, *Harper's Magazine*, May 1996.

[26]Rifkin, Jeremy, *The Green Lifestyle Handbook*, Henry Holt and Co., New York: 1990, pg 67.

[27]Schumacher, as per note 16.

[28]Rifkin, Jeremy, *Time Wars*, Simon and Schuster, New York: 1989.

[29]Gold, Matea and Ferrell, David, "Going for Broke," *Los Angeles Times*, Dec 13, 1998.

[30]Gold and Ferrell, as per note 29.

[31]Gold and Ferrell, as per note 29.

[32]The Harwood Group; "Yearning for Balance," a 1995 study of citizen perspectives on the issue of consumption, commissioned by the Merck Family Fund.

[33]Leider, Richard J. and Shapiro, David A., *Repacking Your Bags, Lighten Your Load for the Rest of Your Life*, Berret-Koehln Publishers, San Francisco: 1994, pg 12.

[34]McLaughlin and Davidson, as per note 1, pg 13.

[35]Schumacher, as per note 16, pgs 159 and 160.

[36]Hawkin, Paul, *The Ecology of Commerce*, HarperCollins, New York: 1993, pgs 126-127.

[37]Schumacher, as per note 16.

[38]Rifkin, as per note 26, pgs 119-124.

[39]Tillman, David, "Global environmental impacts of agricultural expansion: The need for sustainable and efficient practices," *Proc. Natl. Acad. Sci. USA*; Vol. 96, May 1999, pp. 5995-6000.

[40]Tillman, David, "Causes. Consequences and ethics of biodiversity," *NATURE;* Vol. 405, May 2000, pp. 208-210.

[41]Mooney, Pat R., *Seeds of the Earth,* Inter_Pares_for the Canadian Council for International Coalition for Development Action, Ottawa: 1979.

[42]Rifkin, as per note 26, pg 121.

[43]Mooney, Pat, as quoted in the *Earth Chronicles* website under "Environment and Development, http/www.docker.com/~katten-burgd/envdev.htm.

[44]Daniels, Cletus, *Bitter Harvest,* Cornell University Press, Ithica N.Y., 1987.

[45]Rifkin, as per note 26, pg 113.

[46]Pimental, David, et al, *Handbook of Pest Management in Agriculture,* 2nd edition, CRC Press, Boca Raton, FL: 1990.

[47]David Pimental, Cornell University, as quoted by Lisa Y. Lefferts and Roger Blobaum, "Eating as if the Earth mattered," *E Magazine,* Jan/Feb 1992, pg 32.

[48]Pimental, as per note 46.

[49]Pimental, as per note 46.

[50]McLaughlin and Davidson, as per note 1, pg 27.

[51]Cimons, Marlene, "Teachers Often Left to Deal with Pupils' Medical Needs," *Los Angeles Times,* Nov 17, 1996.

CHAPTER 5:

[1]McLaughlin, Corrine and Davidson, Gorden, *Builders of the Dawn,* Sirius Publishing, Shutesbury, Massachusetts, 1986, pg 6.

CHAPTER 6

[1]Motavelli, Jim, "Enough! (Dissatisfaction with the consumer culture)," *E Magazine,* Mar-Apr 1996 v7 n2, p. 28.

[2]Gordon, Anita, *It's a Matter of Survival*, Harvard University Press, Cambridge, Mass., 1991, pg 218.

[3]Gordon, as per note 2, pg 220.

[4]Hawkin, *The Ecology of Commerce,* HarperCollins, New York: 1993, pg 21.

[5]Lewis, Stephen, as quoted in the CBC Radio series, "It's a Matter of Survival," broadcast July/Aug 1989.

[6]Broecher, Wallace S., as quoted by Irving Mintzer in the foreward of "A Matter of Degrees: Potential for Controlling the Greenhouse Effect," *World Institute Report* #5, Apr 1987.

[7]Scott, Doug, as quoted in the CBC Radio series, "It's a Matter of Survival," broadcast July/Aug 1989.

CHAPTER 7

[1]King, Rev. Martin Luther, from his Nobel Prize acceptance speech Dec 10, 1964.

[2]Renner, Michael, *Budgeting for Disarmament: The Costs of War and Peace*, Worldwatch Paper 122, Worldwatch Institute, Washington, D.C., Nov 1995.

[3]Pine, Art, "Military Nears Revolution in Weapons, War Strategy," *Los Angeles Times*, Mar 19, 1996.

[4]*Mindwalk*, a film by Capra, Bernt, Atlas Production Co. in association with Mindwalk Productions; a Lintcshinger/Cohen Production.

[5]McLaughlin, Corrine and Davidson, Gorden, *Builders of the Dawn*, Sirius Publishing, Schutsbury, MA: 1986, pg 91.

[6]Pope John Paul II, as quoted by Fineman, Mark, "Pope Calls for Freedom of Conscience in Cuba," *Los Angeles Times*, Jan 26, 1998.

[7]Hawken, Paul, as quoted by, Hurst, Sam T., "What is it worth to save the Earth?," *Santa Barbara News Press*, Apr 16, 1998.

[8]Brown, Lester, *State of the World 1994*, pg xv.

[9]Gore, Al, as quoted by Hurst, see note 7.

[10]Kapur, Akach, "The Indian State of Kerala has Everything Agianst It—Except Success," *The Atlantic Monthly*, Sep 1, 1998, pg 4.

[11]Mugabe, Robert in a speech to the United Nations as part of the World Commission on Environment and Development's report to the General Assembly, Oct 19, 1987, Document: a/42/PV.41.

[12]Sadik, Nafis, *The State of World Population 1988*, United Nations Population Fund, New York: 1988.

[13]Lewis, Flora, as quoted in *Citizen's Guide to Sustainable Development*, pg 1.

[14]United Nations, *Report of the World Summit for Social Development* (Copenhagen Mar 6-17, 1995), New York, Apr 19, 1995.

[15]Abramson, Ruby and Dolan, "Tension Clouds Beginning of Earth Summit," *Los Angeles Times*, June 4, 1992.

[16]Mugabe, Robert, as per note 11.

[17]Brundtland, Gro Harlem, as per note 11.

[18]World Commission on Environment and Development, *Our Common Future*, Oxford Universaity Press, New York: 1987.

[19]Brundtland, Gro Harlem, as per note 11 .

[20]Pope John Paul II, "The Ecological Crisis: A Common Responsibility," Dec 1989.

[21]His Holiness Bartholomew I addressing a conference on the environment, religion and science at St. Barbara Greek Episcopal Church in Santa Barbara on Nov 8, 1997, as quoted by Parks, Rhonda, "'Green Patriarch' declares pollution of Earth is a sin," *Santa Barbara News Press*, Nov 9, 1997.

[22]Tully, Shawn, "Why Drug Prices Will Go Lower," *Fortune* magazine, May 3, 1993, pg 56.

[23]Cone, Marla, "E.P.A. Proposes Tougher Limits on Soot, Smog," *Los Angeles Times*, Nov 28, 1996.

[24]Cone, Marla, "U.S. Poised to Toughen Air Quality Standards," *Los Angeles Times*, Nov 25, 1996.

[25]*Mindwalk*, as per note 4.

[26]Fuller, Buckminster, as quoted in *Thinking Out Loud*, a Simon and Goodman Picture Co, Film, 1996.

[27]Fuller, as per note 26.

[28]Fuller, as per note 26.

[29]"New World Coming: American Security in the 21st Century, Major Themes and Implications, The Phase 1 Report on the Emerging Global Security Environment for the First Quarter of the 21st Century," *The United States Commission on National Security/21st Century*, Sept. 15, 1999.

[30]"Road Map for National Security: Imperative for Change, The Phase 3 Report of the U.S. Commission on National Security/21st Century," *The United States Commission on National Security/21st Century*, Jan. 31, 2001

CHAPTER 8

[1]World Commission on Environment and Development, *Our Common Future*, Oxford University Press, New York: 1987, pgs 22-23.

[1]WCED, as per note 1, pg 23.

CHAPTER 9

[1]Capra, Fritjof, "Why the Real Issues of our Time Are Not Part of the Political Dialog," *Earth News*, May/June 1992, pg 41.

[2]"Woman loses 3 octuplets; others in peril," *Santa Barbara News Press*, Oct 10, 1996.

[3]*AGENDA 21*, edited by Sitarz, Daniel, Earthpress, Boulder, CO: 1993, pgs 22-23.

The purpose of the Community Planet Foundation (CPF) is the creation and demonstration of planned cooperative ecological Communities that will enable people to live in greater harmony with themselves, each other, and the environment. Imagine living in a Community of loving, nurturing friends who live and work together as one family and live in harmony with all life. Nature flourishes on hundreds of beautiful acres, while most of the food is grown organically, using modern growing techniques and edible landscaping. Since cars are parked at the outskirts of the Community and pavement is used minimally, it's a wonderful place to play outdoors or go for a walk and touch the land. When the residents are done working in supportive, nurturing jobs, the Community offers a full array of growth, creative, and recreational opportunities. Organized sports, music, movies, just hanging out, and other fun and relaxing activities are freely available, and the residents enjoy them with friends within walking distance.

Such a demonstration Community may not be a new idea. However, a Community of this scope, utilizing the latest technology and redefining how people live together, is something that may be an answer to the problems now facing the planet.

Now more than ever we see the need for such a Community. When we look at the world we live in, we see conflict, personal alienation and isolation, hunger, poverty, diminishing resources, and the increasing pollution of our environment that is threatening the survival of our planet. There are so many things that need fixing and these problems are so interconnected that to try to fix them piece by piece is not possible. To heal the planet's imbalances, we must use a systems approach to address these interconnections rather than merely Band-Aiding the symptoms.

But how can we address everything? We do not have to watch the destruction of our planet. We can bring about change by addressing how we as people live and relate together on this planet. There are enough resources and manpower on earth for all of us to live abundantly. So what is the problem?

The way our lives are set up, the way our cities are designed, and the way our economy functions all negatively impact our planet, while also contributing to the isolation and alienation of individuals trying to survive on their own. Our everyone-for-themselves approach has concentrated resources and power in the hands of a few. Our society fosters the idea of happiness coming from the accumulation of wealth, and yet those who get caught up in this pursuit often find themselves subject to this same isolation and alienation.

We have made money the excuse for harming the environment and for not providing basic needs for all. Yet there is more than enough for all of us, and, at this point, the unequal distribution of wealth is affecting the survival of the planet.

Anyone looking at these problems can see that we must change the way in which we live. We must change how we live together so that our lives work for the Highest Good Of All Life. A model of a successful cooperative Community will enable people to see what is possible. People can change the world when they see and experience a better way.

The vision of the CPF has been established in a 45 page document and in the book *The Next Evolution: a Blueprint for Transforming the Planet*. We call this first model Community Planet.

COMMUNITY PLANET
What it is:
• A Community of 400-500 non-denominational, multi-ethnic, diverse people.
• A sustainable Community: keeping the planet's resources intact for future generations.
• A Community that shows how state-of-the-art, positive technology can create better living for all life.
• A Community designed to be energy self-sufficient.
• A cooperative Community where everyone has more through sharing resources. Wealth is redefined as use and access rather than as possession.
• A Community where residents take care of one another as if they were one family.
• A pedestrian Community with parking on the outskirts and few roadways.
• A Community with income producing, socially responsible businesses, enabling most residents to walk to work.

• A place where people regain control, through consensus decision making, of the key decisions that affect their lives.
• More than simply an ecological city, rather, a model that addresses the economic, cooperation, and separation issues that are the basis of our current environmental and social problems.
What it is not:
• A place where one has to sacrifice quality of life.
• A haven for people living on the fringe. Community Planet is designed to impact society, not to escape it.

The way we live together and relate together in Community is the basic building block that is needed to transform the planet. The creation of Community Planet will enable others to see how we can all cooperate and enjoy a higher, healthier, and happier standard of living. With media exposure, millions will be able to see and hear about a life-style that they, too, can enjoy. Future Communities built along CPF guidelines will support individuals in their personal growth and in obtaining their personal goals, providing them with a prosperous life-style through the sharing of resources while, at the same time, addressing our global challenges. Eventually we envision how the replication of our models around the world will have a transformational effect on the environment, world peace, and the prosperity of all humankind as we finally learn the benefit of choosing to live together for the Highest Good Of All.

Since the first printing, many people have now read *The Next Evolution*, and I've made several presentations and been on the air a couple of times. Some of the people who have caught the vision that this model could transform the planet have contacted me and are ready and willing to take action. To that end, the Community Planet Foundation is starting to compile a list of those people. As stated in the "Community Clusters" chapter, it would just take one cluster of these Highest Good For All Communities to start the transformation of the planet. When we get the first 300 to 500 people who are committed to doing this, we will create a conference where we can come together and start the process. By the time you read this, our website, communityplanet.org, may be up and running. If not, then please email me at jack@community-planet.org

I think that those of us who would like to transform the planet would agree that we need a new paradigm. But, with the challenges facing our planet, especially the environmental imbalances, we no longer have the luxury of acting out of againstness towards the government and towards the money/power brokers. Also, with the Systems Theory telling us that all things are interconnected, we cannot really change what must be changed by simply rallying against one or a couple of issues. There are so many challenges and problems the planet faces that we would use up all our time and energy being against this or that, and still the planet will have moved a little closer to ecological disaster. Do I support what those crusaders, who go against the status quo by seeking to expose the harm being done to our planet, are doing? Yes, I do, because they are getting some truth out there. Do I want to get involved with my time and energy? No, because againstness will not produce the new paradigm that is needed, and our current form of government will never operate on the level of the Highest Good For All Life.

The new paradigm can only be created by a group of people who absolutely hold the consciousness of the Highest Good For All and have the vision to bring that into manifestation. People need to see that there is another way, that we don't have to continue doing the separation that has bred this everyone-for-themselves approach that has been in place unquestioned for thousands of years. People need to see a Community of people who adopt a way of living together and relating together in Community on the principle of the Highest Good For All. When people see the quality of life and the ecological balance that is possible, they will also want to learn the consciousness and the form it takes to do that, and this is what will ultimately transform the planet.

I have a saying: "The solution for everything is the solution to anything." Virtually every challenge that one can think of can be resolved by the creation of worldwide Communities such as has been described in this book. Also, one of our leading futurists, my friend Barbara Marx Hubbard, once asked me how much it would take to create the first Community. I responded with a dollar figure, but later I realized that the answer was really that it would take just one person. One person with the resources and the vision could help us to create this, and there are many good people out there who have the resources and are looking for what they can do to help humanity out of the mess we're in. Who knows, maybe you will be the one who gets this vision to them.

I may as well take a shot at this too: I have a movie idea based on the book. It's an engaging fictional story that would get our vision out to the mainstream. Most people have not even thought about how the world could be, and this story would address that need. If you have a contact, I can email you the description.

Again, if you hold the consciousness of the Highest Good For All and wish to be a part of "3000 To Transform The Planet," contact us.

Love and Light,

Jack   jack@communityplanet.org

HOW TO ENGAGE THE AUTHOR

Jack Reed can be found by emailing him: jack@community-planet.org. He gives interviews and presentations on the vision presented in this book: how we can transform the planet so that it will work for everyone and for all life on Earth. The value of his talks is that he is able to actually present a workable solution to the interconnected crises our planet now faces.

Jack also facilitates groundbreaking consensus trainings for groups of people, ranging from 8 to 36 people, who are serious about truly learning the skills and consciousness necessary to do consensus decision-making.

HOW TO ORDER

Books can be ordered directly from the Community Planet Foundation by:

email orders: jack@communityplanet.org

website: www.communityplanet.org

Postal orders: Community Planet Foundation, 1611 Olive St., Santa Barbara, CA 93101.

The price for overland mail is: US $24 per book including tax and shipping.

Payment: Cheque   Credit Card
Visa   Mastercard   Discover

Card number:

Name on card: Exp. date: /